CLEAR THE TRACK

CLEAR THE TRACK

TRACK

THE EDDIE SHACK STORY

ROSS BREWITT

A Peter Goddard Book

A PETER GODDARD BOOK
Published in 1997 by Stoddart Publishing Co. Limited
34 Lesmill Road, Toronto, Canada M3B 2T6

Distributed in Canada by General Distribution Services Limited
34 Lesmill Road, Toronto, Canada M3B 2T6
Tel. (416) 445-3333 Fax (416) 445-5967 Email
Customer.Service@ccmailgw.genpub.com

Distributed in the U.S. by General Distribution Services Inc.
85 River Rock Drive, Suite 202, Buffalo, New York 14207 Toll-free tel. 1-800-805-1083
Toll-free fax 1-800-481-6207
Email gdsinc@genpub.com

01 00 99 98 97 1 2 3 4 5

Cataloging in Publication Data

Brewitt, Ross, 1936-
    Clear the track

"A Peter Goddard book"
ISBN 0-7737-3049-4

1. Shack, Eddie. 2. Hockey players – Canada – Biography.   I. Title.

GV848.5.S453B73 1997   796.962'092   97-931969-2

Jacket design: Bill Douglas @ The Bang
Text design: Andrew Smith Graphics Inc.
Front cover photos: Mike Burns (left) and Hockey Hall of Fame
PRINTED AND BOUND IN CANADA

We gratefully acknowledge the Canada Council for the Arts and the Ontario Arts Coucil for their support of our publishing program.

Contents

Preface ix

CHAPTER ONE
The Man I

CHAPTER TWO
Sudbury 19

CHAPTER THREE
Guelph 39

CHAPTER FOUR
New York 60

CHAPTER FIVE
The Early Maple Leaf Years 73

CHAPTER SIX
The Later Maple Leaf Years 86

CHAPTER SEVEN
Boston 111

CHAPTER EIGHT
Los Angeles 127

CHAPTER NINE
Buffalo 142

CHAPTER TEN
Pittsburgh 153

CHAPTER ELEVEN
Toronto Again 161

CHAPTER TWELVE
Business 176

CHAPTER THIRTEEN
Family 198

CHAPTER FOURTEEN
Friends 209

CHAPTER FIFTEEN
The Pension Fight 221

CHAPTER SIXTEEN
Life Today 242

Epilogue 260

Index 275

Preface

WHEN DID IT BEGIN? THINKING BACK, I GUESS MY FIRST REAL
discussion with Eddie Shack about doing a biography took place a couple of years ago or so on the balcony of the Angus Glen Golf Club in
Toronto. The occasion was the annual CHUM-FM Charitable Golf
Classic, a much sought-after invitation on the celebrity "nosh and
Nassau" circuit. Although a biography had been mentioned before, this
was the first time Eddie brought up the subject, and as usual he had his
own opinion on how it should be done.

"See, we make a nice deal. You talk about Punch Imlach, Timmy
Horton, the Stanley Cups, Bobby Orr, Phil Esposito, all them guys I
played with, okay? Maybe Pop Shoppe, the golf course, right? You boogie with that stuff like you do, and we promote the shit out of it.
Promote, promote. I can probably sell 10,000 myself."

After I threw the anchor over the side to slow him down, and put a
damper on his understanding of the publishing business, I talked about
what I saw as a story and the important things that had happened in his
life. I also told him, "If we're gonna do it, we better do it right. We won't
get a second chance." There it was, a deal in principle, and it had all
taken shape over a hamburger and a beer.

Another reason I remember that day so well is the little scene that
unfolded as we got up to make our way to the practice fairway. Our host
for the afternoon was Gord James, longtime DJ with CHUM-FM, who
was an unwitting witness to the scene about to unfold. He was sitting
with unquestionably the most incongruous group I had ever encountered on one of these golf workshops: figure skater Kurt Browning, ex-
Blue Jay catcher Ernie Whitt, NHLer Kirk Muller, and the diminutive
Mr. Dressup of CBC-TV fame.

As Eddie and I threaded our way through the rapidly filling lunch
tables, he pointed out Browning's table, roared something obscene, and
referred to him curiously as "that little downhiller." Browning had

heard the routine before and, laughing, beckoned us over to his table. James, of course, was no stranger, nor was Whitt, and Muller couldn't have been if he'd been wearing a false moustache and sunglasses, but Mr. Dressup was new territory. Unfortunately for Whitt, he was attired in plaid shorts, a vertical-striped golf shirt, black-and-white shoes, and a hat that looked like a sombrero out of *The Treasure of the Sierra Madre.*

Make no mistake, Ed Shack is a presence, and on this occasion he was watched by everyone on the upper deck. "Mr. 23, I'd like you to meet Mr. Dressup," Browning announced graciously, thinking Fast Eddie would be impressed by the diminutive and venerable icon of children's programming.

But Shack disregarded the TV personality, thrust a huge hand toward Whitt, and rasped, "How's she going, big boy?" There was an instant of dead quiet, then mouthfuls of hamburger were spit up, beer passed through noses, and tables in all four corners of the balcony were thumped into submission.

That was the last week in June. It took until the end of October to get the agreements in place. In between there were several meetings, a few bordering on humorous, and in particular a Saturday session that set the tone for all the days that followed. It was one of those glorious September mornings, warm with a hint of golf in the air, and we stood in the driveway below the panoramic kitchen window in front of Eddie's house as he explained to me, round-eyed and serious, hands held up as if he were pushing a wall, "Now don't piss too high." No doubt the backwoods analogy implied that I wasn't to take myself too importantly or misconstrue my position in the pecking order. "Never forget I'm the talent."

"No problem, E.S.," I countered. "As long as *you* don't forget, I'm the writer."

From that point on he called me "Arthur," which is as close as Eddie can get to a put-on British pronunciation for "author." As he explained, deadpan, to a flustered, full-of-business, self-important restaurant manager busily pitching in to clean our table during the lunch-hour rush, "I'm a hockey player, you're a busboy, he's an Arthur." We all chuckled at the job descriptions, but I think the man was laughing at the perceived improbability of his being a busboy. I know Eddie was laughing at him, and I was amused by Eddie's instant evaluation of the situation, and Mr. Manager.

During the next weeks and months, Eddie would lead off telephone calls by asking, "Is the Arthur there?" Or he would leave voice-mail messages for "Arthur," and introduce me as "my Arthur" without explanation. Often, after a chance meeting with strangers, people shook my hand and said, "Nice t'meet ya, Art."

But we did it. And what follows is the proof.

CLEAR THE TRACK

CHAPTER ONE

The Man

It is 6:00 a.m. a red van turns into the driveway, right on time. The black cowboy hat with the silver autographs is in place. Twiggy, the little shih tzu, all dressed up in a walking vest for warmth in the winter air, yelps against the front window as I throw a briefcase into the back seat. He knows I'm going to steal his place up front and he doesn't like it one bit. Eddie Shack laughs and says, "Nice little dogie. C'mon, little dogie, get in the back." Twiggy, who according to Shackie is a dogie, not a doggy, jumps two inches into the air with every bark and only succeeds in falling off the seat, having to scramble up on all fours to continue yapping. Shackie considers the whole episode hilarious.

We set out on the long drive up Dixie Road and onto the westbound 401. Three hours and a bit later we pull up in front of Elias Deli on Windsor's Ouellette Street.

"How's the ice cream doin'?" Eddie inquires of a machine in front of one of only two windows in the place looking out to the main street. The short-order cook, a man in a baseball cap who wears the look of someone with a lot of miles behind an apron, only shrugs as he toys with our breakfast orders of bacon and eggs spitting and bubbling on the grill. "We dun know. We joos put it in, whadda we know?" The accent is hard to pinpoint. Could be Greek, could be Jewish. Might be Jewish Greek.

"How the hell do you serve it? Toss it out the window?" Eddie laughs, peering to see if the large thermopane can be raised.

"Nawp. Da licence police say you can no do dat."

"Why not?" Eddie asks, incredulous. "People walkin' on the street need ice cream. Get outta them buildings, eh? Take a goddamn walk, have a little ice cream." The cook just shakes his head, shrugs, and noisily clatters two plates beside the grill.

"Assholes," Eddie says to the absent licence police, with a final look at the machine. A man at a small table, reading one of the many newspapers from the counter, glances up, takes a long, cheek-depressing draw on his cigarette, and fixes Eddie through hangover eyes as if to remind him it's Sunday morning.

"G'day, g'day, how's she goin'? Them goddamn things'll kill yuh," Eddie mumbles, smiling warmly for no apparent reason before sitting down to breakfast.

A short time later, after taking the van for a wash, Eddie pulls up in the lobby area of the hotel, and we begin off-loading a few large framed pictures he's trying to sell, a box of publicity photos, and a few sticks. As we enter the main foyer, a large group of young boys and what appear to be coaches and parents are checking out. The jackets tell us we're in the midst of the Kingston boxing team.

The kids don't waste more than a glance on this big Yosemite Sam in the goofy black cowboy hat and boots. But the parents do. A frail grandmotherly type, with glasses and a cigarette hanging out of her mouth, freezes, staring up at the large person she recognizes but is poorly prepared to greet. Trying to speak through the bobbing cigarette between her lips, she inhales smoke down the wrong way, if such a thing is possible, considering her nicotine-stained fingers, and begins a racking series of coughs, like loud bursts of static from an off-station radio. One of the other women, still gawking at the departing Shack, helps Granny to a lobby couch where she sits, wheezing, unable to talk, still pointing and staring watery-eyed at the departing hockey hero.

It's the Days Inn, not the Chateau Laurier, or the Royal York. It's Windsor, not Ottawa or Toronto, but the act is the same regardless. Twenty or so people forming a ragged line are propped against the walls of the meeting room. A table has been placed at one end of the room to accommodate Eddie, while the promoter flits between there and his own table at the entrance. The setup is time-honoured and proven, much like a beer store. One door in, one door out. Two security guards flank the in and out.

Across the hall is a church service, a congregation without their own place of worship, and from time to time intonations and admonitions can be heard. Realistically you'd have to be deaf not to hear it. The preacher uses a microphone in a room that can't be any larger than the one for the autograph session. A relieved but wary promoter welcomes Eddie Shack to the Rose City.

"Amen," Eddie announces to his flock, drowning out the clergyman on the other side of the hall. "Where's the ribbon cutters? Where's the goddamn mayor?" Shack growls through a rasping laugh, indicating to the suddenly brightened loungers that the scissors and His Worship aren't really necessary. The effect on the attendees is immediate. They listen up, straighten up, loosen up, realizing that this is indeed Sweet Daddy Shackie, the Entertainer, live and in person.

Eddie makes a quiet side deal with the promoter, offering a commission on any items from the inventory belonging to him that the promoter sells. Then he dons one of the name-crested Maple Leaf jerseys for display purposes. The show is about to begin. Eddie goes into his routine, greeting, cajoling, making self-deprecating sport of his playing ability and his shortcomings as a writer and speller.

The promoter notices a difference from past shows. "Geez, he's really good. I mean, I've had guys here who didn't even look up at the fans, never mind talk to them."

Just then one of the faithful in the line turns to his buddy and remarks, "This is great," referring to Eddie's running patter.

"Beats waiting in a bank lineup," his partner replies.

Eddie advises a youngster to continue his schooling and to pay attention in class. "A guy asked me one time, 'How far didja go to school?'" Eddie whines, imitating the supercilious questioner. "Two and a half miles," he answers himself, to the delight of the lineup. "Straightened that bastard out, eh?" he proclaims with big eyes and a silly moustachioed grin. And the people all laugh, including the kids who, almost as one, look up to the parents as if to say, "If he swears it's okay, right?" One man in a Red Wings cap and jacket considers the quip an outright knee-slapper.

A bit later a young man with three earrings creeping up his left lobe approaches with several pictures to sign. "Jeezuz, where the hell did you get those? Did you lose a bet?" Eddie asks, leaning over to his right to get an even better view of the ear hardware.

If the man expected to slide past without a comment, he realizes now that he's been caught and frames a weak, frozen, dry-tooth smile. But his heart isn't in it. "Yeah, well, I could say the same about the cowboy hat," he mumbles tentatively, his defence being that Shack is the only one in the room with a real hat if you exclude the variety of baseball caps worn, both forward and backward, by his fellow patrons. It's obvious he's unsure of the territory and whether it's wise to be challenging the centre of attraction.

The next move by a magnanimous Shack lowers the man's guard. "You know how I got started on these?" Eddie says in a confidential tone, doffing the Hoot Gibson special and revealing thinning hair shooting off in all directions. "When I played in Guelph, they had a hat company there — Biltmore. They sponsored the team, and the owner came to practice one day with a load of hats and said to me, 'Hey, big boy, how 'bout you wearin' a hat?' And I did. Been wearin' hats ever since."

Sitting back in his chair, Eddie murmurs, "Yeah," and pauses briefly to reflect, satisfied that he's explained himself. Then the punch line is launched like an air-to-air missile. "Okay, pal, I've told you my story. Now let's hear yours," and the entire room breaks up laughing, with Eddie pounding the table and braying at the young man's red-faced fluster on being cast into the eye of the storm once more.

Eddie sits through three hours of small talk and opinions on the Leafs, the Original Six, and the way hockey used to be. The pace of the banter is occasionally interrupted by hymns and chants from across the hall. It's a surreal setting, this larger-than-life man in a white Maple Leaf jersey, cowboy hat right out of Tombstone, two rent-a-cops with radios and handcuffs, a full-fledged revival meeting next door, kids, grandmas, people dressed in more colours than Phyllis Diller's worst day, and a skinhead sporting an earring hat trick.

There's also the promoter who's paid for the services of Shack, casting a jaundiced eye toward Eddie as he sneaks in the odd freebie, extra signings of kids' hats, the occasional double dip of cards and pictures. At that point a young fan voices bewilderment about Eddie's reference to "Clear the Track."

"You ever hear of a song like that?" Eddie asks. The boy shakes his head, while his parent nods. Eddie croaks into a few out-of-tune lyrics. "Can you believe it? Number one on the hit parade for six weeks," he says, holding up the appropriate number of large fingers.

"Yeah. And remember to stay in school," Eddie insists, changing subjects without warning and causing the look of innocent bewilderment on the kid's face to deepen. "Put in the time. You gotta put the time in, anyway, so stay in school," he admonishes. "Look at me. Every time the teachers said, 'Do this,' I did that. And when they said, 'Don't do this here,' I did it. I didn't like teachers, and look what happened to me," he adds, tapping himself on the Maple Leaf with an accusing finger. The kid stares at him like he'd just dropped from the ceiling, as if to say, "Who is this big dweeb?"

"Yep," Eddie repeats, flourishing another signature, "stay in school."

As the line shuffles forward, the moment when a fan has the celebrity to himself approaches for a boy and a woman, who studies Eddie as he goes through his shtick. It's obvious she doesn't approve of his borderline rough talk, and when their moment in the spotlight comes, she puts down an eight-by-ten publicity shot, the one with the spanking new uniform, pristine gloves, white skate laces, and a stick without a blemish.

"I sure as hell looked a lot better then, eh?" Eddie admits.

"It's for my husband," the woman says, as though someone had asked.

"He still in bed, or at church?" Eddie asks, jerking a thumb over his shoulder at the sermon coming from across the hall, and lets loose with that low laugh he reserves for those who aren't telling the exact truth.

"He has other duties today," the woman says, full of business as she inspects the "Ed Shack #23" in thick blue ink, making sure it's dry before placing the picture inside a legal-size envelope for safekeeping.

Eddie stares at her for an instant, then shifts to the little boy, who's wearing a Philadelphia Flyers sweater. "How old are yah?" he asks, pointing with the pen.

"Nine," the boy responds shyly.

"Know what I was doin' when I was nine? I was stuffin' sausages and pluckin' chickens. I was a sausage-stuffin' chicken plucker!" The rest of the lineup breaks up at the observation, nodding happily and laughing along. All except the woman.

"Who's your favourite player?" Eddie asks, ignoring her.

"Eric Lindros," the boy replies quickly, as if there was no other choice.

"Hey, Eric Lindros," Eddie exclaims, suddenly interested, sliding forward in his chair to talk to the entire room. "Can you imagine they're all over him about havin' a hangover? Holy sheepshit! I know some guys who couldn't play unless they were half pissed. A goddamn hangover was like part of your equipment. How else didja put up with coaches like Phil Watson? How do you think players can live with guys like Imlach, and Sinden, and Laycoe?" Now he turns directly to the woman, with her perfectly stored photo in hand, and raises his arm to point at her. "Now you look to me like a sensible person who's never had a hangover, right?" The woman makes a distasteful grimace and nods. "Well, let me be the first to tell you. To the best of my recollect'll intellect, *I sure as hell have!*" Eddie roars, flings himself back in the chair, and basks in the laughter of the lineup. Or maybe he's enjoying the prim and proper exit of the starchy woman and the little Lindros fan.

Less than an hour later I'm standing and chatting with Tommy "Bomber" Williams, one of my buddies from the Labatt's NHL Old Stars team that I coached in the late 1970s and early 1980s. Tommy's joined me at a popular Windsor sports bar called The Penalty Box. We're there not out of a sense of the obvious hockey theme, but because it's within a short walking distance of the Days Inn, where Eddie is still hard at work.

Windsor's Tommy Williams is not to be confused with Duluth's Tommy Williams, who played for Boston and Minnesota. Our Tommy played for the New York Rangers and the Los Angeles Kings. The other Tommy is an American; our Tommy is Canadian. Our Tommy was only playing peewee when the other Tommy was turning pro. The reason for all the letters of reference is that, during our time with the Old Stars, the question came up every damn time. People inevitably asked, "Hey, is that the Tommy . . . ?" And we'd never let them finish.

Bomber was a speed merchant on skates, and only 31, when he joined us in 1982. On Eddie's suggestion the team was first called the NHL Old Stars (the name was later changed to the Labatt's Original Six) when we debuted in 1979. Eddie had decided that he still wanted to play hockey, but not with the NHL Oldtimers, the team he was skating with back then.

I met Eddie in the office of Bill May at the Pop Shoppe on Eva Road in Toronto in the days when Eddie was their spokesman and the man with "a nose for value." He was adamant about a team that could "do something, entertain for Christ's sake, get the people off their asses, let the poor bastards enjoy themselves for a change. They wanna see real hockey, not this other boring shit." He went on to exaggerate how between periods the Oldtimers often lit up pipes and talked about what a great time they had baby-sitting their grandchildren, or how much a roll of wallpaper cost.

In short, the team was formed and played six seasons across Canada and the United States against Major A and Junior A and B squads, university teams, NHL alumni, Allan Cup winners, Allan Cup finalists and contenders, plus the occasional local team in places like East Musquodoboit, Nova Scotia, Dawson Creek, British Columbia, and Santa Rosa, California, where we played Charlie Brown cartoonist Charles Schulz's bunch of rich college boys.

The team was capable of handling the workload. In goal were Marv Edwards, Doug Favell, and Gerry Desjardins. The defencemen included Bill White, Pierre Pilote, Pat Stapleton, Darryl Edestrand, Dale Tallon, Dallas Smith, Jim McKenny, Mike Pelyk, Claire Alexander, and Brian Glennie. Up front it was take your pick of the best: Norm Ullman, Fred Stanfield, Pit Martin, Stan Mikita, Chico Maki, Dennis Hull,

Jim Pappin, Mike Walton, Jack Valiquette, Larry Mickey, Keith McCreary, Dean Prentice, Errol Thompson, Bob Nevin, Billy Harris, Derek Sanderson. And Tommy Williams. If any of these people ever talked about their grandchildren, wallpaper, or the cost of Pampers, I never heard it.

Today, on his way to a town across the river in Michigan to play with his new team, the Red Wing Alumni, we remind each other of those never-to-be-forgotten road trips and the camaraderie that existed between players who, in many cases, had never met.

"Jeez, I didn't know anyone on the first trip to Saskatchewan," Bomber insists until I remind him of Windsor pal Pit Martin, the man who recommended Williams join the team. "Oh, yeah, Pitunia. But it was the first time I'd ever been around the kind of stars you had on that club. So many players on one team . . . man, it was awesome," he enthuses. "We had the three-star line, right? Shackie, Shakey [Mike Walton], *and Shitty.*" We both say the last name in unison, then bust out laughing, startling the nearby patrons as Tommy taps on his chest and takes a bow.

"But Shackie," Tommy says, "I only played against him at the end of his career, and he wasn't playing much, injured, too. Then when I got to see him on a regular basis it never failed to amaze me how hard the guy could shoot the puck. Wrist shot like a bazooka. Hell, I'll never forget. We were playing out west against that senior team — B.C., I think," he says, sifting through the names and places.

"First shift, I caught Eddie steamin' up the wing with a rinkwide pass, and he came up on the blueline and wristed it, just wired it under the crossbar, top shelf, from way out there. Somehow the goalie got his glove up, big save, no goal, and we start back up the ice. Next thing I know, they get a whistle and the trainer comes out to take the goalie to the goddamn hospital! Broke his hand. Remember that? First shot of the game, the poor guy never even got to go to the party. That's Shackie." Tommy, 13 years Eddie's junior, shakes his head in disbelief. "Like an armoured truck with a cannon. He musta been a lot of NHLers' worst nightmare in his prime. Where the hell is he, anyway?" Tommy suddenly asks, turning in his seat to glance at the door.

"He's signing his heart out over at the Days Inn," I explain, and Tommy begins to laugh. "Newfoundland," he says and we both laugh at a memory that the mere mention of the word recalls.

As OFTEN AS I'VE WATCHED EDDIE SIGN HIS NAME, WINDSOR IS MY first occasion in a very long time to see him in full-contact autograph action alone, the sole centre of attraction, and I'm impressed. Those who have never signed their name, or have little or no chance of being asked to sign their name, might consider it a thrill, and it is, for all of a few minutes. For the famous, like Eddie, a recognizable figure for more than 40 years, it has lost a lot of its appeal.

If there's a story that puts Ed Shack in the biographical crosshairs, it was when the Old Stars played in Newfoundland, and as in all the other places the team travelled to from 1979 to the mid-1980s, Shackie was our centrepiece. So, safely ensconced among The Penalty Box's patrons, I tell the tale once more.

In all we made five trips to the Rock and, because of the people, it became a favourite stop each year. Newfoundlanders are the friendliest, most generous, most welcoming people in the country, and Eddie, at first inwardly skeptical, mistaking their outward show of hospitality as wanting something, eventually found them not only amusing but his kind of people. Somewhere in those early trips was one that took us to Corner Brook.

Wherever the team played, each fan received a four-page program with the two team lineups and pictures of the Old Star players. Autographs were the order of the day, and the trick was to sign at your picture to avoid the inevitable duplicate requests.

From one end of the country to the other the routine was the same: the players sat by themselves at the postgame function until, liquid courage in place, the locals ventured forth for the signings. But in Newfoundland it seemed as if the fans were even more reluctant to approach, preferring to hang back, smile, and almost require an invitation. In a word, they were polite, to the point of being shy. However, once the ice had been broken by one of the more daring of the citizens, it started a flood and they'd happily crowd around in swarms that moved from one table to the next like picnic ants.

In this situation Eddie considered autographs part of the job, an assignment that had to be filled, nothing more, nothing less. While he was a high-profile member of the group, it wasn't his show entirely like the autograph session in Windsor, and therein lay the difference. On these excursions he wasn't the type to listen and chat like Bobby Hull, nor was he the kind to engage in small talk. In fact, he'd rarely glance up to acknowledge any of the remarks passed his way about the Maple Leafs, Punch Imlach, or anything else for that matter. The only time I ever saw him become animated and perk up was when an autograph seeker confessed to being from Sudbury, or if a fan had played Eddie's golf course in Toronto.

To Eddie autographing was a chore that came with the territory, like backchecking in hockey, but only once in "Somewhere's Else, Newfoundland," as one of the locals called it, did Shackie throw up his hands and break away in impatience. On this occasion one of the throng made the mistake of getting too close and elbowed his cowboy hat. That did it.

"All right, goddamn it," he growled, standing up, threatening in his size, exasperated as he checked his hat for dents. "Line up. Get into line for cripes sake. Get along the wall here and straighten up. When you get to the table, you put down your program and start here," he said, pointing to Fred Stanfield. "Freddie, two Stanley Cups with Boston, then Chico [Maki]," he admonished the intently watching fans. "He got one with Chicago. Next, Roscoe," he said, waving haphazardly at me. "Then I'm last. And don't screw it up. After that take yer goddamn program and go bother those other guys."

For their part the fans, by now lined up halfway around the hall, were happy to see somebody, anybody, take charge and bring a sense of order to the proceedings.

If you've ever received an autograph from Eddie, it's always the same memento: "Ed Shack #23." Not Eddie Shack, not E. Shack, and not a scrawl, either, but a more than passable piece of penmanship. Things were going along fine as Eddie started out the procession on the right foot. One woman, watching as her friend's program rounded the table until it was signed by Eddie. observed, "My, my, doesn't he have nice handwritin'?"

I couldn't let that pass. "If you could only write two words in the entire world, lady, wouldn't you be pretty good at it, too?" I asked rhetorically. Eddie was oblivious, handing the first woman her program.

But the guy who caught my attention, about third in line, was a typical Newfoundlander in baseball hat, black-and-red plaid jacket, safety boots, and hydro-company-green, one-size-fits-all pants, with a too-tight belt that drew the fly over to where the pocket would normally be, the kind of pants that made reaching for change look like fondling to anyone else bold enough to stare.

When it came his turn, he watched with interest until the paper came to Shack, then he suddenly became helpful, placing an elbow on the table and staring directly into Eddie's face. "I want it fer Ron. Sign 'er to Ron," he said before straightening and giving the okay sign to someone across the hall.

Eddie only mumbled and routinely put down "Ed Shack #23," then handed back the program over his shoulder. The man picked it out of the air and took only one step before realizing the autograph wasn't personalized. Slapping the program against his thigh, he marched straight to the back of the line. Forty people later he surfaced again and patiently put down the program in front of Stanfield as instructed.

"I've done this one," Freddie murmured, pushing it over to Maki, who acknowledged he had done the same. I knew for a fact I'd signed it and, still studying our man, pushed it over to Shackie. Once again the guy became Mr. Congeniality, elbow on the table, with a friendly if intent look directly into Eddie's oversize moustache.

"Now I ast yuh to put 'er down t'Ron. So put 'er down," the man singsonged almost in a whine. Eddie positioned the program and directly underneath the previous signature put down "Ed Shack #23," again passing it over his shoulder without a word.

"Lord t'underin' Jeezuz," the Newfoundlander growled as he perused the double autograph from behind Shackie, then wheeled and marched to the back of the lineup once more.

This time I kept my eye on him because I figured there was going to be a fight. Hospitable, generous, and friendly as they are, Newfoundlanders, too, have certain limits, and our friend, fuming and upset, wasn't loathe to explain to others in the line that this was his third attempt at a proper signature. I distinctly heard and lip-read his displeasure. "Fuckin' arsehole" was one curse that came through loud and clear, and "beat da be-Jayzuz" was as plain as the "Seals R Us" hat that he wore. Long ago the inherent difference in the terms "Jeezuz" and "be-Jayzuz" had been explained to me, so I was aware things were getting serious. When the Newfoundlander's turn came again, he put both elbows on the table for effect, not bothering with Freddie, Chico, or me.

"Now see, I'se told ya t'ree times t'put down ta Ron. See any goddamn Rons on dis here?" he demanded, pointing at the program with a gnarled index finger. "What da hell's wrong wit you, boy? Put 'er down fer Jayzuz sake. I ain't askin' fer da fuckin' moon."

With that Eddie looked at him directly. It was the first time he'd seen the man. Then, without even a pause, he pushed the program over to me and I dutifully wrote "To Ron" on top of the two signatures and pushed it back. Shack turned it to a better angle and began writing "Ed Shack #23."

Our little buddy, now beaming from ear to ear, flashed the okay sign, picked up his program, pumped Eddie's big hand, and said, "T'anks very much. I always liked ya as a player. Fer a minute dere I t'ought yuh wuz rotten from appetite t'arsehole."

When I finish the tale, Tommy says he has to make a quick exit from The Penalty Box and drive to another hockey game somewhere in Michigan. As he leaves, he tosses a final remark over his shoulder to the group gathered around me, "True story, boys. I was there."

A little later I'm sitting in a booth with John Ferguson, the Montreal Canadiens tough guy, or Mr. Tough Guy to anyone who ever played against him. It occurs to me as we talk that there's a kind of contrived irony that we're in a booth in a place called The Penalty Box.

"I came up to the NHL in 1963," Ferguson says, "and I'll always remember Toe Blake's instructions to me the very first time we played Toronto. The game hadn't even started. I was sitting on the bench, and Toe came up behind me and said, 'Don't rile the Big M [Frank Mahovlich] and keep Shack settled down. Don't let him drag you into the penalty box with him.' I wasn't even on the ice yet. The Canadiens obviously had some respect for Shackie."

John Ferguson is one of those lucky ones who doesn't change. Whatever the aging process is, it's a lot slower for Big John. He came into the bar dressed as a country gentleman but wearing the familiar no-nonsense appearance of a homicide cop on a tough case. His shoulders hunch up in a way that drew my curiosity years ago when I first met him face-to-face on a golf course. It always made me wonder if he bothered wearing shoulder pads when he played, or did he just leave them on when he left the rink? Now, sitting across the table, he looks around with interest at the sparse Sunday lunchtime clientele and asks, "Where is Eddie, anyway?"

"He's knockin' 'em dead at the Hallelujah Lounge."

Ferguson's only response is a smile, and without waiting he begins talking about his old adversary again. "Eddie was better than most as a player, but a little erratic at times. In fact, there was a saying in Montreal. If a young player could really skate but was having trouble scoring, we'd say he cut in like the Rocket and finished like Shack. Believe me, that's all Eddie needed was a little more 'finish' and he'd have been a hell of a player, an outstanding player. Regardless of what you thought about his play, you could never question his toughness. I remember the night he and Ted Harris collided. This was a heavyweight collision, like two semis, and when I skated over, Shack was on his feet. But there was blood coming out of his ear, so I knew he was in really tough shape. He was hurtin', but he wasn't whinin'. You had to have respect for him."

Which is about as good a compliment as you're going to get because Ferguson, known throughout hockey as the leading practitioner of the "no fraternization" rule, had little regard for anyone who wasn't wearing the red, white, and blue. How serious was he about the unwritten law?

"We arrived on a Monday afternoon to stay over in Toronto for a few days before a Wednesday night game with the Leafs. Dickie Duff and I went to dinner at George's Spaghetti House on Dundas Street, and who walks in but Shackie. Dick and he used to run together when Duff was with the Leafs, and Eddie said his hellos and then sat a few tables away with some other people. We had just ordered our steaks, but they hadn't arrived yet, so I threw my money on the table and walked out. No way I'd sit there with the enemy."

And as a super scout and former coach Ferguson had no trouble answering the question of Shack's reaching the 300-goal plateau.

"He could have done it — absolutely. But Punch only spotted him in certain situations, and hey, we were glad he wasn't a regular. But that's the luxury you have with a team as good as the Leafs were, because on a lot of clubs he'd have been a regular without question. He was such a powerful skater. I wish I could have skated like Eddie. Today he'd be a first-round draft choice. Wait, that's not fair. There's 26 first-round picks. Shack would be in the top five of *any* draft year."

A few minutes later Eddie arrives to a chorus of greetings from complete strangers. He lights up with the big moustache grin and points to several pictures on the wall at the entrance, taken on his last visit. Van Niforos, the owner, joins us and remarks on the photo with his son and Eddie together. "He's eight now so that must have been a couple of years ago."

"How 'bout this one?" Ferguson pipes up suddenly, his memory banks no doubt whirring to locate a choice yarn about Eddie. "Years ago Eddie and me did a commercial for the Alberta Lottery. I was in Winnipeg. It was just after I left the Jets, and Shackie flew out to Calgary. We met at a suburban arena, got dressed in our gear, and they put Eddie and me in this sort of bucket underneath the centre ice logo. I don't know how they rigged this thing, but with the camera angle we looked like we came out of the ice and started fighting in the middle of a bogus game. It was tight down there in the basket, and as I recall, they had to do it a few times because we kept coming up laughing. That commercial won an award."

"Yeah," Eddie says, obviously relishing the memory. "We were in this little thing, like a wire tank. We were nose to nose. I guess I won that fight, too, eh, Ferg?"

Later that afternoon, as we drive home and watch the flat, boring Southwestern Ontario farmland inch past the side windows, Eddie, out of nowhere, suddenly comments on John Ferguson. "Tough, dedicated, he'd never mix on a plane, or train, either. He'd just as soon sucker-punch you. He was with you or against you, 100 percent. Either way it didn't matter to him. And he was a good hockey man. Proved it in New York, Winnipeg, and Ottawa, but they didn't listen to him and they didn't use him right, either." Then, just as quickly, Eddie lapses into silence again.

Ed Shack doesn't talk in sentences and he doesn't paint word pictures. They're more like jigsaw puzzles dumped on a table. If there's any design, it's along the lines of a splotch painter dabbing at a bare wall. As if to underline this premise, he suddenly voices an inner thought as we whiz by the West Lorne exit on the way to London.

"The fans are great, eh? I mean, where are you gonna find better people than hockey fans? No bitchin', no moanin' about waitin' in line, no complaints 'bout the price of a goddamn autograph. Unbelievable."

"You want to stop in London and see that restaurant?" I remind him.

"Naw, let's just boogie it. Another day."

He must be tired, I think, and I ask if he wants me to drive. The question goes unanswered as he jumps on another topic.

"Restaurants and bars can't be that tough, you know. I'm sayin' it's pretty goddamn simple. People are lonely. They wanna get out and have a couple of laughs, meet some friends, pick up some girls. Yuh hire good people, I mean, the person runnin' the place. Help him keep his costs down, put out a good samridge [sandwich], good soup, nothin' to it. You hire the right girl behind the bar who doesn't mind hearin' a good joke and isn't afraid to tell a customer to fuck off. Yuh can't miss!"

By now I'm used to Eddie's simplistic rationalizations of complex business practices. He takes the food-and-beverage game, a diverse, market-driven business, fragile and subject to innumerable pressures and stresses, and sifts it to suit his personal understanding.

To the layman it makes perfect sense, judging by the nods he gets from those trying to curry his favour, or having no experience themselves. But like all explanations that barely scratch the surface, the line between theory and practical application is as wide as the rinks Eddie used to skate in. And while he tends to be like most politicians in his assurances, that given the job, he can straighten out the system, he has very often been correct in his evaluations, and but for some discreditable business support from the people around him, may have been even more successful than he is now.

As we come up on "Guelph — 6 North," the van is totally silent. Even Twiggy only makes the occasional frightened yip as he navigates through a dog's dream.

"How old were you when you went to the Biltmores?" I ask, almost sorry to break the silence.

"Fourteen and a half," Shackie says vacantly to the windshield. I do the math.

The year would be 1951.

GORDIE HOWE WON THE FIRST OF FOUR STRAIGHT SCORING TITLES with 43 goals and 43 assists, 20 points ahead of Rocket Richard, 24 up on Toronto's Max Bentley. Detroit and Howe had finished the regular season in first place, with Toronto second, followed by Montreal, Boston, New York, and Chicago.

On April 21 Toronto defeated Montreal at Maple Leaf Gardens to win the Stanley Cup, staging a stingy, defensive five-game series, the Leafs scoring 13 goals, Montreal 10. Each and every game was decided by a one-goal margin, indicating how fine the talent was spread at the top. Mistakes were few; goals were fewer. In the next 10 seasons Montreal would get its revenge, winning the championship six times, while Toronto only occasionally flirted with success. The

Leafs wouldn't win the Cup again until 1961-62.

Compared to the cities of the NHL's Original Six, Guelph isn't a big-time destination, but in September 1951 a gangly kid away from his hometown of Sudbury for the first time made his auspicious debut in the national pastime. Lots of others had made the same trek, and in a few weeks returned home to talk about that brief grab at the hockey ring for the rest of their days. For most it's only a fleeting illumination on a patch of white ice in a dark and dingy arena. More often than not, it becomes a crushing setback when they find they aren't cut out to be the next winter hero, the next coming of an assault on the record book. For only a very few privileged others, the ones who continue to pass the test, show the growth, talent, and skill required at each new level, it's the beginning of a repetitive process leading ever up the mountain to the top. It's a ritual fire of September that doesn't cease until the player leaves the game.

For Ed Shack Guelph was the start of what would shape his destiny, govern the rest of his life, become the absolute key to his future. But no one knew then, on the day he boarded a train at the Sudbury station, he would be forever changed from a boy pursuing a dream to a man with a national identity, from an aspiring hockey player to a millionaire.

And on that early fall morning when he set out, alone, at 14 years and six months of age, to find his way in the violent world of hockey, he was carrying extra baggage. It was an additional, unseen burden to most of the people whose paths he would cross in years to come.

He could neither read nor write.

Now I look over at him and realize the man behind the wheel, Ed Shack, is an oddity, a living, breathing success story, the kind they make movies about, rendering the melancholic and soft-hearted all warm and damp-eyed as the credits crawl up the screen. The truth is, Ed Shack might play the leading role in his own picture, but he could just as easily be the location carpenter, the key grip, the gaffer, almost any position short of "Miss Stone's cosmetician," and still have had a hell of time doing the job.

Hockey be damned, I think, this is much more than a jockstrap saga.

If there's any parallel to his hockey career and the real Ed Shack, it's only that his before-and-after NHL life has run parallel to the way he played the game. His brand of hockey came from the playground, the outdoor rink, a loud, scrambling, helter-skelter, endless, tournament-of-the-road variety, and it never varied or wavered.

When Ed Shack left Sudbury, everything changed for him, with the exception of the game. From Guelph to Providence, to the dirty sidewalks of New York and the long, twisting road through the NHL, it remained little more than a street contest, complete with snowbanks, tennis balls, rubber boots, runny noses, yellow snow, and the occasional break when a car rolled through the neutral zone.

His trademark style didn't evolve out of delicate puck-handling skills. He certainly was no Jean Beliveau, or Stan Mikita. He did not, by any stretch of the imagination, portray effortless skating, so he was no Ron Ellis, either. There was none of Ellis's fluid body coordination or sheer sense of technique. If Ron Ellis was considered the Jaguar of the era's skaters, Shackie was a big ol' Land Rover.

His on-ice silhouette came from a driven sense of exuberance applied to a work ethic that knew no limits, a diligence lacking finesse but made up for with the stack-'em-up, head-on enthusiasm of a full-back with an eye on the goal line. He had no problem accepting the game as one where even the very best know "you puts yer money down and takes yer chances."

Yet from those slag-heap, mining-town beginnings to life after hockey, there were always detractors, those anticipating his demise, biding their time by loitering and sniping from the sidelines, only pausing to watch for this unschooled rube's inevitable failure.

To all those naysayers he was a bum waiting to happen. That he outlasted them all, and in the process became an international figure, is the real story of "Ed Shack #23."

CHAPTER TWO

Sudbury

SUDBURY. A HARD-ROCK, HARD-ASS TOWN, ONCE REFERRED TO AS THE closest thing on Earth to a moonscape, is where Eddie Shack was born on February 11, 1937. It's the place where, he has always maintained, "They grow potatoes there, but they gotta blast 'em out." Sudbury wasn't pretty back then, nor was it supposed to be. This was long before the Big Nickel, light-years before environmental studies.

Like Ed Shack, most of the population "arrived" looking for a new start, many looking for a new country to put roots into, and in the years when Canada was digging out of a Depression, the miners dug more holes in the Northern Ontario rock face. It was a place where there were jobs to work and a living to be made, especially for those who didn't have the skills or the education to carve out a place in the sun. Unless it was underground.

Sudbury, and its satellite towns of Falconbridge, Gatchel, Lively, Garson, Azilda, Coniston, and Copper Cliff, was a sprawling field of mines, a collection of stacks, slag piles, and tailing ridges, countryside blackened by the acrid exhausts of the smelters, devoid of vegetation, scarred downwind to only the hardiest of moss on grey rocks. Bill Shack and his wife, Lena, came to live, work, and raise a family here. On their 1932 wedding day he was a 25-year-old Ukrainian immigrant who had come to Canada nine years earlier; Lena was a 15-year-old Ukrainian Canadian from Espanola. A year into the marriage, they began their family with daughter Mary, and Eddie arrived four years later.

Nobody ever promised them a rose garden.

Horobin Street is now Lilac Street, but the geography and homes are the same, although many have gone through the regeneration of aluminum siding, brickwork, patio decks, and bay windows. But the neat bungalows and occasional two-story homes are never mistaken for the "right side of the tracks." If anything, the descriptive words are "typical" and "ordinary," just regular people in routine accommodations, no different than any other community in Canada of the same time frame.

Lena Shack's house is on the corner and looks larger than expected until I realize it is really two places; the addition on the right side is home to daughter Mary and her family. Subtract it and you have an idea of Eddie Shack's first and only residence in the city of Sudbury.

I have never met Lena. When she opens the door, this small 80-year-old woman seems surprised, but certainly not baffled or confused after my explanation, as if to indicate life with Eddie has been a series of surprises. The problem stems from the fact that Mr. Ed was supposed to call and preannounce my arrival. He hasn't, so I suggest she call her wayward son and make sure I'm what I claim to be. To allay any fears, I offer his cell phone number and suggest I wait in the car until she can check me out. She invites me in, but I insist, and moments later she waves to me and I enter, take the house phone, and chastise Eddie, who only laughs and assures me, "She's great. You'll have lotsa fun talking to her."

Within minutes of my unadvertised visit Lena has taken out family photo albums. She speaks openly about her famous son with a frank honesty that is both interesting and disarming, so much so that I find myself more intrigued about the fact she can be so forthright to a total stranger than I am about the details of a boy's life that still puzzles even her after all this time. As we look through page after page, she adds details in chronological order.

"You know that ski guy, Steve Podborski? Eddie was born in his grandmother's house. Uh-huh, Steve Podborski . . . on Queen Street."

There is one particular picture she comments on — a shot of 10-year-old Eddie with his father, lunch pail in hand, off to work for the afternoon shift. "Wax!" she cries out suddenly, pointing at the snapshot. "In the Ukrainian alphabet that was Bill's last name. It looked like Wax, so the immigration guys made a translation, I guess, and it came out Shack. Lots of people want to know how come we got that name," she says, shrugging, then saves me the trouble of asking.

"One of Bill's friends got a job in the smelter as a craneman, and I told him, 'You're as smart as he is. You should apply, too.' The difference was 42 cents an hour to 59 cents. That was lots of money then. When he got the job, he had to have a chest X ray, and they found he had a spot on his lung. Oh, boy! That was tough times, eh? He was 27 then and they shipped him to a sanatorium in Hamilton. The workers took up a collection for him, and Inco took over the mortgage on the house. Paid me $40 plus another $20 for the kids, and to make ends meet I rented a room, then I had to rent the whole house and went to stay with my mother. When Bill came back after 10 months and got back to work, we had money in the bank." She nodded to herself, making the ordeal of a 17-year-old mother with a baby daughter seem almost idyllic in its simplicity. By the time Eddie was born, stability had returned to the Shack household.

If there's a poster boy for the failure of the education system in the 1940s, he's Ed Shack. In his formative years, the ones right after kindergarten, when the most critical learning process begins in earnest, when habits are formed and routines established, Ed Shack moved through grades 1, 2, and 3, although he had missed much of each school year due to a tonsillectomy and a serious bout of appendicitis that was life-threatening ("They said he could have died," Lena says) on top of the usual childhood afflictions of measles and chicken pox. That he was what's referred to today as a slow learner is a given. That he would have been, should have been, put into a remedial class addressing his problem is another accepted fact today, but not there, or then. That he was labelled an incorrigible was a sign of the times.

A school picture shows a gangly boy, large for his age, sitting at the very back of a grade 2 classroom. It's a sad picture, because it depicts a time when what being a kid is all about is on the verge of coming apart.

Children are creatures of conformity. They do what others are doing at the same age. Their common denominators are going to school, playing games, fighting with the complexities of arithmetic and grammar, learning the basic social qualities of following acceptable behaviour, accumulating manners, and developing conversational skills and vocabularies filled with the constant use of terms of the day, vernacular peculiar to children. There are songs to learn, poems to memorize, games to master. For girls it is the singsong lyrics that accompany skipping. For boys it is the rough and tumble at recess. And for both it is a transition period accepted as the norm. For Eddie Shack it was none of these things.

When you consider he missed much of his class time due to illness, and the critical and irreplaceable lessons in phonics, alphabet, and other basics necessary for anyone to cope with what follows in the middle years of elementary school, it isn't hard to understand his lack of enthusiasm. Eddie Shack could not understand what was coming next. They just kept putting him through to the next level.

At an age when being a boy is almost as macho an experience as being a man, he learned to be a tough customer, a kid who was not only bigger physically than most in his age group but unafraid of or not suppressed by rules and penalties, homework, detention, or punitive discipline. He admits he fought a lot, and with reason. Kids can be cruel, and the ones at Wembley Public School in Sudbury were no different than anywhere else. Besides, he was a big dope, wasn't he, who could neither match them in schoolwork nor grades. That he was so cavalier about his plight was his only saving grace among his contemporaries, that and the ability to tough it out with anyone. When a grade 4 kid can beat the hell out of another in grades 6, 7, or 8, the word spreads fast in the school yard underworld.

Kids in the mid-1940s had to contribute to making their own recreation because there was no television, video games, cellular phones, or computers. For most children the only diversion from the real world was in the movie theatres of the day, at what the critics called "horse operas" or "oaters," through the escapades of Hopalong Cassidy, Lash LaRue, the Cisco Kid, Gene Autry, and Roy Rogers, the King of the Cowboys, a sharpshooter with Hall of Fame credentials. Roy fired a pearl-handled silver six-gun from the hip, knocking the desperado's weapon out of his hand, not tearing a finger off or anything so gory, just stinging the "black hat" enough to teach him a lesson. And Roy never ran out of bullets as he travelled the country at a breakneck gallop, his horse seemingly able to sustain Northern Dancer speed over hill and dale for however long it took to reach the next crisis. Roy often ran with Bob Nolan and the Sons of the Pioneers, a five-piece band that could set up and jam, complete with a stand-up bass, at the drop of a road apple.

All the entertainment was lost on Ed Shack, who didn't see many movies as a child, since he was already working on Saturdays and was fascinated by the things adults did. These were easy to accomplish because, for the most part, they were manual and required little in the way of study and nothing in the way of education. All it took was strength and a willingness to accomplish the mundane. That Ed Shack had an adult mind was one of his attractions for other adults whose company he functioned well in. He understood about successfully completing a task, about making ends meet, the rewards of money and all the doors it opened. Was this ability an acquired trait, or was it genetics, an ingrained, natural-born talent, like body structure and temperament?

He had an enthusiasm, a willingness, to succeed and an insatiable drive to get along in the adult world. Because of his character, size, strength, and attitude, coupled with the sheer enjoyment in almost everything he did, there were those who labelled him "a bit off." It's conceivable that in today's "safety-net" society there would be a lengthy list of help avenues to travel for a boy who was passed along the system without concern for his well-being or his education. Back then, though, he was labelled the kind of kid who would amount to no good, the sort of child to be humoured rather than helped.

With the exception of neighbourhood acquaintances, the street games and summer holidays, Ed Shack's world was populated by adults and their talk of business and the concerns of making a living. Long before most of his peers had throwaway cash, usually from Dad, the young Ed Shack was wealthy by any childhood standard, with his own folding money, his own independence.

Aside from hockey, his interaction with other children by the age of 11 was limited to the hours after school or on weekends. His sharing of the concerns over education, his knowledge of ongoing social events relating to school, which was usually the centre of the universe for his peers, was only through what he heard, what he was told, relayed by friends, teammates, and acquaintances. Like most children out of the mainstream, isolated through handicap or illness, he learned to cope with his lot, protect himself through the timeworn childhood defence of indifference. For the young Ed Shack truancy wasn't done on a dare, skipping school wasn't an occasional childhood prank, it was a way of life.

Al Biggs, a schoolboy chum from those early Wembley School days, remembers Eddie's sheer daring. "He was always a big kid, carefree, or so it seemed, because he'd play hooky as soon as the ice froze. He stood out in the hockey crowd in a town where there were some pretty damn good hockey players. Hell, he'd get the strap in the principal's office for playing hooky to go skating, and the next day he'd do it again on the creek right behind the school. You could see him out there from the goddamn school windows. He just didn't give two hoots about school or the strap." Neither boy had any idea at the time that they were destined to meet again 30 years down the road with Pop Shoppe.

For a while Eddie's dilemma may have had an envious appeal for those other children burdened with the mundane issues of homework and the constrictions of getting an education. He didn't have assignments to meet, nor was he operating under the limitations of balancing a budding social schedule with the confines of the classroom and all the responsibility that entailed. And, of course, he had money. From a very early age he was in every sense a free spirit.

But the costs of this autonomy were long-term. The price would reach far into the future and take a sizable cut out of his self-esteem. As Eddie tells it, his mother and father often had arguments over his going to school. Teachers couldn't handle him, and even when the powers that be stationed a teacher at one door and a second at another exit, he'd muscle past them and go home.

Now, as Lena flips through a few more pages, I ask her about Eddie's altercations with his teachers. "Eddie had a fight at school with the principal. They said he could never return, and the choices were to see a doctor or go to reform school in Niagara Falls. I felt so sorry for Eddie.

We took him to Dr. Dixon for an examination, and Eddie said the doctor asked him a lot of questions, told him to write something, and draw something. After all that, Eddie said the doctor thought he was crazy."

But later Dr. Tom Dixon, a local psychiatrist, would enlist the advice of a Toronto colleague, who visited the Shack home and told the parents their son "read backward," to use Lena's words. According to the Toronto doctor, who did no testing, Eddie was dyslexic, which was then a new learning disorder in the medical journals. There was nothing the Shacks could do now, he informed them, but perhaps they could later. He also told them that if the boy wanted to work, then let him. Their son, he said, would never read or write, nor would he ever be a student of any kind.

The question that inevitably comes up today is why would parents allow their child to go through life in such a fashion? Before we are too hard on Lena and Bill Shack, though, we should look at the times and situation in which their predicament occurred.

It was a time when being able to leave school to work, with parental permission, was an accepted practice. Apprenticeships were often started at age 14, and with little more than the basic skills of the three R's a boy could get by, in fact, was considered lucky to start learning on-the-job. In addition, many of the automated machines we now take for granted weren't even in existence, and manual labour wasn't completely in the hit-and-miss, low-level category some place it in today. Girls, for the most part, were considered to be prospective wives.

This was the situation the Shacks found themselves confronted with: a son who was quite frankly a terror to the school system, a kid who was more at home washing cars and learning a trade than he was learning the alphabet. Added to that, they had a "medical opinion" staring them in the face, one that told them their son would never be a student. It was either let him go to work or be the parents of a boy who was about to be institutionalized.

Another picture album brings into focus Eddie's beginnings in hockey, and his exit from schoolwork. A sheaf of clippings from his Maple Leaf days, yellowed and randomly scissored, also slides out onto the table. "Ah, do you want those?" she asks. "Eddie went skating at neighbourhood rinks. There was lots of them all over the place — the Rimsteads', the Campbells'," she says, pointing out the locations as if I knew them myself, "and at Riverside playground. When he tried out for a team, he was put in goal. A goalie! Bill went to watch him play all the time, and when Bill wanted to spend $25 on hockey, I told him he was spending money on foolish things."

When he was 11 or 12 years old, Eddie often told his mother he was going to play for the Toronto Maple Leafs. "Yes," Lena tells me now, putting a hand to her forehead as if to acknowledge an oncoming headache, "he was going to be a Maple Leaf. I felt sad, you know, a kid like that, because I thought, How the hell is he ever going to play professional hockey? I didn't even want him to play that stupid game. They were always getting hurt. I never saw him play as a boy. Bob Davidson, a scout for Toronto, came to the house when Eddie was 14 to talk to him about the Marlies, the Leafs' Junior A team. Davidson never came back, though, and we got the letter a week later, but Eddie couldn't wait." She turns the page of the photo album, then looks up as another thought crosses her mind. "He didn't play baseball. The coach told him not to even bother."

After a while we stop looking at the photo albums and move into the small kitchen. Wearing slacks, a T-shirt, and a pair of soft tennis shoes, Lena shuffles happily around the newly renovated room, telling me she's got a sore foot today. Quickly and confidently she rolls dough, then cuts the flattened ring of white into strips and again into squares. Her daughter Mary, who has joined us, fills each square with a spoonful of blended cheese and potato, folds them over, then seals the edges by crimping the two sides together. In a few minutes the table is covered with 200 perogies. Watching, I grin, remembering Eddie's story one afternoon about how as a boy he'd help his mother close up the perogies. "Every time I made a mistake," he told me, pointing at his much-publicized beak, "she'd pull my nose. Can you imagine me at a coke party? I'd be the first guy to go broke."

Just then Lena looks at me and says, with a sense of accomplishment, "It's a business. I've been doing it for nine years. I bought a new roof, an air conditioner, rebuilt this kitchen. Eddie said to me, 'Don't be chintzy. I'll give you the money.' But I told him no way. He's got two kids." Still thinking of Eddie's children, Cathy and Jimmy, as youngsters. "Eddie said, 'Don't save it for me. I got lots.'" Lena nods to herself, agreeing with this fact, but is still determined to underline how she can look after her own affairs. "I told Eddie it's a loan. That's it, a loan. It's what I do," she adds, waving a hand at the rows of perogies filling the kitchen table. Then she smiles and says, "It keeps me independent.

"In the old days," she continues, beginning on a new track, switching subjects on me yet again, "we used to cook gifts, little gifts, you know, bread or cabbage rolls, to give to people. What else could we afford? That's what people needed, but now I give the kids money. I'm not a good shopper. I tell them, 'I don't care what you do with it, otherwise I have to go out and buy something, and you think I'm gonna prowl the streets looking for a gift?' They say, 'You shouldn't send us money. You need it.' But I go by what my granddaughter told me a long time ago — do you know Cathy?"

I nod. Satisfied that I'm following the conversation, she goes back to work and resumes the story. 'You give me money, Baba,' Cathy said to me. 'I'll be able to have my own money and I can spend it.'" Lena chuckles at this notion of liberty. "So that's what I do. I give the kids money. I remember one Christmas when Norma and Eddie called and said they were drinking the wine I bought for them. I didn't buy no wine. I gave them $100. I said, 'Why did you buy that stuff for, anyway?'" (Later Eddie and Norma tell me they bought wine glasses, not wine.)

It's only now that I realize "the kids" include Norma, Eddie, and Mary, who sits silently across the table. To Lena Shack, a woman of 80, "kids" will always include her offspring as well as the grandchildren.

"So you give *Eddie* money?" I ask, incredulous.

"Yes, sure!" she says, waggling the rolling pin for emphasis. "For Christmas and on his birthday," Lena says with finality, switching once more to the topic of her son, "that's what he gets. That's it."

It's obvious that since our introduction only an hour earlier, Mary has been listening but has chosen not to participate in the conversation. From interviews with other people, I knew to expect this, since relations between Mary and Ed weren't as good as they might be. Still, I was hoping her curiosity might prompt her to speak. Then, suddenly, without being questioned, she offers an observation. "I never knew my brother. First of all, I was four years older than him, then he went away to play hockey at 14. My dad looked after him." Her last remark has a contentious tone.

"Dad would say to me, 'You'll lose your virginity if you have a bike. A girl doesn't need a bike.' Same thing with school. I needed money for a course to be a lab technician, but he said no. He said I didn't need to go to university, that girls didn't need that much education, that I would get married and have a family. To him it was a waste of time. But I can remember my dad saying, 'Here, take this cheque to Eddie. He's buying a car.'"

"When Bill said we should buy a car," Lena interjects quickly, "Eddie told him, 'Don't worry, Dad, I'll do all the driving.' Imagine, he was just a kid then, maybe 10, maybe younger, moving trucks in Dan Rain's back lane. He was with Dan all the time. He'd watch them work, then move the trucks and wash them. Now you can't get a kid to do that.

"Eddie was always working at Rain's meat market or at the Dominion supermarket [where he worked in the meat department under supervisor Chester Wilcox], and one summer, when he was 18, he came home from Guelph and his dad got him a job at Inco. The foreman came to Bill one day and said, 'Hey, remind that kid of yours that he's here to work, not sleep on the job.'" Lena shrugs. "Eddie ran around with girls too much. He had a white convertible at 16."

AT EXACTLY 12:00 NOON DAN RAIN KNOCKS AND COMES THROUGH the front door of the Shack residence, wearing a light jacket, green work clothes, boots, and a cap that he removes as soon as he's inside. Lena and he exchange greetings, an inside track that people who have known each other for years can use to make outsiders feel like fifth wheels because so much is read into so few words. By this time Mary has returned to her own house.

Dan Rain is a solid-looking man, not particularly tall or oversize, but compact and much fitter than you'd expect for a man in his seventies. The handshake tells it all: a large hand, firm and with the knowledge that there is more strength there if needed. His manner of speaking is precise and measured, and he appears to be at odds with the interview, almost as if I were from the *National Enquirer*. He seems reluctant and wonders what I'd like to know, then where I'd like to start, once he's satisfied I'm just looking for Eddie's beginnings.

Rain had an old-fashioned butcher shop that dealt in wholesale and retail meat. He also had a stall in the downtown Sudbury market and slaughtered seven or eight head of beef a week, plus chickens and pigs. Rain says Eddie's father was strict about his son having time to play hockey, but as soon as it was over, Eddie would run across the street to help wash the cars and three trucks and clean the refrigerators. Although Rain had three teenagers working for him, Eddie was by far the youngest. Saturday mornings were the start of a busy weekend. By 5:30 a.m. they'd load the trucks with meat, freshly killed chickens, smoked meat, bacon, ham, and sausages. It was hard work. A quarter of beef was between 125 to 200 pounds, and they'd load almost three tons into the trucks.

By 7:00 a.m. Rain's mother would cook up a big breakfast, and the young helpers would eat and eat. "When the kids took their lunch break, the restaurants around the market let them bring their own pork chops or veal and cooked it for them. Half a dozen chops for lunch was nothing to those boys."

At one point Rain employed 21 meat cutters, a half dozen behind the counter at the market, and that was where Eddie learned to read the scales, back in the days before digital readouts when you had to know where to look and which lines to follow. He learned quickly because his heart was in it, and he was good with the customers, entertaining in his own way, giving them the price with a little spiel, a smile, and a giggle. Right from the first time he went behind the counter Eddie gained regular customers, people who came to the market and waited for him to serve them. They loved to see him on Saturday mornings, and it didn't matter what the price was; they'd wait for the kid with a brush cut in a white butcher's smock.

Rain offers no explanation why he, a successful small businessman, took a chance putting a hooky-playing kid behind the counter, except to admit, "That's what Eddie wanted." Rain has no conclusion to draw from his prize salesman's lack of school deportment. Sitting in Lena's living room, he frowns only briefly, then begins to talk about Eddie's illiteracy as if he's considered it many times but given up trying to solve the problem.

"Eddie showed me very early on that he was ambitious, that he wanted to work. There was never any question about that. But it seemed he simply had no patience for learning to read or write." Rain spreads his hands to show puzzlement; the gesture is an unasked question. "You can't say he wasn't smart. I had lots of fellows who worked at the shop over the years who were good students yet couldn't seem to grasp reading scales or following instructions, but Eddie had very little problem, and when you told him once, he'd do it right time after time. He had something in him, something that was there as a kid behind the counter at the market, and he still does. He relates to people. I always trusted him, especially with the trucks. He wasn't reckless. He was reliable, and he was very honest, with himself and to others. He proved himself over and over."

Rain's sincere remarks take me back to a recent morning with Eddie as we drove along Toronto's Avenue Road. We had to slow down as we came up to a struggling trucker who was fighting the wheel, his eyes working over both mirrors as he tried to navigate a tight delivery in a small driveway. Eddie guffawed at the man's plight and recalled the time he was "reckless."

"I'm just a little guy, right, and I'm backing up Dan's truck after washing it. I can't see behind me very good as I reach for the clutch, and I hook the headlight and fender onto something. I don't know what's hangin' me up. I can't see it and I'm tryin' to turn the goddamn thing away from whatever it is, but it keeps soundin' worse. Holy sheepshit, I'm a nervous wreck by the time Dan gets there. But Dan, he don't get mad. Dan Rain doesn't bounce around from pillar to post. He'll always reason with you, sit down and talk things out. He was great.

"See, I'd wash the trucks and help Dan when we'd go out to the farms. He had one truck, I had the other. We'd be on the road comin' down a long hill and Dan would probably say, 'Oh, shit, I hope Eddie can make this corner.'" At that point Eddie did his best impression of steering a truck and working the clutch and brake, laughing uproariously. "But I could double clutch, eh? I'd go out to the gravel pit for him by myself, shovel a load onto the truck, and one time when I was going back to Dan's, the goddamn cows got in the road, so I blew the horn and scattered them bastards, all except one that I hit, breaking the headlight. Holy sheepshit, another talking session."

I smile to myself, then focus my attention on Dan Rain again, who now modestly acknowledges the indirect responsibility he had in shaping Eddie's life. He tells me how proud Eddie was to have his own money at a very young age. He didn't spend it on pop or candy. Instead, Rain taught him to keep his money in order, to be careful and cautious with it. Perhaps, I think to myself, this is the origin of Eddie's considerable respect for money.

During the time Rain "courted," as he puts it, his wife, Eddie would tag along with the couple when they drove out to the country to look at cattle. In 1949 when Rain married Helen, Eddie drove Dan's 1933 Ford in the wedding procession, blowing the horn. Dan grunts rather than laughs at the dusty memory, then reveals a rare grin, and my math tells me that Eddie was 12 at the time. "He's a good friend," Rain says quietly, keeping his private amusement private. "He comes to see Helen and me all the time — every time he's here. I know there were people who doubted him, but I was never surprised at his success."

Dan Rain gets ready to leave, but he waits for Lena to come from the kitchen so he can say goodbye. His hat still in his hand, he asks her if she has written to Santa Claus yet.

"Yes, I told him I want a young man," she says emphatically, and they both chuckle.

"We can dream, can't we, Lena?" Rain says. He doesn't put on his hat until he makes his way down the outside stairs.

AFTER A PEROGIE LUNCH, DURING WHICH I PRACTISE MY BROKEN Ukrainian, much to Lena's amusement, we get back to business. Sitting in a kitchen chair in front of the sink, a small knife in her rubber-gloved hands, potatoes in one large pail, peels in another, smaller one, she tosses the naked spuds into a colander in the sink. These will be tomorrow's batch.

"The potatoes come from a farm here," she tells me, nodding at the window. "Eddie came here one time and I told him that I had a farmer guy to go see, and I had to pick up a few bags of potatoes." She turns sideways to face me as if she's remembered an important item. "That time Eddie came here to visit he had a little black car, a Lexus, I think, and I said, 'What the hell did you buy a two-door car for? You're a family man.' Then I thought, He must have paid a lot of money for it and here's his mother not approving. So I didn't say anything else, but I wondered how we were gonna get three sacks into this little thing."

Lena resumes her work, sizing the growing pile of potatoes in the sink with a practised eye. "We went out there. As soon as we pull up, the man recognizes Eddie, and they talk hockey. Then Eddie says to him, 'Can you deliver these to my mom's house for that price?' And the farmer agreed. Mr. Rainville is his name, and for nine years he brings me my potatoes. A few times I've been asked to buy somewhere else for a better price, too, but I say no. I stick with him."

Looking at the pile of peeled potatoes soaking in a large pot, I'm reminded from personal experience in my mother-in-law's kitchen just how much hard work and arm strength are needed to turn them smooth, and I ask about it.

"I hand-mash them," she says. "How else? When I started, I used a mix master thing, see?" She opens one of the new kitchen storage drawers and points to a Hobart machine. "But it took me more damn time to clean it every day than it was worth. Besides, it made the potatoes . . . too whippy." She rubs her thumb and index finger together as if talking about money. "Then the kids got me a masher, a new one, but it didn't last. The handle broke, the wire thing bent, it was no good. I went back to using my old masher." She holds up the utensil that has obviously seen a lot spuds in its career. "This is the one I've been using for years. They don't make them like this anymore."

Once again Lena abruptly changes the subject. "There was a guy lived over there," she says, pointing, as if I might have some idea where "over there" is. "Jack Haddow was his name. He had a garage and Eddie knew him. His car was already full of young players going to Guelph for hockey tryouts, so he gave Eddie a train ticket."

Back in the early 1950s a local hockey scout would gather up a bunch of likely prospects and take them to a junior training camp. If the player made the team, the scout would get $50. It wasn't a draft, though, just a tryout. Apparently Haddow informed the Guelph Biltmores about Eddie's arrival, and even though Shack hadn't been specifically · invited, because of his age, his reputation had preceded him. So although he went to the tryout on speculation, he still travelled with impressive credentials. He had to change trains in Toronto and got on the wrong one. For some reason he threw away the lunch his mother made for him, but he did hang on to his skates. When he finally arrived in Guelph, it was 9:00 p.m. The Biltmores figured he had decided not to show up. Obviously they didn't know Eddie.

For the next while Lena and I sit quietly in the kitchen. The only sound is the potatoes boinking into the pot of water on a regular basis. Then, out of the blue, she says, "Eddie could have been a bad boy and turned out wrong. There was a time he was home in the summer, from Guelph, and I remember him and his friend at the time — Gary — stole some hubcaps, and Bill found out.

"Bill was so mad. He said Eddie couldn't do that kind of thing if he wanted to be a hockey player. Eddie told Bill they hadn't stolen the hubcaps off Sudbury people, but Americans. Tourists, I guess. Eddie said they figured they'd never see those people again. Little buggers, eh?

First, Eddie said they had hidden them in the garage, then he admitted he'd sold them to Mr. Penn, a neighbour. Bill made him get the $10 he'd gotten for them and took him over to Penn's to return the money and get the hubcaps. Then Bill put them in a sack and made Eddie toss them off a bridge into the river. He was so angry with Eddie, and Eddie didn't like his buddy Gary anymore.

"Yes, he could have gone wrong so easily," she repeats softly, pausing to think of how things might have been. Then she chuckles. Satisfied that the pail is full, she packs the peels into a bag and stores them on the countertop. "I'll take them out later," she reminds herself, wagging a finger as if I were her assistant. At that moment I realize it's time to go. I've taken up enough of Lena's day.

Returning to Toronto, I hook up with Bob Nevin and Jim "the Bird" Pappin, two of Eddie's former Maple Leaf teammates. We drink a few beers in Soupy's, a bar on Dundas Street. A hockey game is on the television and the constant clack of billiard balls intrudes from a table in the corner. Pappin sports a brown fedora turned up in front, which gives him the appearance of a taller Slip Mahoney from the Bowery Boys.

Like Eddie, Pappin is another Northern Ontario boy. Back in the 1960s the Leafs' lineup was dotted with northern kids. There was Dick Duff and Larry Hillman from Kirkland Lake, Frank Mahovlich from Timmins, and Tim Horton, George Armstrong, Al Arbour, Shack, and Pappin from the Sudbury area. Our conversation focuses on the standards for playing hockey in "Sooseberry."

"Nevvie," Pappin says, taking the tone of a patient teacher with an obstinate student, "you had to be an Inco kid to play at the arena in Copper Cliff. To be an Inco kid cost $8 a year and you had to be a card-carrying member to be eligible to play. For us kids it was like having a goddamn driver's licence, and only a handful of Sudbury boys were in the league at Copper Cliff. Eddie was one of them. He was a big, always friendly kid, whose dad, Bill, came to every game and practice. Jay McCarthy was Eddie's first coach, probably everybody's first coach."

"Get out," Nevin says, feigning astonishment.

"I remember the last year Eddie played in Copper Cliff. His team lost in the Northern Ontario Midget championships. They got beat by Noranda, Kent Douglas's team. Rollie Giacomin was in goal for Copper Cliff, but Eddie was their best player."

Pappin then takes us down a tortuous trail, pointing out that Douglas and Shack went their separate ways before meeting again. Shack headed to Guelph, Providence, the Rangers, then Toronto, while Douglas began with the Weston Dodgers and Kitchener Juniors, then did a stint in the Western Hockey League and four seasons with Eddie Shore, learning to be a defenceman at Springfield in the AHL. In 1962-63 Douglas came to Toronto and won the Calder Trophy as the rookie of the year. He also won a Stanley Cup with Shack.

"Eddie's family was very close," Pappin recalls. "His sister Mary was a great athlete, too, a speed skater, and probably the best female golfer in the area at one time. Lena cooked all that great Ukrainian food. They lived over on Horobin Street. Yeah, in fact, that was quite a neighbour-hood. Timmy [Horton] was there, Bryan Campbell's place was right behind Eddie's, and Paul Rimstead [the former *Toronto Sun* columnist] lived on Ontario Street.

"Back in Sudbury you rarely saw Eddie when you didn't see Irv Spencer. During the week, the two of them played pool, three hours at a time. They never left each other's side. We'd hang out at the International Hotel owned by Adam Borovich, a place they'd call a sports bar today. It was an ethnic area, you know, all immigrants, all miners." He shrugs and puts his hands out to indicate life doesn't get much better than that.

At that moment the front door of Soupy's groans open and the sub-ject of the history lesson marches in, complete with black cowboy hat, fashionable sport jacket over black leather slacks, and western boots. Across the horseshoe bar sits a guy named Dougie in a red Amstel hat, a Canadian Legion jacket, and no teeth. "I misplaced them. Two years ago," he advised us earlier. Dougie decides he wants to tell Shackie, who has parked himself directly across the way, a "fascinatin' story" about

King Clancy. After the fourth time Eddie has ignored him, and following a warning from Eddie to quiet down, Dougie admits loudly over the hubbub he's created that, yes, he is a bit hard of hearing. Eddie raises his voice, which is hardly necessary, and bellows, "Well, okay, but the rest of us ain't fuckin' deaf, y'know." Then Eddie buys Dougie a beer. Suitably fortified, Dougie sighs through a cheek-filling belch and settles in to observe quietly.

The conversation moves to playing in New York and the fact that the Rangers were rarely able to practise on the big ice in their home arena, using smaller facilities in Rye, New York, or a small rink above the Garden instead. Eventually the topic of discussion zeroes in on junior playing when Nevin produces a newspaper clipping he's brought along for the occasion. It shows the faces of the 1957 Ontario Hockey Association All-Stars, including Bob Nevin (right wing, Toronto Marlboros); Frank Mahovlich (centre, St. Michael's); Eddie Shack (left wing, Guelph Biltmores); Harry Neale (defence, Marlboros); Ron Casey (defence, Marlboros); and Bruce Gamble (goalie, Biltmores).

"Nevvie, you ever get sent down?" Eddie asks, tossing the clipping onto the bar without comment.

Pappin's fedora jerks up, and he points proudly to his chest, indicating he's been sent down. "I was. All the goddamn time."

Nevin only offers a slight grin and shakes his head. "Went right from the Marlies to the Leafs."

"Yeah, but everybody liked you. You were henpecked," Eddie says. Even understanding Eddie and his limited vocabulary, the three of us look at one another with puzzlement, wondering which word was supposed to be used in place of "henpecked." By this time the newspaper clipping has found its way into the hands of Dougie across the bar.

"Mahovlich was good," Dougie agrees in a voice that probably startled people in the washrooms.

Eddie looks up, his green eyes piercing and sparkling. "My last year of junior I was better than Frank. I had more goals than Bobby Hull or Stan Mikita, then I went to the Rangers and got fucked by Phil Watson.

He sent me down to Providence and he sent me down to Springfield for bein' honest."

Even Dougie is a bit taken aback, and he returns to his free beer.

A man in an expensive leather jacket has been watching the trio of ex-Leafs. Out of curiosity he asks, "Was Tim Horton from Sudbury?"

"Same block," Eddie advises without looking at the man. "There was me, Horton, Soupy Campbell, and Rimmer, who lived down the alley. Even back in Sudbury Horton was always running around the block, joggin', yuh know, stayin' in shape. Snooty guy, too. He couldn't fight, though."

"That's not the Soupy that has this place, is it?" Dougie blurts out, having patiently waited his turn in the conversation. The man in the leather jacket snorts, knowing full well it isn't, and just Eddie waves a disgusted hand at Dougie.

I'm reminded of a phone conversation with Bryan "Soupy" Campbell, ex-Sudbury grad, now living in Florida, who remembered Eddie Shack very well, although he was seven years Shack's junior. Soupy told me that every winter his father made an outdoor rink in his backyard, and that's where Eddie practised, hour after hour. Soupy recalled the constant *boom-boom-boom* of Eddie's shot hitting the side of the house. He said it drove his father crazy. One time they looked out their kitchen window and saw Eddie stretched out on the ice. Apparently he had been zipping around so hard that he had somehow knocked himself out. Soupy's father carried Eddie inside, and when he came to, warned him to take it easy. Eddie just said, "No, I should be out there playin' hockey." But perhaps the most interesting thing Soupy told me was that when Eddie was playing for Copper Cliff the league banned his slap shot. Apparently he was tearing up the goalies, nets, screens, seats, walls, and spectators.

Eddie's har-har-har jolts me back to the bar on Dundas Street. He's now regaling Nevin and Pappin with the story of that fateful train trip to Guelph in September 1951. I'm sure they've heard it before. But after hearing it from Eddie's mother's perspective, it's interesting to listen to the man tell it himself.

"Mom made me a big lunch. She had everything in there — cabbage rolls, sandwiches, the works. It was embarrassing. I got to Union Station and asked a guy which train to Guelph. He pointed to the track, but I got on the wrong coach, and next thing I know, I'm heading for Hamilton. The conductor told me to get off at the next stop, Mimico, or Port Credit, somewhere in the west end, and I had to hitchhike back. The asshole who picked me up didn't take me all the way, and when I was walkin' across the Spadina Bridge, I took the lunch and tossed it over the side."

Despite the many years that have passed, I still hear a note of regret in Eddie's voice. Little did he know crossing the bridge that day what awaited him. Guelph was only the beginning.

CHAPTER THREE

Guelph

It's early January, one of those days that reminds you the world isn't battleship grey. There's enough sunshine to make you remember summer.

"Turn the oven down to bake. It's getting to me," I request, snapping out of a heater-induced daydream.

Reaching for the control, Eddie asks softly, detached, "You got hooks for hands?"

We make the turn onto Campbellville Road at the Mohawk Inn and pass the raceway. While Eddie is pictured as a loud, nonstop talker, he can be rigged for silent running behind the wheel.

"Shackie, you ever play baseball?" I ask.

He only smiles wanly and grunts in answer. Then I remind myself about Eddie's mother's remark concerning the Sudbury coach who told Eddie he'd never be a ballplayer.

The countryside rolls by steadily and the comments come in a regular pattern. "Look at that place," Eddie says. "What do these people do all day for Christ's sake? They ain't farmers. What the hell's that?"

A sign comes up on the right. "Electrical Museum," I read out.

Eddie snorts and shrugs. "I thought it said Mushroom Farm."

Now we come to the area he's familiar with. "Yeah, this is it, Ronnie Joyce's place," he says, pointing a little finger without his hand leaving the wheel. "Holy sheepshit, what's *that* say?"

Once again I read for him. "Tim Horton Children's Foundation Offices."

"That's a pretty good deal, eh? It used to be Joyce's house, and he tried to flog it for years and couldn't, so he sells the place to himself." Eddie shakes his head at the sheer genius of the move. "Cagey, eh?" He chuckles as we make a hard, wheel-squealing left turn into the driveway.

"They used to have parties here." We crawl around the circular drive and head back onto Campbellville Road. The wheels are turning in Shack's mind. "Goddamn," he says, and slips into silence once more.

As we pull into Lou Fontinato's driveway, Eddie's former teammate on the Rangers and another graduate of the Guelph Biltmores, I relate how Leapin' Lou decided he didn't "want to say anything about Eddie, nothin' good, nothin' bad, just nothin'" when I drove down before Christmas for an interview date. "He felt bad because he didn't have my number, couldn't call and cancel, but he was great. Offered me a coffee . . . with a little hook in it."

"What?" Eddie asks, looking up suddenly as if I've said a key password.

"You know, a little shot of rye, I'd guess."

"Did he tell you about the time I ran him at practice?"

I nod as we pull up to the house.

"He's still tellin' everybody about that." Eddie chuckles and dismisses the incident with a brushaway hand. "He always thought he was so fuckin' tough, and if yuh hit him, he had to hit you back harder, right? We just kept it up until I ran him, hurt his goddamn knee. Back then he wouldn't say anything, but now he tells everybody about that hit."

Eddie interrupts himself as he gets out of the van to ring the doorbell, which goes unanswered, and gives up after peering through the porch windows. We drive across the road to the feeding barn, searching the outbuildings for signs of life. As we cruise by slowly, a line of indifferent cattle glance at us, and we head back onto the highway.

A little later we're holding the speed limit on York Road pointed toward downtown Guelph when Eddie inquires absently, "You seen Louie lately?"

"Hmmm," I mumble, instead of reminding him that we've done this bit already.

"Jeezuz, does he look like the *raft* of God or what?"

I've taught myself not to laugh, just write. Another Shackism for the record.

Only seconds slip by when he spots a small white house on the left side of the road. "Yeah, that's it. That's where Mickey McMillan sent me to school. A guy named Mel somethin'. He was a teacher at the 'formatory. I went there two times a week for private teaching. Long way to go to school, eh? Jeezuz, I had t'have a car to get an education." He hawhaws at his unnatural situation as a 15-year-old.

GUELPH'S DOWNTOWN STREETS CRISSCROSS THE URBAN HILLS AND valleys of pavement as if the engineers who made them had been coming off a four-day bender. No grid system here. The spires of Cathedral of Our Lady dominate the Guelph "skyline" from almost every angle, and that's not a bad thing. It gives you a central point to cling to, because streets change names if not directions.

The van rolls through the main streets, and although the city has grown, it's not long before we double back, make a turn on Carden, and crawl past the Guelph Memorial Gardens. "Look the same?" I inquire.

Shack bobs his head once and glances the other way, across the street. He points at a building, then says quietly as if we've intruded on a funeral procession, "That used to be the Green Rooster Restaurant where we hung out." The Via Rail station is next, I point at it and he only answers, "Uh-huh."

Then it dawns on me. He walked to the arena to start his career as a hockey player in Guelph, and I experience a strange feeling, as if reliving a late, late movie, the one with "comedy/drama — 1951" beside it in the listings. Suddenly, when I realize the train depot and the arena are close together, it strikes me how fortunate that must have been. It could have been much harder for the 14-year-old who found himself in a strange city on a dark September night, particularly since there was no one to meet him and he couldn't read.

Vague memories and yellowed clippings report that upon Eddie's arrival there were questions about what to do with a kid who didn't go to school or, as rumoured, had no education whatsoever. What kind of job should he be assigned? What would he do with all his free time?

Those first few days turned out to be a whirlwind of billets, tryout practices, and training-table meals. Although the Biltmores' management — Roy Mason, the GM of the Biltmores, and his son "Swat," who held the same position with the B team — liked what they saw of this Sudbury bumpkin, they waited as long as possible before they considered exactly what kind of work they should find for their newest player. When the question was finally posed, Eddie advised them not to bother. Since his arrival, he had already found himself not one but two jobs on his own.

In the early 1950s the league rules governing the Junior A teams said you could only have six players per team making $60 a week. In Guelph $15 went toward room and board, $25 was given to the player in cash, and the balance, $20, was banked. To Eddie the economics were even simpler if he intended to keep up the lifestyle to which he was accustomed.

"You either made $20 a week in Junior B, or $30 to $60 in A. So I got a job at a meat market, then I got another job on a coal truck. I was real strong for my age, working like that, carrying quarters of beef, half a pig, boxes of chicken, bags of coal — sumbitch!" Eddie shakes his head as he muses over the workload.

We take a circuitous route through the downtown streets, past the old Royal Hotel, to a restaurant still doing business at a corner location. "I think it was called the Trinnan," he says, unsure as he sometimes is when it comes to pronunciation. The name is Trianon, a fact I discovered in earlier interviews, but now the sign is different, something even Eddie is able to discern as I advise him the Trianon is now Van Gogh's Ear. When he hears that, he does a double take.

"The *what*?" he roars. I tell the story of the world-renowned artist, and for a brief instant Eddie squints at me with blue-green eyes and grins with a look that says, "Get outta here." Then he begins the har-har-har he uses when he finds things difficult to accept or a little overstated.

"Oh, my God," he snuffles, thinking over Vincent Van G's predicament. "I gotta tell yuh. Get a little pouty, big boy, sulk a bit, yuh know things ain't always gonna go just the way you want them to, but holy sheepshit, leave yer fuckin' ears alone." Then he breaks into howls of laughter once more. "You 'arthurs' are goddamn dangerous. I'm glad I never got an education."

As Eddie brakes for a stop sign, an elderly man with a cane slowly crosses in front of the van. When Shack rolls down the window, the light of recognition spreads across the man's face.

"How the hell yah doin'? Got a bad wheel, eh?" Eddie barks, drawing every eye on the street with the volume. The man waves and grins broadly. "See, I knew that old bastard would know me. Probably paid to watch me play and thought I was a big dummy, too," he adds, his moustache twitching blissfully.

We drift up to the traffic lights at Woolwich and Fountain. The police station is dead ahead, and as the light turns green, Eddie eases out into the intersection to make a left turn. A woman approaching the other way is also making a left turn ever so carefully while trying to see around our van. As she accelerates, so does Shack, going around her passenger side door, then making a quick right to continue straight ahead rather than complete the turn.

Eddie howls with laughter and briefly covers his eyes. "She's probably sayin', 'That stupe's a worse driver than me.'" He cackles, his eyes almost disappearing into his animated grin. At the police station he makes a U-turn under the No U-turn sign and parks directly in front of the main doors beside one of four No Parking standards.

Inside, a young constable gets up from his desk, approaches the counter, and asks, "And what can we do for you, Mr. Shack?" Meanwhile, his desk sergeant, who's on the phone, waves a greeting and nods. Obviously no introductions are necessary. They go to considerable trouble to reach John Gillis, a retired cop, and one of Eddie's former Guelph Biltmore teammates, but can only come up with a home phone number.

"Yep, we had to listen to John tell us all those stories about you and him," the senior man observes as we get ready to leave, telephone number in hand.

"John was a good player, you know. He wasn't just chopped chickenshit," Eddie says, intending a serious compliment, although the policemen don't look convinced. After we say goodbye, we step out into the sunny but brisk January afternoon in time to hold the door for two officers leading a handcuffed man into the station.

"G'day, g'day," Shackie greets the prisoner, "how she goin' t'day. Fuckin' cold, eh?" The culprit breaks into a smile while the officers try to hide theirs. There's no ticket on our van.

DURING A HOCKEY CAREER, A PLAYER ENCOUNTERS A STRING OF improbable roomies, from kids' tournaments where the "boys" get to stay up all night, to the Junior A and B training camps where it's usually a lottery and total strangers are paired for the first time. Next come the boarding houses with substitute families, places where limited "freedom of the house" doesn't include run of the rec room TV. On the road it's buses and who sits with whom. Then, moving up hockey's ladder, there are shared apartments, sometimes entire houses, and a never-ending string of cookie-cutter hotel rooms of the chain variety.

Team management policies differ at the pro level. The stars get their own choice, usually a combo of veterans, while naive management puts negative and positive influences together, hoping the apple's worm will turn. Usually, though, good loses to bad, and the team wins two worms for the aggravation of one.

Coaches prefer to match those long on experience with the blatantly gullible, the rebellious with the studious. They want defence partners to live, eat, and snore together; goalies to cry on each other's shoulder, and link left and right wingers to wonder about paired centres.

Rarely does a team allow a player to select a roomie. Even rarer still is consideration for one, or the other, cellmate ever part of the equation. The exception is with the exceptional, the senior, more experienced players. The stars get to pick their roommates.

In the case of John Gillis and Eddie Shack it was only Sudbury geography that made them partners in residence. Gillis arrived as a right winger, one of the kids who came down from Sudbury in Jack Haddow's carload of prospects, the ride Shack missed. From Garson, just outside Sudbury, and two years older than Eddie, Gillis had also come to the Biltmores' camp on speculation, looking for something other than northern hockey and a career in the mines. He made the A team coached by Alf Pike, who had won the Memorial Cup the year before, while Eddie started with the Bs. But it wasn't long before they were teammates. Gillis, of course, had no idea then that his roomie would become one of the most recognizable faces in the country. But he did have an inkling that there were bigger things in store.

The Biltmore club policy was weekly room-and-board allotments plus educational support. Those going to high school had their books and other essentials looked after, and in the case of John Gillis, the team paid his tuition to business school, a fact that became significant as a career choice later in life. Gillis played two seasons with the Biltmores and one year with the Montreal Royals in the Quebec Pro league, but a detached retina ended his career and he moved back to Guelph, eventually joining the police force and serving for 34 years until his retirement as an inspector with the Criminal Investigation Division.

When it came to team policy in Eddie's case, Mickey McMillan, the team president as well as the head honcho at Biltmore Hats, was appalled to find he had a player who could neither read nor write. So he personally arranged to have Eddie see a private tutor, an English instructor at the Guelph Reformatory.

A FEW WEEKS LATER I FINALLY CONNECT WITH JOHN GILLIS AT HIS turn-of-the-century farmhouse off the Eramosa Highway outside Guelph. I'm comfortably seated in Gillis's living room which, with its honey-coloured, tongue-and-groove walls wrapped around a large stone fireplace, is something out of a "gracious country homes" magazine. And as I settle into the warmth of my new surroundings, my host launches into his recollections of those early junior hockey days.

"Our first rooming house together was on York Street. I can remember we'd sit around on Sunday night and watch *The Ed Sullivan Show*. But our landlady got us out of there, claiming we were rude. Hard to believe, huh? Next we went to a place on Glasgow Street. They had an upstairs shower, but you had to light the gas heater to get hot water. One day, after Eddie had his shower, I announced I was going to take one, too. I went in and turned on the gas, or so I thought, but Eddie had never turned it off. All I'd done was turn it up a notch. When I lit the match, *kaboom*! It was really some kind of explosion. My eyebrows were gone, the door to the heater blew off, and the force knocked me flat on my ass. That was it for the landlady. She told us to leave before we wrecked her house any further. Same thing happened on Elizabeth Street. No explosion, but we didn't stay too long there, either. The landlady said we ate like horses."

Gillis tells me that Joe Verone, the Biltmores' trainer, always waited until 10:00 or 10:30 p.m. to check if his players were at home. As soon as they got the call from Joe, Shack and Gillis would take off and do whatever they wanted. Still, it was around this time that Eddie began to get more serious about learning to read. He laboured over 'Mary, Jane, and, Peter' primers and was tutored by a private teacher paid for by the team, but it was tough. Buses didn't run out to where the teacher lived, so Eddie had to drive. Actually Shack was the only player coach Eddie Bush allowed to have his *own* car. He was also the only player with a job and the bucks to own one.

As for the schooling, Eddie got more and more frustrated at the slow progress, then embarrassed, and eventually gave up altogether. According to Gillis, though, he had tremendous potential as a junior, thanks to his size, strength, and speed.

In those days Guelph was an even smaller town and the players usually had to supply their own entertainment. There wasn't much to do except play hockey and certainly little in the way of night life. Mostly they hung out at restaurants such as the Green Rooster, Trianon's, and the Voorvis, and there were Wednesday dance nights in a place over Ryan's clothing store on the main street. For the most part, though, they lived and breathed hockey full-time. Still, when the opportunity presented itself, the young Biltmores weren't afraid to go farther afield, say, Buffalo or New York City.

"If I remember correctly," Gillis says, "myself, Glen Ramsay, Bill Sweeney, and Shackie went to this club in Buffalo we'd heard about where a major singer of the day was working — Julius La Rosa." He shrugs off my grin. "What can I tell you? This was the early 1950s before rock and roll. We had a Sunday off with nothing to do, and Ramsay borrowed a car. We didn't think it was a good idea to let Eddie drive down there, which turned out to be a great idea.

"When we arrived, we marched right in and they treated us like royalty. Nobody asked for any ID, we ate like horses and, of course, there was lots of beer. We were determined to be big shots and leave the waitress a large tip because she'd been so good to us. Then the bill came. For openers there was a cover charge. We'd never even heard of a cover charge in Sudbury or Guelph. I think we had $60 between us, and the bill came to $80. You should have seen the faces on the *big shots* then."

Gillis grins sheepishly at me and shakes his head. "First, they were going to call the cops and arrest us. Then we started pooling our valuables. Hell, can you see four dummies like us with 'valuables'? Our money was our 'valuables.' But between the watches and rings, which at first they didn't want anything to do with, we got the manager to agree to let us off the hook and we'd come back with the money. He was really cheesed off with us. And I suppose it wasn't difficult to figure out we were underage, if not borderline, and calling the police wasn't going to look good for him. So he gave us shit, took the money we had, and gave us back our 'valuables.' I don't remember him inviting us to drop in on our next trip back, either."

The last year Gillis and Shack played together, Gillis worked during the summer in the Falconbridge timber yard with Al Arbour, who was with the Detroit Red Wings at the time. Eddie and Gillis would often go back to the beach at Grand Bend on weekends. They'd drive down from Sudbury on Saturday, get a room at the hotel, and be back to work on Monday morning. On Sunday they'd hold out as long as possible and drive home at the last minute. In order to do so, they worked out a driving arrangement. Eddie had a clock on his dashboard, and they agreed, since they were both whacked out and tired, that they'd drive in one-hour shifts. Gillis won the toss and got into the back seat first. An hour later Eddie woke him up and said, "Your turn." Then Gillis drove for an hour, woke up Eddie, and they'd follow the routine again. It took Gillis a couple of times to realize they weren't making much headway when Eddie was driving. He watched Shack the next time, pretending to sleep, even faking a little snore, and sure enough, Eddie was turning the clock ahead as soon as he figured Gillis was asleep.

We take a tour of his known rooming houses and jobs. He supplies a play-by-play, impressing me with the memory process that after more than 40 years still allows him to find places without the benefit of street signs, as if he were a huge Canada goose in a cowboy hat and snakeskin boots.

"Is this Howitt Street?" he asks. "Mrs. White's, I think it was the first year." Next we proceed to the small brick bungalow of Frank and Vi Lapard, on Yorkshire, followed by a little white bungalow on a slight rise facing the park on Kathleen Street. "The club was paying those poor people $15 a week for room and board. Geez, the way we ate, no wonder there were a lot of moves."

He remembers the jobs, as well: Palmer Coal on Exhibition Street and the Hales Meat Market. "Monday was slaughtering day. We'd go over to the stock pen and kill a dozen, maybe 15, head of cattle. Bleed 'em an' gut 'em. Then, late in the afternoon, I'd go to practice."

Our next stop on the tour is Barber Building Blocks. "They made cinder blocks. Don't think bench-pressin' those buggers onto a flatbed truck wasn't hard work. That was some kinda muscle-buildin' job for a 16-year-old. But they had this one job where a guy ran a mechanized dolly that brought the bricks for the dummies to lift onto the truck," he says, pointing to himself and raising his eyebrows, ready to laugh. "Kiss my ass, pal. I was only there a week and I'm runnin' the dolly. Hell-oooooo, Dolly. Show me the money.

"I had a Meteor Rideau when I was here, pale green and cream, but I did some customizing, y'know, made the chrome come around and join. Then I had them paint a black patch in between the chrome. Frank Lapard was really good at fixing things, and we lowered it two inches. It had dual mufflers, whitewalls, a three-colour paint job. Whooooo-eeee. I was a hotshot then.

"Later came a convertible, with dual exhausts, Hollywood mufflers, fender skirts, exterior-mounted sun visor. I'd put her in low and goose the shit out of it down the hill to the little curve and make a U-turn. See?" he asks, pointing down the road to a sign that says No U-turns. "Then I'd do it all over again. I liked it when it rained. Those mufflers really barked.

"Sometimes, when the Bilts had a team meeting, I'd be drivin' the coal truck, so I'd double-park in front of Ron McNaughton's smoke shop across the street from the rink and leave the keys in the truck in case I was boxin' anybody in. Jeez, sometimes I'd come out and the fuckin' truck would be a block away from where I'd left it. Naw, I never worried about it bein' gone. Who the hell would steal a coal truck? It'd cost yuh a goddamn fortune in dry cleanin' just gettin' in and out. Come to think of it, I used to take Ron's car and wash it, then go for a little spin. He had a brand-new '54 two-door Meteor hardtop, a beautiful car. At the time I was drivin' a 1927 two-door Chev, one of them old-time shitboxes. It even had curtains in the windows, the works. You had to retard the spark, stuff like that, and it wasn't too fast, but I used to drive it to school when I was goin' to that tutor's place by the 'formatory.

"Back then all the extras you needed in a car were a defroster fan and a car radio with 12 push buttons, and you were the man. I had one of those radios, and believe me, I was the happiest guy this side of North Cobalt. I had a 1938 Dodge six-cylinder. I couldn't afford a V-8, but I decked it out in plaid fender skirts, yeah, plaid, with the word *Ed* on them. I'm tellin' yuh, I was *twice* as goddamn happy as the dope from North Cobalt."

One summer Eddie went home to Sudbury and worked on the natural gas line going through the city. Jim Pappin recalls, "That summer Eddie was all over town, leaning on a shovel, with no shirt, plenty of muscles, and a great suntan. He was always laughing and seemed as happy as a lark. By then everybody in Sudbury knew Eddie Shack, the 16-year-old with a convertible and pockets full of money."

About that summer with the pipeline, Eddie says, "I was on the shovel for a while, but you know me, I wanted to get on the machines. They had this one piece of equipment called a cutter, I think. It looked like a giant knife blade and it sliced down through the sod and shit. You'd go along cutting a line one way, turn around and come back to make a line the other way about two feet apart, then the back hoe dug the ditch for the pipe. *Ka-chung, ka-chung, ka-chung.* I'd ride that sumbitch all day, and every once in a while when we were going through concrete, the chips would start to fly, landin' on people's cars. But I'd just say, 'Fuck it!' and keep on going. The best was when we were behind John Bizar's jewellery store and he came runnin' out the door, screamin at me and wavin' his arms like a lunatic, 'cause the good china was fallin' off the shelves. *Ka-chung, ka-chung, ka-chung,*" he mimics again, rocking back and forth as he haw-haws.

We cut off Gordon Street, turn into a crescent, and stop at a house. All Eddie says is, "Joe Verone's place," then he walks up to the door and rings the bell. After a brief wait, a young man who looks like a student parks his bike and goes up the steps of the house next door. "D'ya know if the people livin' here are around?" Eddie asks the student.

The kid just shrugs. He doesn't recognize Ed Shack.

"Maybe Joe's gone to Florida," I suggest as Eddie settles in behind the wheel.

"Joe Verone's dead," Eddie responds matter-of-factly. For some unknown reason, perhaps because of a tugging memory or due to a sense of association, Eddie felt it necessary to stop by "and shoot the shit" with the people who now live in the former Biltmore trainer's house.

We return to the corner of Wellington and Gordon where Tailgate Charlie's sits on the lot once occupied by Hillbilly Shack's, one of two bars Shack formerly owned. Now the only common ground they have is the empty parking lot. Both names are defunct, null and void, dead. Still, it's a busy area set between a Taco Bell and a Wendy's and sharing the street and main intersection with Kentucky Fried Chicken, McDonald's, and Red Lobster.

The closing of Hillbilly Shack's and another place of the same name in Orangeville is still a sore spot with Shack, and he confesses little about the reasons other than that he got screwed and relates how he padlocked the places himself, rescuing all the TVs and salvageable items he could. Any questions regarding the dispensation of justice only bring a gruff response.

But for the time being he's preoccupied again, looking for a landmark and searching for a point of reference as we make our way to a place called Amici's for lunch. Sitting at the bar, he remarks how good the soup is and opts for seconds. A patron asks him for an autograph, which piques the interest of our waitress. Eddie jokes with her after she asks him how he likes his bloody Caesar. "No, no, how do *you* like it?" he shoots back. When he sees she isn't following him, he answers for her. "I thought you were gonna say, 'In the morning.'" Then he guffaws at his own line. "You gotta watch these days, eh? I could get two minutes for harassing."

Later, as we get ready to leave, he tells me what he was searching for before we arrived at Amici's. "One night I was speedin' down Woolwich Street right outside here," he says, pointing to the door, "and I saw a cop hidin' in a driveway. As soon as I blew by him, his lights come on and I put it to the floor, barrellin' down the street until I got a good lead. Then I switched off the lights and made a left turn into a gravel pit. There I was bouncin' around, sand and pebbles flyin', water, mud, cow shit, everything, until I got behind a ridge. I got out, climbed to the top, watched the cop go by, then ran back to the car and drove downtown.

"The cop picked me up walkin' along Wyndham Street and asked if that was me speedin' on Woolwich. A real Sherlock Holmes. Like I'm gonna say yah. I said nope. Then the cop asks me, 'How come your car is so dirty?' I looked really stunned, which isn't tough for me, and said I had no fuckin' idea. He knew he had me, but he couldn't prove it. Them bastards wanted to get me so bad after that." He chuckles as he searches for a sleeve in his jacket.

"Eddie, you can't read or write, you can't fill out the application, how the hell did you ever get a licence?"

"Ah, no problem. When I went for my licence, there was a $100 fine for lyin'," he says, taking out his money clip, peeling off an imaginary bill, and pretending to stick it in my shirt pocket. "I got the tester to fill out the form. I didn't know left from right. All I knew is he'd say, 'Turn,' and I'd turn, I had to guess which way he wanted to go, and I passed."

When we get into the van, Twiggy is so happy to see us again after 90 minutes in solitary that he forgets to bark at me for stealing his seat. Eddie is now in full throttle, and he continues his story as he scratches Twiggy's ears.

"The real reason I didn't stop for the cops that time in Guelph is one day in Sudbury I was in my '38 Dodge with a buddy named Emile Lavar an' this other guy with a car comes along an' we get to yakkin'. He says he can beat me. I tell him bullshit, and we get out on Highway 17, headin' for North Bay. Next thing, I look in the mirror, and Jeezuz, it's a cop. So I say, 'Let's get outta here.' Emile starts wailin', 'No, no, pull over and we'll plead insanity.' They give me a ticket. Sumbitch didn't even have'ta chase me. Cost me $87, and I lost my licence for three months. No big deal, though. I was workin' at Dominion [supermarket] that summer, so I had it paid off before I was even able to get the goddamn licence back. But my poor mom was so worried, scared shitless, in fact. She musta thought her little Eddie was goin' to the 'formatory. Hell, I was only 13.

"My poor mother," he repeats, shaking his head and winding down to a low chuckle. "She felt sorry for me. Every time I went out the door she musta thought to herself, There he goes. I hope he comes back." Then, as though he's been tapped on the shoulder, he picks up on the discarded chain of thought. "But I learned my lesson back in Sudbury. There's no goddamn way I was gonna pull over on Woolwich and wait for that fuckin' cop."

As we leave Amici's parking lot, Eddie aims the car a short distance down the street to a Speedy Auto Glass shop, climbs out of the van, and strolls in with Twiggy a shoe length behind. The store manager is surprised, as are a customer whose car is being worked on and an employee who, almost frozen in place, openly gawks at Shack.

"Remember I had'ta come in here?" Eddie asks by way of introduction, and the manager nods, still skeptical, still unconvinced that this is just a visit, suspecting a glitch in whatever window problem was serviced. By the time we leave, the manager has loosened up considerably but maintains the attitude of a man waiting for the punch line of a joke. Meanwhile his assistant has relaxed a bit, too, but continues to stare as he leans on the perplexed customer's car. The latter is in his early twenties and is obviously not a hockey fan. He clearly has no idea who the stray cowboy is or why he's here.

In the van Eddie offers an explanation. "You gotta stop in and say hello, right? Every time you show up it shouldn't be with your goddamn hand out looking for a favour, or some help, eh?"

EDDIE'S HOCKEY TIME IN THE ROYAL CITY SPANNED FIVE SEASONS. IT was a junior career that gained momentum with each passing summer until he turned professional in the fall of 1957. For Shack it was a period of success, injuries, recognition that far outstripped that of his teammates, and notoriety as a maverick. A borderline delinquent, he was a player with much promise travelling a road with many pitfalls.

The parent club in New York considered him a diamond in the rough and their chief scout, Jack Humphreys, and others within the organization regularly monitored and scrutinized all avenues of progress. Eddie's status as a junior climbed to the level of "untouchable," and by the time he reached his final year he was touted as one the best prospects in Canada, if not *the* best.

Not lost in the annual ratings of players with ability was Shack's talent for playing the kind of hockey that drew exultant cheering from the hometown fans, and strident booing from those in the cities around the league. He was a marketable commodity, and the fans came to see him even as a teenager. It was never dull when Shack was in the game, or on the ice.

In all the musty clippings and tattered cutouts of Shack's past, one noteworthy squib in particular, on December 30, 1954, was a column by Al Austin in the *Guelph Mercury*, after Shack, age 17, had missed 16 games of the season with a broken ankle. Austin wrote: "Shack is another one who is playing much more thoughtfully. He generally looks before passing now, and he is slowly approaching a gracefulness that one day might well make him a great player." This may be the only time the words *graceful* and *Shack* were used in the same story. But other hockey people were taking notice, too.

Billy Harris, another young player at the time and an NHL-bound chattel of the Leafs, had no idea that Ed Shack, the up-and-coming star of the New York Rangers, would ever suit up as a teammate on a line with him. They would play together on three Stanley Cup-winning teams.

"I was with the Marlies in 1955 when we won the Memorial Cup, Shackie would have been 18 when we beat Guelph in one quarter final. I think Eddie and Tommy McCarthy were in the hospital, and I remember the story about Eddie Bush saying the Biltmores would have given us a better battle if we had Tommy in the lineup. Apparently Eddie heard the comment in their hospital room, and Shackie is supposed to have thrown the radio out the window."

Brian Webber, a right winger who played the wrong side just like Shack, says, "We all came up from 'Swat' Mason's Junior B Biltmores, The Masons owned a grocery and pharmacy store up the hill on Gordon Street, right by the college. Eddie came up to the A team first, but by the time we finished, the scoring leaders were Bill Sweeney, Shack, Frank Mahovlich, and me. Friday night was hockey night in Guelph. Four thousand people turned up like clockwork. When we went to Toronto to play the Marlies, the other end of a doubleheader would be St. Mike's and the Ottawa Junior Habs, and there'd be 16,000 people at a game. It was a different time and a different age."

Webber remembers Shack's influence in the city with both young and old. "My mom, Velma, always laughed and said, 'That Eddie, he'd fight with his own shadow.' She went to all the games. Then there was the Guelph parent who called Eddie Bush to complain that kids at the school were smoking cigars and blamed it on the fact Eddie was going around town smoking them. He had that kind of impact, because as a player he was so damn exciting. He picked up the puck behind our net and flew down the ice like a runaway tank. He was a full load, I'll tell you."

As for coach Eddie Bush, Webber recalls that in one of their much-publicized dustups, Shack was taking off his equipment in the dressing room when Bush fired a pair of skates toward Shack, hitting the wall just above his head. "I think it was in Barrie, but wherever it was, *that* was scary stuff." Another morning, after a lost playoff game in St. Catharines, Bush tore a strip off Eddie, telling him that he'd seen him cruising the downtown streets at midnight. Bush kept screaming at Eddie, who finally got up to leave. But Bush wouldn't let it go and kept yelling into Eddie's face. They almost came to blows. Shack was either benched or suspended; Webber can't remember exactly anymore. At the next game the team went out for the start of the first period without Eddie, but word came to the bench that Shack was in the dressing room with Jack Humphreys, the Rangers' chief scout. Humphreys said the Rangers wanted Shack on the ice, so that's what happened.

At that point in his career, if not sooner, Shack had come to understand the professional way. He knew that he was good enough to force the issue, that he could afford to let his ability do the talking, and to hell with dictatorial directives by coaches. He had learned to appeal to the higher court of talent over procedure, value over principle. The New York Rangers had a gold nugget, and Eddie Bush was a junior coach, a custodian, an interim guardian, nothing more and nothing less.

On another occasion the Biltmores played the Waterloo Siskins and Eddie took a city bus for a ride around the parking lot. The driver went ballistic. This prank must have been a Biltmore tradition, because three years later, in Geneva, Switzerland, aspiring centre Bill Sweeney took a bus for a preemptive tour while Muzz Patrick, Phil Watson, and the Rangers cooled their heels in the hotel lobby. Sweeney's shoulder pads never touched the inside of a Ranger jersey again. As Sweeney's friend Don Cherry points out, "In those days the Rangers held all the cards. What the NHL didn't have to put up with was a smartass, and Billy was a smartass. And Eddie was as talented as Sweeney, but it didn't matter." There were other ways to snap people into line.

Webber concedes that Eddie Bush was tough. One New Year's Day the Biltmores had a game at home with the Peterborough Petes, and

Bush told the players to report to the arena dressing room at 11:55 p.m., the night before.

"He once told me, no make that threatened me, 'How'd you like to finish your schooling in Barrie?' That was the kind of thing you said to kids in those days, to scare the hell out of them. I know it scared the hell out of me. I lived in Guelph, what the hell did I want with room and board in Barrie? Then one Sunday we played the Marlies in Toronto at the Gardens and to this day I still don't know what it was I had done, or he thought I had done, but he was ticked at me for something. Bush was shouting at me from the doorway while I was in the shower, saying he wasn't going to let me on the team bus, and saying since I was so goddamn smart maybe I'd better get dressed, get out on Carlton Street, and start looking for a ride home.

"Hell I was a kid, he was God. If he said you weren't on the bus, well, you weren't on the damn bus. But Shackie came up chin-to-chin and said, 'Leave him alone,' deflecting the tirade away from me and onto him. And that's exactly what Bush did, started in on Eddie. I managed to get on bus, but it was close. That's the kind of guy Eddie Shack was, a great teammate, and I've often gone back and thought over that particular incident."

Bush was of the old school, the kind of coach who believed you had to play through the pain. When Eddie crashed into the boards during a game and hurt his foot badly, Bush told him to keep his skate on so the ankle wouldn't swell. Of course, Eddie being Eddie, he still somehow managed to limp to Billy McCreary's place for dinner after the game, thinking the foot was just sprained. But when he had it X-rayed at a hospital the next day, he found out that his ankle was broken. As for Eddie Bush, he was quoted as saying, "You know how tough that kid Shack is? He played a whole period for me on a broken ankle."

The two Eddies had a typical coach/player love/hate relationship. Junior coaches have always had an affinity for their stars, the ones who make them look good, the ones with the most talent, the guys who keep the people upstairs interested in what the coach is doing with the team's blue-ribbon mustangs. Bush was the personification of "crusty," a hard-nosed, no-nonsense man who didn't take kindly to snotty kids or wise guys.

If there are those who remember Bush as a man of the times, a tyrannical coach, a despot in a suit, Shack himself doesn't see it that way, certainly not in retrospect. "He was good for me, made me get serious. He was the one who told me I could make it in the NHL. The time we had that blowout at the team meetin', I got in the car and drove to Kitchener or somewhere down the road to cool off, because it wasn't just Bush. In Junior you want to do well, and the club, they expect so much. There's a lot of pressure on both sides."

John Gillis says, "With Eddie Bush you knew where you stood, and he played you when he thought you were playing your best. He didn't like showboats, and Shack wasn't a showboat, contrary as that may seem in light of what transpired later in his hockey career. In Guelph he may have started the 'entertainer' label, but it was only because he played full-bore all the time, not because he was into antics, playing the fool, or clowning around."

Ron Wicks, another Sudbury native who went on to star in the NHL as a referee, remembers talking with Eddie Bush and gaining some insight into the relationship between the two. "Seems every Monday Eddie bought a car from Bush, who managed a car lot. There he'd pick up a load of cut-rate hats at Biltmore and drive back to Sudbury, making stops along the way — diners, gas stations, those kinds of places — flogging the hats. He'd either sell the car to a waiting buyer, or to Sam Sutton, a dealer up there, then hitchhike or catch a ride back to Guelph in time for Wednesday practice. One time Bush told me Shackie came into the dealership with a wad of money, profits from selling hats and cars, and asked, 'How much is that convertible?' Bush told him what it was worth. 'Will this cover it?' Shackie asked, and when the coach finished counting the roll, he had the price plus a thousand to spare. Bush said there was never any doubt in his mind that Eddie would go a long way."

There also wasn't any doubt that Eddie had counted the money before he handed it over to Bush, probably testing him. If there was one thing Eddie didn't need any lessons in, it was finance, plus he'd had a lengthy background in the vagaries of folding money, courtesy of Dan Rain.

As his time in Guelph drew to a close, Shack was touted as one of the best, a surefire NHL prospect who couldn't miss. The *Globe and Mail* had this to say on February 27, 1957:

> Turk Broda rated the top pro prospects as Mahovlich, Nevin, and Shack. There were some raised eyebrows over the selection of Nevin over Shack. "Nevin had as good a season, and he's a year younger than Shack," [Broda said] but added why he still thought Shack was no worse than the top three. "He's improved tremendously, because he was on the chippy side last year, now he's settled down."
>
> Eddie Bush disputed the rating. "No, sir, I don't consider Mahovlich a better prospect and I can tell you why in one word. Temperament. The other teams ride Mahovlich and he puts on the brakes. They gang up on Shack, too, but he controls his temper. That makes him a better team man." Bush went on to rate his own picks as Shack, Mahovlich, Ken Girard of the Marlies, and Nevin.

Bob Nevin agrees with Bush's comments. "When I played against Eddie in his last year, he got 50 plus goals. So did Mahovlich and me, but Eddie was physically dominating — big, strong, and tough. And he could skate and had a great shot. If he were coming up today, he'd be drafted in the first two without question."

That final spring the *Toronto Star* described Shack as "a Ranger-bound speedster" and a runner-up to Frank Mahovlich for MVP. And, as mentioned before, Shack made the OHA Junior A All-Star team. The future looked good.

ON OUR WAY BACK TO TORONTO FROM GUELPH, EDDIE AND I TRY Lou Fontinato's farm once more. We rap on the door of the house, then drive across to the outbuildings and barn and along the row of cattle still feeding contentedly at the trough. Thirty huge, curly-headed sides of beef follow our every move in unison, as if on a single swivel control, lower jaws making munching circles on the grain. Eddie lowers the van window and grins at them as we crawl along the line.

"WHERE'S LOUIE?" he suddenly bellows, scaring me and the closest three of the huge animals which stumbled back from the trough, startled, spooked, and wild-eyed. Eddie just speeds up and drives away, laughing happily.

Watching him roar with glee, I think of the news I got from Norma in Eddie's kitchen in Toronto less than two weeks earlier, just after Christmas. "I'm going to tell you something," she told me, "but you can't let anyone else know, or let Eddie know you know." And then she informed me that Eddie would be going into the hospital for prostate cancer surgery.

Now I ask him, "So you'll be in Florida for February?" I know the answer already, but I'm forced to play this waiting game.

"Naw. I'm not goin' now. I gotta go to the doctor. You know that thing Normie [Ullman] had? I gotta have that done." He pauses. "Prostate."

"Jesus, Eddie, what the hell . . .?"

"Yeah, I was talkin' to Normie. He knows. You know. Normie was tellin' me about the exercises. Piss a little, hold it, piss a little more. He said he did that after the operation, but my doctor said I should do it now, get in shape. Just like playin' hockey, eh? Stops and starts."

His slight smile fades quickly and we're quiet for a while. Then he speaks again without being asked. "I gotta go and give blood. Four times, I think. My own blood for the operation." He glances at me. "Did you?" he asks, referring to my quadruple bypass.

"No," I answer absently.

"I gotta go and have a scat cam," he adds as a final comment. I write down the Shackism, but the fun is outside the van, pale in the patchy snow of the fields.

As we roll southbound along Campbellville Road, I realize I've been reduced to being a knowing conspirator in the plot to keep who knew, and when they knew it, from a guy who must be going through hell. I know Eddie has to be fighting the devils that prey upon the afflicted: reminders of his father, Bill, who died from colon cancer, the death of his dear friend, Billy Parrish, and soon his friend Gerry Paxton would be gone, too.

Although the day has been cold and blustery, laced with sleet and snow squalls, it's still been a series of laughs — parking in front of the police station, the tale of the car chase at Amici's . . . but as we roll by the "Mushroom Farm" sign again, the grey sky takes on an even colder face.

CHAPTER FOUR

New York

SINCE 1950 THE NEW YORK RANGERS HAD FINISHED FIFTH, FIFTH, sixth, fifth, and fifth in the six-team NHL. In 1955-56 they vaulted to third under Muzz Patrick, who moved upstairs to the GM's office and replaced himself as coach with rookie Phil Watson. The following year the team managed to get into fourth, and the season Eddie Shack turned up for his first Ranger training camp in 1957-58, it went on to post its highest ranking for the next 10 years, finishing in second place.

There were two main factors in the Shack situation. First, he was a prospect who had all the elements of stardom, including Junior A All-Star ranking and a second-place finish in the scoring race. In that respect he held much promise for the Rangers, a team that was starting to show some life.

The second factor was his rebellious nature. While the issue in Guelph concerning his dressing room confrontations was water under the bridge to happy-go-lucky Shack, his argumentative behaviour wasn't passed over in Jack Humphrey's reports, or Muzz Patrick's personal discussions with Eddie Bush. Even though Shack had suddenly seen the light, as he claimed at the age of 19, and had turned his considerable talents to the game, the people in the front office of Madison Square Garden had already tagged him with words such as *malcontent* and *maverick*. Along with his rumoured inability to read, he was also labelled as a young eccentric, proof once again, if any corroboration was needed, that reputations are easy to acquire but tough to lose.

As far as the big team was concerned, their prize stock of Bill Sweeney and Ed Shack weren't needed on that second-place finisher. The Rangers were deep enough to afford the luxury of sharpening their newest talent one more year in the minors. There, it seems, Sweeney only confirmed and added to his legend as a "black sheep" in the organization, and although he put up big numbers in the AHL and eventually got a brief four-game whirl with New York, he was small at five foot ten and 165 pounds. He never really figured in the plans of Patrick and Watson.

Like Sweeney, Ed Shack was stereotyped on his arrival in the NHL, and it became a fact of his hockey life, too. In the NHL you are told what to do. Shack was no longer the up-and-comer, the big fish in a small pond. The kid stuff of his junior days wouldn't cut it on the big pond. As far as the Rangers were concerned, the time had arrived. In the case of this young, powerful, illiterate rookie from Guelph, there wasn't any farther to go other than down and out, back to the meat lockers of Sudbury and the prospect of sharpening knives and wearing a white smock over a heavy sweater.

But all of that wouldn't matter, anyway. In his first professional year Eddie watched the Rangers from Providence, wearing a plaster cast and crutches.

COACHES BY DEFINITION ARE UPTIGHT PEOPLE WITH UNSTABLE JOB prospects even at the best of times, and in the six-team NHL, smartass players were cowed into submission or demoted. A coach's number one priority was to establish control, and to see that, win or lose, the team's players had his mark tattooed on their butts. Any infringement on that territory was deemed a personal attack, the precursor of revolution, the prelude to anarchy.

To Eddie coaches were bronc riders, the people who tried to break and tame him so that they could program him for future use. By all accounts, having Phil Watson as his first NHL coach wasn't a plus.

Despite wearing the patriotic colours of the New York Rangers, Eddie was a Johnny Reb. That he would play himself out of an on-ice role, out of a position of favour with the coach, was a given. When you're that young, headstrong, unflinching, and unassailable with a no-fear attitude, you take your arrival in the pros as a given, as the natural evolution of a hockey player. At least that was what Eddie thought. But this was the 1950s and Phil Watson wasn't Eddie Bush. Shack's problem was that he never saw it that way.

To Watson, an NHL coach since 1954, Shack was a challenge to his authority at a time when a coach's jurisdiction was sacrosanct. Watson balked at this big, goofy, kid who couldn't read a plane ticket and who was also the subject of glowing assessments on Watson's desk, plus a significant sheaf of negative reports as long as a hockey stick. Who did this unruly clown think he was? Teaching him to knuckle under, to conform, seemed to be the order of march. Given Watson's dictatorial views and Shack's unbridled mustang mind-set, it isn't surprising that their everyday dealings over the next three years were confrontational.

And so in the fall of 1957 the Rangers shipped their Guelph one-two punch of Bill Sweeney and Eddie Shack to their AHL team in Providence. There, under the tutelage of Johnny Crawford, who Shack referred to many times as "a really nice guy," the two did everything expected of them and lived up to their advance billing. Sweeney played in 70 games with 31 goals and 46 assists for 77 points, and a predictably timid 28 minutes in penalties. On the other side, Shack maintained his Mad Hatter reputation, but his year was cut short by a broken leg, "a fibular," to use Shack's orthopedic knowledge, the same left leg that now sports metal pins in its ankle. But injuries aside, Patrick and Watson in New York were smiling. Shack was their prize and was well on pace with 16 goals, 18 assists, and a rambunctious 98 minutes in the penalty box in only 35 games. Nothing had changed. Eddie was still "Eddie," and the scouts heaped praise on this tough kid from Northern Ontario.

For the remainder of that initial season Shack was relatively happy in Providence. "I used to go to Smokey Cerone's car lot. He bought used cars, and when I had time between games, I'd go to Albany or New York, pick them up, and drive them back to Providence. It was somethin' to do. Then we'd go to his house and eat spaghetti."

Shack's requirements, as evidenced by that summary statement of his one full season in the AHL, were plain and simple. And it was when playing for Providence at a game in Springfield that he collided with Jack Bionda, breaking his leg. It's what's known in the business as a good break. Punch Imlach, the coach in Springfield, got his first look at Eddie Shack in action.

With the opening of the 1958-59 season at the Niagara Falls training camp, Watson was quoted as saying, "If the Falls is one of the seven wonders of the world, we've got the eighth in Eddie Shack." Unknown to both men at the time, Shack would spend so much time on the bench that around the league he would be nicknamed the "Lone Ranger."

The plain truth is that, as the months rolled by, the New York City experience, and Phil Watson in particular, undermined the one thing any young hockey player needs to crack the big time: confidence.

If anything, New York City was a prison with an oversize exercise yard. The gregarious kid from Sudbury via Guelph was overmatched and overwhelmed. For other players New York was a place where leisure time could be well spent, consumed by the best of theatres, museums, art galleries, restaurants, and a myriad of places to go and things to see. The catch? Ed Shack didn't know what the word myriad meant.

For the first time he was ordered to report to meetings where he was obligated to show up. No more could he simply jump into his car and drive away to let the storm pass. The alternative wasn't a whitewash from big brother, or the option of going somewhere else. This was the NHL, and the next step was suspension. Whether he liked it or not, he was a professional, and these people were calling the shots.

Today Eddie says, "I'd go up to the office when they called me in for a little talkin' to and I'd tell Patrick, Watson, or both of them that, plain and simple, I didn't want to play in New York. They just told me I was a problem child. Watson said I was uncoachable." Watson's cutting remark was something Eddie never forgot. Only a few years later when Shack was in Toronto celebrating his first Stanley Cup (1961-62) he was heard to say about Watson, now the coach of the sixth-place Bruins: "I guess they musta had a bunch of uncoachables there, too."

Eddie is blunt about his New York experience: "They almost ruined me, like they ruined Billy Sweeney. Shit, we should have come up together, but they had a hard-on for him. He could score, I could score. We should have come up together, but no, Watson had his way. I asked for a $500 raise and they fought with me like I was askin' for $50,000. I was only makin' $7,500 at the time, livin' in a shithole, holed up like a rat in the goddamn Bronx. And they said no. Nothin', no reason, no offer of a bonus, nothin', just no. So Sweeney went back to the minors, and they turned me into a checker.

"I hated New York somethin' terrible. I always fell asleep on the subway. Everybody did, like a bunch of dopey, drugged-up addicts. Then you'd wake up, have to get off, cross over to the other side, get on, and ride back. Shit, half the time I didn't even know where the hell I was goin', and sometimes I'd fall asleep again and have to do it all over. It seemed I was always tired in New York. The heat in the subway — what a goddamn place to play hockey. Then, as if that wasn't bad enough, you'd get to the dressing room, get your stuff on, and practise in the rink above Madison Square Garden. They had tin boards for Christ's sake. It was like playin' inside a garbage can. Another boring practice, go home, sleep, watch TV, cook, eat. Nobody knew nothin' about hockey. A goddamn boring life. Once in a while my mom came down and she'd cook for us, and that was a relief. Shit, even in Sudbury they had wooden boards."

But help was on the way by the end of the 1958-59 season in the form of a 22-game European trip, featuring the Boston Bruins and Rangers plus a few Chicago Blackhawk first-round losers in the play-offs. Eddie joined up on a line with Bobby Hull and Ed Litzenberger.

Concerning that European series, Hull himself says, "I played against Eddie for two years in junior when he was one of the premier players in the OHA. He was big and strong and could skate and shoot. He was a goal scorer. I would have liked to have had him on the Blackhawks anytime. He'd have been a 50-goal scorer absolutely. Phil Watson likely did ruin him.

"But when I played with him in Europe at the end of the 1958-59 season, I had to tell him not every game, not every period, but every damn shift that when he got the puck he should stay wide and go down the right side and not the middle. I also had to keep telling him that if he couldn't cut in to the net that he should look in the slot and I'd be there to get the puck from him. Well, that worked like gangbusters, but one shift I thought, Hell, I don't have to tell him anymore. He's got the idea now. God, he almost killed us, running through the middle, so we had to start all over again. I scored 50-some goals over there, and I came back and told my dad I was going to win the scoring title that year, and I did, in 1960, for the first time.

"But to me the surprise of that trip was how terrific an offensive player Eddie could be, and that's why I've always said he could easily have scored 300 goals in his career, without a doubt. Truthfully, if I had him on my team, he would have been a big-time offensive threat, and I mean it. I saw him in junior, and you don't change that much from junior to pro. I wondered what the hell were they doing to this guy. Just another example of how the NHL didn't know how to handle talent. Phil Watson would fight with players, and there was no one to take Eddie in tow and tell him how things were done, how to handle situations, and how to get along. There was no one to say, 'Sure, we'll have our fun, but when it comes to working. we plug for a couple of hours.'"

As for Eddie, about Bobby Hull, he says, "I played junior against him, and he was like me, strong like bull, smart like streetcar, and a hard worker. I remember when he came with us to Europe on that tour — we got $1,000 and a goddamn blazer — he won the scoring over there and then got 'kidnapped' in Geneva. He didn't show up for a few days, so those two Einsteins, Muzz [Patrick] and [Phil] Watson, kept his trophy."

The good word of Shack's European performance preceded him to the Rangers' training camp, both verbally and in print, but it was within the New York ranks where the consensus was positive. It hadn't always been that way among his teammates. It was said that among the established Rangers Shack had a bad reputation as a hotshot, snot-nosed kid who wouldn't take advice. But at training camp other Rangers noted an improved attitude, and the new-look Shack was attributed to the European tour. Shack may have gained final approval that he was a bona fide major leaguer when he outslugged the Bruins' top heavyweight, Fern Flaman, in a toe-to-toe bout during the final game of the tour.

Jerry Toppazzini, one of the Bruins on that trip and a fellow Sudbury native, verifies Shack's status: "When we played the 22 games in Europe, it was wide open and Shackie was really motoring, plus he had unbelievable energy. I got to see a new side of Shackie on that trip, began to see what he could do when he got down to playing hockey, and for the first time I thought to myself, Goddamn, he can be a great player. But I also remember Milt Schmidt once telling me the problem with Eddie was that he lost the game plan between the dressing room and the bench. Ever since then I've always said, with all his ability, I'll bet if he had to do it all over again he'd forget that clowning crap, because it'd be so goddamn easy to be remembered and respected as a great player. Make no mistake, he could do it, too."

Phil Watson was questioned by the New York newspapers about Shack's disappointing NHL rookie season of seven goals. The Ranger coach answered, "He's completely changed, well, not quite completely. But he's changed. And I think he'll help us more than he did last season. The bad year may have helped Shack wake up to the fact that he's not going to run through this league like he did in junior and the minors." Chicago's general manager Tommy Ivan was quoted in the same article: "He's got too much ability to be a flop. The way he can skate and drive he's bound to be a star. I wish some of my guys had that ability."

Eddie approached his second season in New York with as much anticipation as he could muster after the success of the European trip, but it didn't take long for both Watson and the environment in the city to put a damper on things. Within the first few weeks Shack wanted out of New York City and away from the Rangers. He continued to cross swords with Watson and Patrick, and soon the team was struggling again. Finally, in Montreal, a team meeting was called; it became one of those defining moments people always refer to when speaking of career-altering moves.

As Shack recalls, "Watson and Muzz Patrick called a meeting after a loss against the Canadiens. They said it'd be an open meeting, that we could say whatever we wanted about what should be changed and that nothing would be held against us. You know, show and tell. When nobody else volunteered to speak up, I figured, What the hell? Let's get everything out in the open. I told Watson to his face that everything he said went in one ear and out the other. Nobody else said nothin'. Next thing I know, Frank Paice [the Rangers' trainer] tells me I'm being sent down to the Springfield Indians, that I had to get on a bus and report to Eddie Shore. I said, 'What the fuck happened to nothing will be held against you?'"

For Shack it was the culmination of a summer of pressure and anxiety over the direction of his career, and whether he admitted it or not, he was going to bring things to a head. Shack liked Eddie Shore. For one thing they had the same first name and initials. But after two weeks in Springfield (nine games, three goals, and four assists) Watson called and told him to come back to the Rangers. Shack told Watson he liked it fine in Springfield with a real coach like Eddie Shore. Watson nearly had a fit and ordered Shack back to the team. Eddie had no choice.

Andy Bathgate, who had come from the Guelph Biltmores, too, and who was one of Eddie's teammates on the Rangers, had a ringside seat on the Shack-Watson fight. Bathgate was one of the NHL's finest players. He won the Hart Trophy as the NHL's most valuable player in the 1958-59 season, was among the top ten in scoring nine times, and after a 17-season career was inducted into the Hockey Hall of Fame. A friend of Shack's in the younger player's New York days, Bathgate was also a teammate of Eddie's when they won a Stanley Cup with the Leafs in 1964.

When Bathgate speaks, you listen: "In that famous Montreal team meeting when Eddie pointed at his ears, indicating anything Watson told him was going straight through, well, those are the kinds of things that aggravated Phil. But that was just Eddie's way of saying, 'What do I know? Just let me play hockey and don't ask me to analyze the game.' That's the way he is to this day. All he was saying is just get rid of all this frustration and play the game on the ice."

On the subject of whether Bill Sweeney and Shack should have come up to the Rangers from Guelph together, Bathgate says, "Yes, they should have kept them together, let them develop just like Dean Prentice and I did when we played together as Biltmores, then came up to the Rangers. We were with other linemates from time to time, but with Larry Popein, we clicked. Sweeney could have provided that same spark with Eddie, and most of us on the Rangers back then knew it, but we were afraid to speak up. You just never did that then as a player. Look what happened to me when the Rangers wanted to trade Jean Ratelle. I was captain by that time and felt I had something to say. I really put a case forward for keeping Ratelle. Muzz Patrick told me right then and there, 'You're getting too big for your britches.' Right after that conversation I was history. The Rangers traded me to the Leafs in February 1964 for speaking up about a guy they claimed wasn't tough enough. I don't think Jean Ratelle ever had a fight in the NHL, but for winning face-offs and coming out of the corner with the puck, there weren't too many better at the job. And I felt the same about Eddie.

"Out there on the ice where it counts he never eased off, and I've often said Ed would give you the hardest jolt of anybody, at least anyone I ever ran into, You ask Gordie [Howe] or Bobby [Hull] and they'll say the same thing. When you ran into Eddie, you bumped into a tree. He'd hurt you. Even when you tried to hit him, had him lined up, or so you thought, he had a habit of jumping into the check, and sometimes he'd bring his stick up a little, on the borderline. Can you imagine if he was using one of those aluminum shafts they have today? Hell, he'd break your arms. When he carried the puck with his head almost down and you thought you had him, at that last instant he'd see you and everything would come up, the stick, the knee, and Eddie. He could break your ribs, because he'd be in full flight by that time and it'd be too damn late to get out of his way.

"Tough? Without question, and he got in his share of scraps, but he wasn't a real puncher. If he had a choice, he'd just as soon run over you. He was so solid and strong, like John Ferguson, and though Fergie could throw punches better, Eddie knew how to take care of himself. I know Gordie Howe and Eddie tangled a lot, and they finally made some sort of pact. And even when Eddie hit big Bert Olmstead, his own teammate, in a game at Maple Leaf Gardens, Bert said he'd never been hit that hard before.

"Eddie would take me out, too, always with that grunt of his. But I like to believe because we were friends that he never really ran me. Still,

I can remember Rod Gilbert once saying, 'Eddie was my teammate and he almost killed me a couple of times . . . at practice.' Believe me, if you were hit by Shack, you'd remember it."

As for whether or not Shack had the skills to be a 300-goal scorer at the NHL level, Bathgate says, "Oh, sure, definitely. You could tell he was a scorer from the first day he arrived at training camp. Hell, of the 239 he got over his career, most of them were even-strength goals, which is a point a lot of so-called experts fail to consider, because you have to remember he was rarely on the power play. In today's game he'd be more than a force. He'd park his ass in front of the net and be too tough to move out of there. I don't care how big these guys are now. You can't move a player of Eddie's leg power, strength, and size.

Red Sullivan, a former captain and coach of the Rangers, and a teammate and roommate of Eddie's, confirms that Shack was immediately sent down to the minors because of his speaking out at the supposedly "open" meeting in Montreal. "Watson took advantage of Shack," he says, "at least I always thought so. Probably because of the literacy thing, figuring if Eddie couldn't read or write, he must be a dummy. I can't recall Watson ever giving credit to Eddie for anything he ever did on the ice, not a pat on the back, nor a kind word, nothing. On the other hand, Eddie went out of his way to drive Watson nuts. We used to practise upstairs at the Garden and the rink had metal boards. Eddie would fire shots at the boards while Phil was talking or trying to coach some player one-on-one, and Watson would yell at him, no, he'd have to scream at him, to cut it out."

Sullivan feels that the Rangers, and Eddie, would have performed better without Watson as coach. Still, he thinks Eddie wasn't ready for New York, or that the Rangers weren't ready for Shack. There's no doubt in his mind that Eddie was terribly unhappy back then. One day, Sullivan says, Dave Anderson of the *New York Times* called Eddie and asked him to comment on a rumour that he was going to be traded to the Red Wings for Red Kelly. Anderson also wanted to know what Eddie thought about the Rangers. Shack gave the reporter an earful, telling him, "The city stinks, the coach stinks, the management stinks."

Sullivan tried to restrain Eddie, but was unsuccessful. The trade never happened, but the story came out and, unlike Eddie, Phil Watson and Muzz Patrick could read.

After Eddie returned to New York from Springfield, he moved into the Sullivans' house on Long Island for what was supposed to be a few weeks but which turned out to be the rest of the season. Irv Spencer, a friend from Sudbury and a teammate of Eddie's, also moved to Long Island, bunking with the Bathgates. Marion Sullivan, Red's wife, recalls that time fondly, and mentions that Spencer and Shack promised to take them and the Bathgates out to dinner to repay their hospitality. "It was supposed to be on them," she says, "but when we got to this fancy place, a gentleman recognized Red and Andy. He was a fan of theirs and the Rangers and he paid the entire bill. Eddie and Irv got off scot-free, and they laughed all the way home."

But the season wasn't really much fun for the two buddies from Sudbury. Andy Bathgate says, "The whole setup in New York was tough on Ed. He was a single guy, and where do you go in New York? To a bar? Eddie couldn't go home and read, couldn't go to a museum. He had to get rid of that energy somehow. He didn't have anywhere to go to take his mind off the game, certainly none of the places he would have liked to see. In a smaller place, like Providence, he could go to the car lots and dealerships or drive around in his car, but in New York he was like a duck out of water."

One morning Irv Spencer was badly injured in practice. He ran into a goal post and fractured his jaw, sustained a minor concussion, and split his ear for 14 stitches. That may have been the end of Eddie as a Ranger. They were close friends, and now he felt really isolated. On the road, with Irv not playing, Eddie would lounge around the lobby of the hotel like a lost soul. He had nothing to do and nobody to run with. On top of that, he was the kind of player who only needed four hours of sleep. After the other players ate their game steaks, they would go back to their rooms and relax, have a sleep, or just lie down and watch TV. Eddie meanwhile would pace the lobby because he was so hyper and pumped that he couldn't relax. The same sort of thing happened at home, too.

Eddie, of course, has a lot to say about his situation in New York: "I coulda been a Red Wing, you know. The Rangers made a deal with Detroit. Me and Bill Gadsby for Red Kelly and Billy McNeill, but Red refused to report and the deal fell through. When I first heard the deal was a deal, I started yappin' on the bus, tellin' Watson what I thought of him as a coach, and I guess that didn't sit too well."

On the subject of Phil Watson, Shack doesn't mince his words: "He had a rule that said all bars on Manhattan Island were off-limits. Why? We were 20 Canadians mixed in with millions of guys who didn't know shit about hockey, and couldn't care less. Nobody knew who you were 30 feet outside the dressing room door. The two years I was there Watson took us to fifth, then sixth place. Yeah, we were very popular, real fuckin' celebrities.

"In junior I was a scorer, over 50 goals in my last year. That was my job. Hell, in my first year as a pro [Providence] I spent half the season injured and scored 16 goals in 35 games. Then I come to New York, and Watson, the wizard, has me checkin' all these big, tough bastards."

Eddie feels Watson ruined him as a player in his early years. According to him, the Rangers took away his confidence. Every night, he says, they had him tramping up and down the wing against the likes of Gordie Howe and Rocket Richard, so it shouldn't have been surprising that he only scored seven goals in his rookie year and not much more in his second season.

Leo Labine, another of those Northern Ontario boys who carved himself a spot on the Boston Bruins with body checks and a grinder's work ethic, remembers those days in with Eddie Shack as a New York opponent.

"Sometimes we thought he was playing for us! Honest to God. When I had to check him I just stayed on my wing . . . hey, it's not up to me to psychoanalyse the guy I'm matched against. If Eddie wanted to wander off all over the ice, all that means is *I'm* free.

"The first year he came up, New York sent him down even though he was better than half the guys on the Rangers. That was Watson, and Muzz Patrick's doing, I suppose. Hell, we always felt if Watson was coaching, we had a better chance to win. Anyhow, let's put it this way, Phil Watson wasn't good for Eddie Shack."

By the time the 1960-61 training camp came around, Phil Watson had been shuffled off to scouting, but Muzz Patrick remained as general manager. He installed Alf Pike behind the bench. Alf was an organization man who had once coached the Guelph Biltmores to a Memorial Cup, but that didn't cut any ice with Shack. The battle lines had been drawn, something that should have been obvious from a New York news item that appeared around this time: "Alf Pike thought Shack could read. He gave Eddie a contract and he said Shack looked at it long and hard, turning the pages and giving all the appearance of being able to read. Later, Pike was stunned to discover that wasn't the case."

Pike shouldn't have been surprised, nor should he have felt singled out. Brian Webber, Eddie's linemate in Guelph, says, "I remember going to the Ranger training camp in 1958, and Bill Sweeney was reading Eddie's mail for him. That was the first time I came face-to-face with the fact that Eddie was illiterate. Up until then it was only a rumour to me. Amazing. You play hockey with a guy for that long and you don't know, at least I know I wasn't really sure until that training camp."

At the 1960-61 Ranger training camp Eddie decided he'd had enough. He went home to Sudbury, where he dropped in on manager Chester Wilcox at the Dominion supermarket. Wilcox was surprised to see him and asked what was going on, so Eddie gave him an earful. Wilcox listened to the tirade, then took Eddie aside and said, "Think about it. Do you want to be wearing a bloody smock all the time, half frozen, cleaning chopping blocks, in and out of the cooler lugging sides of beef? You practise a couple of hours a day, travel first-class, stay in the best hotels, eat the best steaks, get to go to Toronto, Montreal, Chicago. Are you nuts? You can work here anytime. Get the hell out of here. Go back to New York."

But soon that wouldn't be an option for Eddie Shack anymore. A column by Dink Carroll in the Montreal *Gazette* made the Rangers' feelings about Shack loud and clear:

> Phil Watson said Eddie Shack couldn't miss because he was fast, aggressive, and could drill the puck. But Watson was the first to give up on Shack, to be followed by Muzz Patrick, who said, "I'd pay to watch Shack skate, but I wouldn't pay a dime to watch him play."

CHAPTER FIVE

The Early Maple Leaf Years

THE GREAT DAY ARRIVED ON NOVEMBER 8, 1960. IN A NONDESCRIPT trade that sent Johnny Wilson and Pat Hannigan to New York, Eddie Shack came to Toronto.

For an obscure player, one who was rapidly gaining a reputation for being an object of team disunity in New York, much was made of Shack's New York statistics: 141 games with only 16 goals. Fred Cedarburg, in the Toronto *Telegram*, stated at the time that "cold, hard statistics say that Shack, a highly regarded junior performer, has been an NHL flop."

Punch Imlach, though, had listened and sniffed out the situation in New York and, remembering his one good look at Shack in the Providence-Springfield game, felt he had a chance to make the Toronto Maple Leafs a better team with little or no risk. Imlach was quoted as saying, "I'm just gonna move him around and see how he fits in. He never showed anything with the Rangers, but his record as a junior impressed me. He's a big, strong skater, and he's tough. But he's still going to have to make his place on this team."

Today Shack says it didn't matter what he had to do as long as he was leaving the Big Apple. "When Red Sullivan told me I'd been traded to Toronto, I said, 'If I am, point me in the right direction and I'll start walking right now. When I got to Toronto, I didn't even know who Punch Imlach was, didn't give a shit, either. I was just happy to get out of New York. I remember the first time I met Punch. I came into his office and he was all business, not very friendly, like he had somethin' on me. He said, 'Shack, you won't have any problems with me if you do what the hell I tell ya.'"

For reasons unknown at the time Ed recalls he felt it important to inform Imlach right up front that he could neither read nor write. Imlach, never one to show concern openly for a hockey player, told Eddie that he didn't care if his new player could read. All he was concerned about was whether or not he could play hockey. Still, Imlach did offer to send Shack to school and pick up the tab. Unfortunately this attempt failed, too.

"Punch was good to me," Eddie says. "I was mouthy in New York, but when I got to Toronto I put on the brakes. Toronto had a young team, and I wanted to make it, so I worked extra hard and tried to get myself and the club going. For a young player I think I was good in the dressing room because of how I could read people. Maybe it was because of all the selling I had done in the meat business."

Eddie had now fulfilled his prediction to his mother by arriving in the city of his childhood dreams with some fanfare. His answer to the copy-hungry media on whether he wanted to be a Leaf was simply: "Doesn't everybody?" Ironically an ominous rumour came in the wake of the Shack trade, one that caught the interest of the Toronto newspapers. Some were saying that Punch Imlach was seriously considering hiring Phil Watson as his coach. Luckily for Eddie, the rumour was unfounded.

However, when Shack began his first season in a Maple Leaf uniform, one ongoing problem remained the same: he was still assigned to shadow the Red Wings' Gordie Howe. In a December 1960 magazine article Howe accused Shack of "holding, boarding, and high-sticking me for the past three years." Then, on January 4, 1961, the two collided in a game at Maple Leaf Gardens, an event, according to the newspapers of the day, that was "witnessed by 12,750 fans, the smallest crowd of the year." Howe suffered a concussion and a 10-stitch cut.

In the dressing room after the game Shack said, "I saw him charging at me and jumped higher to protect myself. I didn't hit him with my stick. It was my glove that hit him in the face." The newspaper report went on to say that film of the incident clearly showed Howe injured his head when he struck the ice, following the collision. It also verified Shack's contention that there was no stickwork involved.

Former Leaf Billy Harris remembers the Crash of 1961, too: "Howe was rocked all right. He spent 10 days in the hospital, as I recall. It happened right in front of the Red Wing bench, but I never heard a word out of the Detroit team, or Howe for that matter. No crap whatsoever, and there was no penalty called. Hey, when a pair of 200-pound-plus guys are looking the other way heading north and south, chips are gonna fly."

Shack's 55 games for Toronto in the 1960-61 season was a start, not a big start, but an auspicious debut on a team with the Leafs' style of play. He scored 14 goals, made 14 assists, and racked up a truculent 90 minutes in the penalty box. Added to his 12 games in New York, he had a total of 117 penalty minutes, the second-highest season total of his 17-year career. The Leafs finished second in 1960-61 and lost in the semifinals to Detroit in four straight games; Shack went 0 for 4 at the plate.

In Shack's next season with the Leafs two major events would occur in his life: he would win his first Stanley Cup and meet his future wife, Norma. On the marital side the go-between was fellow Sudbury native Jim Pappin, who wasn't an official Maple Leaf at the time, just a young Toronto foot soldier stationed in Rochester.

Pappin recalls the Leafs' 1961-62 training camp in Peterborough with distaste, but relishes the memory of his role in introducing Norma to Eddie. "Back then training camps were six weeks long, like a freakin' boot camp, the same thing they do to goddamn Marines. But on our first day off in a month we were gonna go golfing at the Kawartha course. I was taking a girl I was seeing, and I asked Eddie if he wanted me to find out if she had a friend. Eddie said, 'Wait, there's one girl I want to ask first, so hold on until I see her.' He went down the street to Eaton's, but she wasn't there, so that's when I asked my date to bring along her pal. When we met Eddie, he said to me, all hush-hush, 'That's her. That's the girl I was going to ask.' It was Norma Given." The following year Norma and Eddie were married in a Ukrainian Catholic ceremony.

The 1961-62 season was a long, tough, haul, even for the veterans, and as was becoming commonplace, it was the hard-nosed Chicago

Blackhawks, the reigning Stanley Cup champions, who provided much of the rivalry in the 1960s for the Leafs. Aside from his pal Bobby Hull, Shack had a close battling relationship with three Hawks: Reggie Fleming, Pierre Pilote, and Stan Mikita, the flinty, menacing centre who asked and gave no quarter, unless it was yours.

At Christmas the Leafs visited Chicago Stadium, and Shack suffered torn left knee ligaments in a collision observers say had everything to do with Reggie Fleming. Shack was on the shelf for four weeks. and later, on February 18 at Maple Leaf Gardens, to add insult to injury, he was hit by defenceman Pete Goegan, then with the Rangers, on the same left knee. Eddie spent another three weeks in sick bay, cutting his season to 44 games.

On March 12, it's back to Chicago for another go-round. "I spear Pierrre Pilote at the blueline and he swings his stick at me. Bert Olmstead goes after Pierre and it starts. Larry Hillman goes after 'Cementhead' (Reggie) Fleming, so I figure I better get into it since I started the whole thing, and in the scramble to grab somebody I get . . .?" — Eddie's moustache goes horizontal over a big smile — "Stan Mikita. He was a little dirty fucker, always hackin' and choppin' people, and since he's the closest, I kick the livin' shit out of him. They told me later that's when Stash got the idea to change his ways. Did ya know he won two Lady Byng trophies after that?"

On that evening in Chicago in 1962 Shack had two fights for the price of one when he was suckered from the side by Fleming, who broke Shack's nose. It was a feud that had been heating up for a long time, one that had Punch Imlach worried. "I was afraid that [NHL president] Campbell was gonna come down hard on the both of them. I didn't care about Fleming — he was a small-time player for the Hawks, a fourth-liner at best — but Shack was a regular for us."

Today Stan Mikita has mellowed somewhat on the subject of Ed Shack: "I always considered Eddie a package of controlled mayhem. Thank God, though, he was around for some fun. And the guy could play, too. We came from an era where it was a job, sure, but we had more fun, and more heartaches, I suppose."

By this time Shack had already earned several of the many colourful titles he would eventually be tagged with in professional hockey. Reporters referred to him as "Pugnacious Pinocchio" and "The Man on Left Wing — and Right." And a feature magazine piece of the day blared in big, black type: "Shack, Rattle and Roll." But if Eddie was the darling of the fans and every beat reporter's and columnist's idea of nirvana, he wasn't gaining any stature with his boss, Punch Imlach. In Imlach's view Shack's play was beginning to take on a dismaying pattern as he evolved into the consummate "role player."

In 1961-62 the Leafs finished second to the Canadiens, beat the Rangers 4-2 in the semifinals, topped Chicago 4-2 in the final round, and won their first Stanley Cup since 1950-51. In nine playoff games Shack failed to get any points and largely sat on the bench because he hurt the team with penalties. For Eddie it was the continuance of a disturbing trend. In his two seasons with Toronto he had now played in 13 Stanley Cup contests and his statistics read zero. He might as well have been in New York; the statistics were zero across the board there, too.

"When we won the first Cup," Eddie says, "we were in Chicago Stadium wahooin' an' havin' a beer in the downstairs dressing room, and Imlach comes in all cranky and pissed off like we just lost. Then he says, 'If you aren't on the goddamn bus in 15 minutes, you won't be on this team next year.' No congratulations, no nice goin', or anythin'. Whatta crabby bastard. He couldn't even loosen up and have a beer with us."

JUST BEFORE THE 1962-63 SEASON BEGAN, THE STANLEY CUP champions set out on a western exhibition game tour. Defenceman Allan Stanley recalls a deviation from the norm: "At one of the games Punch set up a fourth line of Eddie, Kent Douglas, and me at centre. We scored four goals. Nothing to it. We'd dig the puck out in our own end, I'd get it over to Eddie barrelling down the wing, then just trail over the blueline, stepping over bodies and debris, and score. Imlach busted up that potent line," Stanley says, sighing, thinking of what might have been. "Too embarrassing, I suppose."

Eddie remembers that exhibition game tour, too. "We lost a game to the Portland Buckaroos. Timmy Horton put one into our own net, and Punch had a goddamn fit. He slapped us with an eleven o'clock curfew. What the hell can you do after a game in 45 minutes? But we power-drank some beers at some goddamn place, and later, Bobby Baun, Carl Brewer, and a few of the others went into the hotel pool in their suits, then went up to their rooms. There was water everywhere, and Punch comes up rantin' and ravin' and has an even bigger shit fit. Imlach was the boss, a goddamn sergeant major. You had to know after somethin' like that he was gonna have you skatin' 100 times of this, 100 times of that, the next day."

Centreman Dave Keon has even more details to add: "That night the entire team was invited to a place called The Worst House in the Cellar run by a couple of college kids. I'll never forget the name. Of course, Imlach had us on the clock with a curfew, and we had just been humili-ated by the Buckaroos. Having been there before, I knew practice the next morning would be hell, so a few of us left early.

"At about 1:30 a.m. there was a knock on my hotel door, and when I asked, 'Who is it?' I heard this snuffling and snorting and I recognized the voices of Carl Brewer and Billy Harris. Being a suspicious person and a veteran of the prank wars, I got down and looked under the door, but all I could see were shoes . . . and dripping water. I wasn't about to open the door, so I asked them what they wanted.

"At that point the phone rang. It was Punch, ranting and raving and demanding, 'Is that goddamn Duff around?' I said the first thing I could think of, which was 'He's in the shower.' 'Well,' Punch roars, 'tell him to get a towel on 'cause I'm comin' down to see for myself.' So I ran back to the door and told the clowns outside that Punch was on his way, and they scattered. Right after they left, Duffie came home and jumped into bed just as Punch pounded on the door.

"As soon as I opened the door, Punch yelled, 'You buggers been swimming lately? Maybe paddlin' around in the goddamn pool?' We denied it while he checked our clothes in the closet, which were dry. 'Is that water outside your door, or did somebody take a piss?' he demanded. We told him we didn't know anything. So Punch took out his room list, used our phone, and called down to the front desk.

"'I want 7:00 a.m. wake-up calls for these goddamn rooms,' he barked, and started rhyming off the the names of the AWOLs from his bed check. 'Shack, Harris, Brewer, Baun, Nevin.' Then the night clerk, who obviously had never had a curfew, asked, 'Do you want to talk to them directly? A bunch of them just came running into the lobby now.' That was one hell of an early practice the next day."

Despite the synchronized swimming events, though, by the time the Leafs returned to Toronto, they were ready. The annual All-Star game was played between the Stanley Cup champions and the All-Star squad on October 6, 1962. Toronto defeated Blackhawk coach Rudy Pilous's All-Stars 4-1. It seemed no matter who Pilous had on his team he still couldn't get past the Leafs. Shack was the game MVP, nosing out Bobby Hull and Gordie Howe and scoring one goal while typically taking two minor penalties in what was supposed to be a kiss-and-giggle game. When asked what he received for his efforts, he replies, "Same as everybody else — a jewellery case with no jewellery." Reminded that today's players get a car, Shack only grins and says, "Ah, we only needed one car at the time, anyway."

That season Shack and Kent Douglas were reunited, this time on the same side. "He was a hard case, you know, tough with a good shot," says Eddie. "I'd use his sticks in practice. They had real thick handles, sorta like lugging a two-by-four. Use them bastards for a couple of days and by the time you got to a game your own stick felt like a pool cue."

On January 20, 1963, Shack and Mikita went at it again. This time Mikita already sported a stitched and leaking cut over his eye. Today Mikita claims Shack "always wanted to go at me. Him and that [Henri] Richard and [Lou] Fontinato. When Eddie and I got to the penalty box, I pointed at my eye and said, 'Ya picked a good time to sucker me, asshole.' And Eddie just grinned and said, 'I felt like fighting.' Can you believe it? Who the hell 'feels' like fighting?"

In a late February loss to Boston, Leo Boivin hip-checked Shack, restretching his left knee ligaments and putting him out for two weeks. But the pain was worth it when the Leafs won their first regular-season championship in 15 years, nosing out the Blackhawks by one point and Montreal by three. In postseason play the Leafs racked up their second Stanley Cup in as many years, beating Montreal in the semifinals 4-1 and Detroit in the finals 4-1.

The amazing statistic about the Maple Leaf Cup-winning team of 1962-63 is that the club did it with one less man on its roster than the previous year. Bert Olmstead had retired. In the early 1960s it was particularly hard to crack the Leaf lineup and there were few personnel movements. The only other change from 1961-62 was Kent Douglas replacing Al Arbour.

IN THE OFF-SEASON THE SHACKS BECAME A FAMILY WHEN DAUGHTER Cathy was born. With this added responsibility came a need for new living quarters. Norma recalls they had been living in an upstairs apartment on the shore of Lake Ontario "where the angle of the roof cut into the space. Eddie couldn't stand up in the living room," she laughed. Soon, however, circumstances and Eddie's fast-growing fame provided a roof over their heads in a pastoral setting.

Eddie describes what happened next: "M. J. Boylen was a rich guy who named a racehorse after me. He had mining investments. When I met him, he took me out to his place at Dixie and Derry roads in Mississauga. It was a great big place, a huge mansion, and it had an indoor track, pool, the works. M.J. had this other house on the grounds for his horse trainer, I guess, but nobody was using it. So I said I'd rent it and how much would it cost. He said $125 a month. Can yuh believe it? A goddamn bargain. I put a trampoline in the backyard, and the boys on the team would come out, get pissed, and jump on it, doin' back flips, front flips, outta control. M.J. also gave me some market advice. He told me to buy Brunswick Mining and Engineering stuff. Whatta tip. It was his company.

"And that dumb horse. Remember them Air Canada Lifesavers they used to pass out all the time? Well, I'd get a load of those candies and bring 'em to the horse, hand them over the fence and he'd eat them, real nice. So one day I figure what the hell, we're pals, and I went over the fence with a fistful of these candies. Holy sheepshit, he come snortin' after me, snappin' at my ass, and I had to jump the goddamn fence . . . That goddamn Eddie Shack," he moans.

As the 1963-64 season got under way, Imlach stood pat with his lineup; only an injury made room for Jim Pappin. "My first NHL game was an on-again, off-again thing," Pappin now recalls. "First Imlach called Rochester to send me up, then he called back and said never mind. The next day, November 22, I'll never forget because it was the day President Kennedy was assassinated. The Leafs called again and told me to get to Toronto as fast as I could. There was an injury or something, Ron Stewart, I think. I got to the Gardens for my first big-league game against the Bruins right in the middle of the Kennedy thing. That was all you could get on the news. Who cared about hockey? After the game, we left for New York, and the Kennedy assassination was the only topic of conversation. Everybody on the team was interested, of course, and we wanted to get back to our rooms after the game meal at the hotel. I mean, it was absolutely the only thing on our minds. Except Shackie's.

"Typical for the NHL, I was put in a room with Eddie. Why? Because we were both from Sudbury. Eddie didn't give a shit about what was on TV. He growled at me, 'Turn that goddamn set off. Go to sleep. We gotta game tonight. You need your rest.' Just about that time Oswald was brought up from the cells and Jack Ruby popped him. I told Eddie what happened and that we had to watch. He got out of bed, shut off the TV, and said, 'It's all bullshit. TV is bullshit. We gotta play tonight.' So there I was lying in bed, eyes wide open, too pumped up and wondering what was happening in the world outside the hotel. Meanwhile my roomie was hibernating like a grizzly, and I was afraid to turn the damn set on. Today's players' association rules allow you to get your own room if you don't like your roomie. All you have to do is pay the extra charge. I woulda paid just about anything that night in 1963, whatever it took, but back then rookie roomies didn't do that kind of thing."

December 9 marked the infamous fight staged by the benches of both the Leafs and Blackhawks. According to Stan Mikita, it was one of the more memorable Toronto-Chicago dustups: "I'll always remember that night we had the brawl at the Gardens before Christmas. Murray Balfour chased Carl Brewer around the ice like a greyhound after a rabbit. Twice, I think. He finally caught up to him near the Leaf bench, stuffed him through the gate, and proceeded to punch the snot out of him. It was a riot. People came out of the seats to join in, and I think one of them was Argonaut running back Dick Shatto. For Maple Leaf Gardens it was unbelievable. Meanwhile, we were out on the ice, trying to pair up, everybody latching onto somebody, and who do you think grabbed me? Eddie. He popped me one, and I was out like a goddamn light. I was 165 pounds and he was pushing 210. But I think I scared the crap out of him. He thought he'd killed me."

In February 1964 Imlach made a trade, which turned out to be a fateful decision. Andy Bathgate and Don McKenney came in from New York, while Bob Nevin and Dick Duff went off to the Rangers. During the balance of the season, Shack stayed in his role, playing 64 games, scoring 11 goals, making 10 assists, and amassing his highest total in penalty minutes at 128. According to Imlach, who wasn't too happy with some of his players, Shack "had a great year," bringing up the perennial question: Did the Leaf coach really want a slambang Shack, or a more genteel, goal-scoring Shack? It was a question that continued to puzzle Eddie, too. The Leafs finished third, six points behind second-place Chicago and seven ahead of Detroit.

In the semifinals the Leafs faced Montreal again, and with the series 2-1 in favour of the Canadiens, a piece of comical hockey history unfolded in game four at Maple Leaf Gardens. It was the setting for the "coco-bonking" of Henri Richard, the night when the Canadiens went home beaten on the ice and beaten in the alley. Frank Mahovlich was in on all the Toronto scoring in a 5-3 Leaf victory that evened the best-of-seven series at two wins each.

The other hero of the night was Shack. The incident started when the so-called "mild-mannered" Ron Stewart thumped Dave Balon, which led to the "confrontation" between Shack and Richard. "He called

Eddie, age 10, with his father Bill in Sudbury.

Eddie's grade three class photo. Eddie is in the back lefthand corner, in a plaid shirt. His future business associate, Al Biggs, sits in the front row, in white shirt and bow tie.

B. Shack

Name of school you attend   *Wembley*

KINSMEN'S KIDHOCKEY LEAGUE

MINOR BANTAM: Age group 10-11 years. Must be 10 years old not later than Nov. 1 and 11 years old on or before Oct. 31, 1947.

Pupil's Name   *Eddy Shack*

Address   *629 Horobin St*

Phone No. at home   *8-8690*   School Grade   *III*

Age *10*   Born *11*   Day *Feb.* Month *1937* Year

Teacher's Name *M. J. Stephen*   Phone *3-2187*

Name of team you played for last winter *Miners (St. Alphonse)*

Are you a member of a cadet corps? *No.*   Boy Scouts? *No.*

If so, what night do you attend? *N/a.*   Hour? *N/a.*

Do you sell papers? *No.*   What hours? *N/a.*

Have you signed up or agreed to play with any other hockey team or club? *No.*   If so, what team? *N/a.*

If you have played before, what position did you play?   Goal

Left wing   Right wing   Right Defence   Left Defence   Centre

CONTRACT

1. That I will not smoke.
2. That I will not neglect my school studies.
3. That I will return home as soon as my game or practise is finished.
4. That I will get plenty of sleep.
5. That I will always be on time for practises and games. If I cannot, I will notify my coach in plenty of time.
6. That I will always play the game to the very best of my ability.
7. That I will not swear or use bad language. (Any boy doing so will be immediately suspended.)
8. That I will accept my coach's decision on all matters concerning my team.

PENALTIES FOR BREAKING ANY OF THE ABOVE RULES:

First offence, one-game suspension; second offence, two-game suspension; 3rd offence, must appear before Kinsmen's Kidhockey League.

I do hereby promise and pledge myself in good faith to keep the above terms.

Signed *Eddy Shack*   Witness *M. J. Stephen*
     Name of Player

PARENT'S or GUARDIAN'S CONSENT

I, *B. Shack* do hereby consent to *Eddy Shack* taking part in hockey supervised by the Kinsmen's Club and in the event of any injury I understand that I cannot hold the Kinsmen's Club of Sudbury responsible.

     FATHERS: Would you consider offering your services as a coach for one of our boys' teams? *No* If so, what evening or evenings could ~~you coach?~~ *no* Hours _____ Games will be played ~~every~~ evening between 4.30 to 8.00, and on Saturdays. All games must ~~finis~~hed by 8.00 p.m.

Eddie's first minor hockey "contract," as a goaltender. Note his printing at top and again at "Name of Player," spelled "Eddy" by Eddie himself and by his father.

Ed Shack in 1957 as a Guelph Biltmore, selected to the OHA All-Star team. TORONTO STAR

The Guelph Biltmores Junior team, 1952-53: Eddie is in the middle row, fourth from left. John Gillis (front row, third from left) was Eddie's good friend and Junior roommate.

The prized white Chrysler convertible Eddie drove as a Guelph Junior, one of many cars he owned as a teenager.

Shack, 20 years old, in his first season of pro, in front of the Providence Reds arena. At mid-season he suffered a broken leg.

With coach George "Punch" Imlach as a Maple Leaf, in 1962. Shack's left knee received three serious injuries over his career. Shack also broke his ankle and tibia. MICHAEL BURNS, TORONTO STAR

In play typical of his style, Shack hurdles over the Bruins' Guy Gendron.

Ed and Bill Shack in 1973.

Eddie was willing to shed his moustache in one of his many post-hockey promotions, 1987. BORIS SPREMO, TORONTO STAR

me names I'd never heard before," Shack said in the dressing room reporters' scrum after the game. Since Richard was probably speaking his native French, it isn't hard to fathom why Eddie was confused. Although Shack fired off the two best punches of the fight, the matchup degenerated into a standoff when the fire-hydrant Richard held Shack's arms helpless and vice versa. As they shuffled around in the corner, Shack suddenly decided to take matters into his own hands and head-butted Richard twice. The result? Richard was cut over the right eye for six stitches and cooled out for the night.

According to Eddie, Richard had been "showing off" early in the game. "Yeah, you know," Shack now says, "he was out there zippin' around like he didn't have a goddamn care in the world, so I decided to bring him down to us. But the little bugger was strong, so I hadda watch my step. A fight started and I grabbed Richard, and bing, bing, I got in two good ones real quick and we started waltzin'. He had me by the arms and I had ahold of his and we'd take two steps over here, two steps over there. So what else could I do? I said piss on this and I banged him with my head."

That wasn't the only highlight of the night. Still revved up in the second period, still in the game after a foul that today would send you to the NHL offices in New York for a tribunal, Shack may have sealed the Canadiens' fate when he rattled Jean Beliveau into the boards in the second period, sending the Montreal superstar into a two-game gimp.

But the story of the Richard head-butting didn't end there. Like all such hockey stories, it continued into the next matchup, which was scheduled for the Montreal Forum, with a day off in between games for the news to settle in, spread, and grow. Shack approached the next game with predictable concern, which was felt by a lot of the Leafs, including linemate Billy Harris. "I know Eddie was concerned about Fergie [John Ferguson] after the coco-bonk incident. He musta had sleepless nights over those kinds of things. Hey, we all did."

Shack was greeted in the early warm-up at the Forum with the predictable booing, but by the time the skate was over and the players were heading to the dressing room for the ice resurfacing prior to the start of the game, Eddie faced a new challenge. Maurice "Rocket" Richard was sitting in his customary seat above the exit walkway to the visitors' dressing room. Richard, who at the best of times looked like Charles Manson on steroids, glared down at the Leafs as they left the ice.

Shack admits he "ducked behind a couple of the big guys, Mahovlich or Stanley." At six foot one and 210 pounds, Eddie might as well have been a cruiser trying to hide behind a battleship. Needless to say, he didn't go unnoticed by the beady, Bela Lugosi eyes of the Rocket. "'Ey, Shack, good t'ing you never 'it my brudder wit your nose, eh? You coulda split 'im in 'alf," Richard cracked.

But Ed Shack and the Leafs had the last laugh. Toronto won the game and the series, then polished off Detroit four games to three in a much tougher final than the previous one, winning their third Stanley Cup in a row. For Eddie it must have been a great feeling, sitting in a convertible and wearing his Leaf blazer alongside trench-coated Dave Keon, signing autographs in the Stanley Cup parade on April 19, 1963. Six hundred Toronto police officers on motorcycles, horses, and foot lined Bay Street for the trip to the Old City Hall, where Mayor Phil Givens said to the 5,000 fans standing and cheering, shoulder to shoulder, "We have the greatest hockey team in the world."

When it came time for Leaf captain George Armstrong to reply, all he could say before the roaring drowned him out was, "We have the best fans in the world." Certainly for Eddie Shack those words rang true, for all along the ticker-tape parade route up Bay Street from Wellington to Queen, the loudest cheers were raised when Shack appeared. According to news reports of the day, the mayor's closing speech was drowned out by unified cries of "We want Shack! We want Shack!" which befuddled Eddie's detractors. He had played in 13 more Stanley Cup games and and had picked up only one assist.

Interestingly enough, around this time, when Shack's stock among the Leafs' fans seemed to reach greater and greater heights, Frank Selke, the Montreal Canadiens' retiring general manager, revealed he had once had the opportunity to secure Shack for his team. According to Selke, he was offered the winger in a trade with the Rangers back in the late

1950s. "I hesitated," he remembered, "and then counselled the Rangers to have some patience with Shack. My misdirected generosity resulted in his going to Toronto where he has the determination and ability to be the kind of player to stick in the league for a dozen years." Of course, at the time, Selke couldn't know that the NHL would expand in six years, allowing Shack to extend his career well beyond a dozen seasons.

In April of 1964, though, Eddie Shack was definitely a Toronto Maple Leaf, and how sweet it was.

CHAPTER SIX

The Later
Maple Leaf Years

IN 1964-65 EDDIE SHACK, AFTER SIX SEASONS IN THE NHL, FOUR OF them as a Leaf, experienced his worst numbers of any NHL season: five goals, nine assists, and 68 penalty minutes in 67 games. Even compared to his time in New York, the previous standard setter, it was a dismal year. To add to his woes, one of those five markers was punched into the Boston net by Bruin winger Dean Prentice after Shack made an innocent pass-out from behind the goal.

In short, the 1964-65 season is one that's best forgotten by Shack, and the Leafs, who finished fourth with 74 points only because the fifth-place Rangers could barely muster enough offence to finish 22 points behind Toronto. The nondescript year came to a close early as the defending Stanley Cup champions lost to Montreal in the semifinals, four games to one, a quick and concise reversal of the previous year's meeting.

But while the season was over in a hurry, the controversy, trade rumours, and growing story behind the Imlach-Shack feud simmered at Carlton and Church streets. As the September 1965 training camp packed up in Peterborough, the news broke that Eddie was heading to the minors. In a September 25, 1965, article in the *Toronto Star*, Jim Proudfoot wrote:

> If you want my opinion, Eddie Shack is a terrible hockey player. His incompetence irritates me, but not as much as the cheers he draws for doing things incorrectly, but enthusiastically.
>
> Still, I don't believe he deserves what's being done to him this fall by his Maple Leaf bosses. As a matter of fact, I contend he's entitled to better treatment.
>
> Shack seems to be accepting the deal he's being given, although he may be hard to get along with when the time comes to talk money. But

those close to him say he's puzzled and bitter. He's skating over top of players who happen to get in his way.

Shack wouldn't place very high in a popularity poll among Leaf regulars. In that group of serious professionals, he's out of place. His boyishness can wear thin, but his exuberance can be catching, too. And there are those who think his toughness is a Leaf asset, even though it's an unused deterrent. There are those, too, who think he could win the job if he got the opportunity.

He won't, though.

Proudfoot was right on the money. Shack wasn't given the chance to win his job with the Leafs.

It was a time of serfdom for hockey players, no free agency, no need to clear waivers, no one-way contracts, and roster players could still be sent down to the minors. It wasn't as bad as the era of Conn Smythe, the father of the Maple Leafs, who was given to visiting the dressing room before games with a sheaf of train tickets to places like Pittsburgh, Rochester, and other destinations with a minor-league ring to them. Play well, you take the train to Chicago; play badly, and it's pick a ticket, any ticket.

Shack was about to be used in what many in the media reported as nothing more than a con game concocted by Stafford Smythe, and implemented by his GM and coach, Punch Imlach. Eddie was going to the minors. Eddie was the designated dupe.

There were others who could have worn the collar, players who also had less than eye-popping statistics, but none of them had the charisma, the fan appeal, to put people in the seats, and that was the sting in the scam.

Rochester was the American Hockey League Leaf affiliate. The Americans were having problems at the gate; they also had to leave their building for two weeks in the early part of the season, bumped from their home ice by a professional bowling tournament. To say the Americans were in trouble, all you had to do was realize it was the only occasion on record when "Bowling for Dollars" replaced the action of pro hockey.

The smell of a rat the newshounds got downwind of was wafted north by the fact that the Leafs decided to have Rochester's home games played in Toronto. What better way to (a) fill the seats in attendance-weak Rochester, and (b) fill them again with Shack-starved fans when the team played those scheduled games in Maple Leaf Gardens? It all came back to asses in seats, money in the bank, a plain and simple piece of business.

Given the rules of the day, Eddie had no other choice, and reluctantly he agreed to report. His only alternative was to quit. But he attached a string of his own. He gave the experiment two weeks, otherwise, he cheekily told Imlach, he was "outta there," which was tantamount to waving a red bed sheet in front of a bull. It was something that wasn't done, serving up ultimatums to management. Too many willing bodies were available to fill the slot, too many rules were slanted in favour of the bosses. Look what had happened to Red Kelly and Ted Lindsay in Detroit, players with considerably better credentials than Shack's. Eddie was threatened with the last and most obvious rule of engagement: you couldn't buck the system and expect to stay in it.

It was a time of slings and arrows between the media and the Leafs' hierarchy, volleys of accusations followed by salvos of denials, but in the end it came down to Ed Shack. "The bastards put me on a minor-league salary," he now says, "and after two weeks I told them I wasn't making enough to eat in restaurants, that I could make more money selling hats, cars, or fuckin' sausages, that they had another 14 days and if I wasn't up with the Leafs, I'd quit hockey." In eight games with the Americans he had three goals and four assists. And although he didn't know it at the time, he would help Smythe and Imlach cover their tracks by having his greatest season as a Leaf. In doing so, he made Imlach look like a genius, the man who smartened up a class clown and put him on the path of atonement and redemption.

In fact, with the help of the constant badgering of his supporters, as well as that of some former detractors in the media, Eddie called management's bluff. One of those who blew the whistle on the Leafs was Milt Dunnell of the *Toronto Star*, accomplished through his humorous style and gently prodding column. Today, taking a break from his retirement, Dunnell has this to say about the injustice of the Leafs ver-sus Shack: "With all due respect to the principals in that fiasco, it was nothing more than a flagrant misuse when they sent Eddie to Rochester to set up the gate. In fact, when you look at Shack, you have to say, gen-erally speaking, hockey misused Eddie.

"The counterbalance to all this was that hockey had everything to do with making him 'The Entertainer' so, in his case, he owes a lot to hockey, too. There simply weren't many places for a guy in his situation to go. Still, Shack deserves most of the credit because he turned his handicap into an asset. When the talent wouldn't play, he was there to put on a show. In summary, what the Leafs did on that occasion was not right, because, although rugged and undisciplined, he was a lot better player than he ever got credit for.

"And as the saying goes, perhaps he was born too soon. Television made Eddie a national figure, but in his glory days TV coverage was lim-ited. With today's communication systems he'd have been a celebrity across North America, probably internationally."

The Leafs relented in the face of the threat. Shack was called up and proceeded to turn the tables. The night he fired the 3-2 winner over the Rangers in New York, his fifth goal, it equalled his output for the entire 1964-65 season, and he accomplished it in 11 games. At the time only Dave Keon, with seven, had scored more.

It was a dedicated, more humble and subdued Eddie Shack, who sat still for an article by George Gross in the *Toronto Telegram*:

> "I really came up here [from Rochester] to have a good year as a Leaf. I had my sights set on 20 goals, but . . ." If he had suggested a 20-goal year before the opening of the campaign, it would have been generally regarded as another of his jokes. Now it doesn't sound silly at all.
>
> "Shack is a different player," said Rangers' GM Emile Francis. "He's no longer giving the puck away, and he's got his size going for him. He's always been a good skater. Now he seems to be settling down to serious business. But don't think he didn't have talent before. When he played junior in Guelph, fans were standing on their feet and many of them said Shack was the best junior they had ever seen."

On December 7, Pearl Harbor Day, Shack suffered an elbow from behind by Ted Harris, and while X rays dispelled any severe injury, he sustained a 15-stitch cut when his head struck the ice. Eddie remained in a Montreal hospital overnight, and assistant trainer Tommy Naylor brought him back to Toronto the next day.

But Shack bounced back, and picture proof of his return to his search-and-destroy ways was confirmed by the *Telegram*'s December 20 front-page story of Shack cutting through the Rangers like a sabre. The headline read: "The White Tornado Strikes Again — Twice." It referred to the night Shack dropped two Rangers to the ice on the same play. In the photo Rod Gilbert and centre Phil Goyette are stretched out like sunbathers on the ice of Maple Leaf Gardens as the play moves away. Another picture shows Shack, who scored a goal and an assist in the 8-4 win, cruising like a circling shark as the victims are administered to by players from both sides, and referee Bill Friday stands surrounded by other Rangers demanding a penalty.

At the time a less charitable Emile Francis railed that Shack had hit Gilbert from behind, then cross-checked Goyette across the head. In the initial newspaper report Eddie didn't recall even running into either Gilbert or Goyette, but later admitted to elbowing both of them. The Shack was back!

In his very next game he scored two more goals against Boston, giving him 13 in 19 games since his return ride up I-90 from Rochester. And the Leafs were 10-6-3 in that stretch. Now the newspaper clippings began to swell and fill out the scrapbooks. On December 21, 1965, Milt Dunnell wrote an article entitled "Shack the Great Silencer" in the *Toronto Star*:

> The quietest items in town these days are "Silent Night," and critics of Mr. Edward Shack, the shinny player. Even Punch Imlach, who exiled Eddie to the pastures of the Leaf farm in Rochester, is afraid to suggest what must be in his mind. That Shack should be given a saliva test.
>
> If Shack were a thoroughbred, some trainer would be taking the bows for making him a winner. It would be explained the transformation actually was simple. They put a blinker over one eye. That's how Whirlaway

was persuaded to run through the stretch without going around by way of Paducah.

Shack's weakness used to be that he played both wings on the same shift. He came pretty close to becoming the first man to rendezvous with himself in orbit.

There were some Leafs who listed Edward among the occupational hazards of their profession. Getting hit by him was like getting run down by your own automobile.

On March 27 the lady known as Justice sneaked a peek from under her blindfold and gave Eddie the big wink in a game with the Red Wings. Shack scored two goals, the winner and the insurance marker, in a 3-1 win over Detroit. Eddie was given credit for the second goal, which guaranteed the Leafs third place and a $10,500 bonus from the league, although there was some controversy about whether Shack, cruising in front of Roger Crozier, had even touched Red Kelly's shot. For many spectactors the puck had appeared to go straight in. Nevertheless, Art Skov awarded the goal to Shack. While the goal was his 25th of the season, reason enough to celebrate since he had a $100 bonus for every goal over 15. It was a goal that haunted Eddie for many years to come.

Despite the rocky beginnings, the 1965-66 season turned out to be a glorious one for Shack. He turned in his highest single NHL goal output (26) in a career that still had eight years to run, and accumulated his most interesting penalty time in that, without registering a major or misconduct, he finished with 88 minutes.

In the playoff semifinals Shack played four games and scored two goals in the same game, but the third-place Leafs lost to first-place Montreal four straight. Adding to the lustre of his season laurels, Shack's 1966 playoff record matched his previous best playoff year, with only one blemish. He took 33 minutes in penalties in four games, which meant two things: his fans were ecstatic; his boss wasn't.

COMING OFF A PERSONAL BEST SEASON, EDDIE SHOULD HAVE BEEN AT the top of his game, but the fall of 1965 appeared to repeat itself. In the summer of 1966 Shack was 29, and the headlines shouted: "Imlach Ships Shack to Victoria." The huffing and puffing on both sides started all over again.

Imlach claimed in a newspaper report that Shack's demotion to Victoria wasn't a repeat of the previous year's 'Rochester' experiment in which Shack was banished to promote attendance, even though Victoria was another Maple Leaf farm club. "This has nothing to do with boosting tickets sales in Victoria," Imlach insisted, bristling.

When it was suggested the Leafs could ill afford to start without the winger who was third in team goals behind Bob Pulford and Frank Mahovlich, the media underlined the difference a year had made. Shack had five goals and nine assists in 1964-65, 26 and 17 in 1965-66. Imlach's only reaction was to counter by damning Shack with faint praise: "There's no question he had a good year . . . for him."

The crux of the problem was rumoured to be a misdemeanour that Imlach, for the moment, refused to make public. "He started off this situation through things he did over the summer" was Imlach's comment. "As far as I'm concerned, he will not be at the Maple Leaf training camp. What I do is for the good of my team. The decisions are mine, final, and that's that."

If this was Imlach's idea to throw the newsies off the trail, it backfired. Media speculation throbbed and centred on one event that was suspected had raised the blood pressure of the aggravated Imlach. Shack had played a benefit game with some other NHLers in Kelowna, British Columbia, without receiving Imlach's pulpit dispensation.

Shack, of course, had a different version of the reason. He claimed he was banished because he wouldn't do an off-season activity that Imlach had arranged. According to Eddie, he and some other Leafs were supposed to do a spot for Imperial Oil through MacLaren, its ad agency. The selected Leafs were told they would receive $150 each for their trouble. Eddie balked and demanded $500. Predictably Imlach hit the roof, and the next thing Shack knew he was headed for Victoria.

Even though Imlach was well aware Eddie couldn't read, he sent a letter to Shack about the Imperial Oil gig instead of calling him. The newspapers reported that Eddie was glad and ready to go to Victoria if only to get away from Imlach, that he'd take his family this time and enjoy himself. Wife Norma, however, had her doubts: "I don't think I want to go there," she confessed.

As it turned out, however, the two parties got together, Imperial Oil got its recording session, and Shack, although late, began practising with the Tulsa minor leaguers before opening the 1966-67 season on time with the Leafs. Norma was spared packing the family bags.

The season turned out to be run-of-the-mill for the Leafs; the fun came in the postseason, although not for Shack. Toronto finished third with 75 points, two behind the Canadiens and a distant 19 back of Chicago, the runaway leader from gate to wire. Eddie suited up for 63 games, scored 11 goals, added 14 assists, and got on the ice long enough to collect 58 minutes in the penalty box. He played in eight of the 12 playoff games but failed to notch any points, nor did he receive any penalties. The Leafs beat the stunned Blackhawks four games to two in the semifinal, then did the same to the Canadiens in the finals to win their fourth Stanley Cup of the decade. It would prove to be Toronto's last Cup to date.

In his farewell postseason with the Leafs, Shack ran afoul of Imlach for the last time. Experiencing a miserable semifinal during which he rode the bench for the most part, he then missed the team plane to Chicago, and even though he arrived in time for the game, he definitely made the top of Imlach's shit list.

Dave Keon recalls another little event that grated Imlach the wrong way: "The first game of the Stanley Cup final we lost 6-2 in Montreal, with all kinds of power plays, but hadn't scored. The reason? We rarely worked on having the man advantage, but the next day at a Forum practice Punch wanted nothing but power plays. Eddie, being the leader of the 'Black Aces,' was playing on the shorthanded team, killing penalties. By the time Punch called a halt to the drill, it was 6-1 for the 'Black Aces.' Eddie, proud as a peacock, skated around the ice, announcing in his loudest voice, 'The only goddamn problem with the power play is I should be on it.' Punch just skated away to the dressing room, completely pissed off."

Imlach had let it be known that aside from being unable to follow an airline schedule, Shack wasn't going to be given the opportunity to sit in the penalty box, either.

"I'd sit on the bench and be rarin' to go," Eddie groused at the time, "and when Punch wanted some checkin' and he'd throw me and [Billy] Harris and whoever out there, I'd be more worried about gettin' a penalty, any kind of penalty, than I was about doin' my job. You know, sometimes you didn't give one iota, and other times you wanna kick your own ass."

Shack's last celebration, his last yahoo with the boys in blue, his last chugalug from the Stanley Cup, was at the team party held in Stafford Smythe's house. "He had an indoor pool," Eddie says now. "[Tim] Horton and Pully [Bob Pulford] were carrying Stafford, pretending they were gonna throw him into the pool, clothes, wallet, watch, the fuckin' works. So while they were makin' a big show for everybody, I came runnin' up behind and pushed all three of them in. Oh-oh, I'm thinkin'. I don't give a shit about Smythe — serves him right for sending me to Rochester — and Pully, who cares, but Timmy was a handful. When he drank, everybody drank. When he told a joke, everybody laughed. The best thing to do when he got pissed was to stay out of his way. Now I'm lookin' over my shoulder for goddamn days, right, knowin' Horton's gonna get me. But he never got the chance. I got traded."

An era had truly come to an end.

IT'S DOUBTFUL THERE HAS EVER BEEN ANOTHER "REGULAR" PLAYER, with the exception of goalies, who dressed and spent more time on the bench than Eddie Shack did while still remaining a prominent player in the NHL. Even from that difficult position he commanded attention, the respect of his teammates, the concern of opponents, and the regard of the fans. Even though he was made a role player for all of his peak years, he never became passé or pigeonholed. Shack was much more than a faceless body in a uniform. If anything, he represented that much used cliché about professional athletes "having fun."

If the NHL is famous among its workforce for anything, it would be as a "no fun zone," a place where the only laughs come from the players, the boys in the trenches, the people whistling past the graveyard. A sense of humour is a required staple to fend off depressionists, coaches, and management, not to mention fickle fans and the hardhearted, spiteful media. To the uninformed fan professional hockey is a fun place, the ultimate carousel. To insiders it's a lot less.

When professional players and coaches talk about a winning attitude, "having fun" often comes up. It is equated with winning, or with a mind-set that has to be developed in those aspiring to be winners. But few players, and even fewer coaches, can look back on their careers and find much to do with having fun. With the exception of dressing room pranks, on-the-road and year-end parties, or the momentous occasion and euphoria of winning the Stanley Cup, there is no fun in professional hockey. It's a violent world where injuries and pain aren't just common but expected, part of the lifestyle.

Winning is a lot better than losing, true, but for the most part it's fifty-fifty at best. Life in pro hockey is a constant struggle for the individual player to make the team, to stay on the team, to sacrifice for the team, to produce more, to attain bigger numbers and larger contracts, to salt away cash for the irrevocable day of reckoning on that inevitable morning when daybreak and realization dawn at the same time and retirement is the only option. Only then, when it's all over, does a player really get a chance to look back and enjoy his career and the special moments that it brought.

The exception to that theory, the lone example of a man playing a kid's game and enjoying every minute, including the injuries, pain, setbacks, and coaches, was Eddie Shack, "The Entertainer."

Shack himself sums up his attitude to life best: "I've always thought like this. If it's snowin', we'll have some fun in the snow. If we're at the beach, we'll have fun in the sand. If it's rainin', we don't give a shit. We'll have fun gettin' wet. What the hell's the difference? If that's the way it is when you get up in the morning, just get out there and enjoy it."

Shack's career is the equivalent of his own experience as a young rookie riding a hot subway in New York, insulated from the world outside, only keeping abreast of goings-on through the conversation of his fellow passengers who continually get on and off. The stations along the subway line are much like the stops he eventually makes in his passage through life. Next stop Boston, next stop Los Angeles, and today the only thing Eddie vaguely remembers are some coaches, a few Stanley Cups, a smattering of teammates, and the occasional incident, good or bad, that's he's embroidered to suit his story line.

In my various talks with Eddie I found him to be unsure of years, never mind months. He mixed players and teams together, particularly in the Toronto years the first time around, and he never, ever, used injuries as signposts. There are players who can only put things into perspective based on the sequence of their medical record, guys who say things like, "That was after the broken arm in Calgary and before the hamstring in St. Louis."

Eddie doesn't recall injuries. He can't remember the broken ankle in Guelph. Nor can he remember whether "the fibular" in Providence was the same leg with the pinned ankle. He never mentions his serious knee injuries, a couple of them in the same season, checks that were administered to that same left leg by heavy hitters such as Pete Goegan, Reggie Fleming, and Leo Boivin. He doesn't recall a cut around his eye in Rochester, one that Don Cherry says *he'll* never forget. Nor does he place any importance on the injuries inflicted on others with the exception of the one he delivered to Lou Fontinato, and even then he chooses not to remember exactly what happened in the collision.

For instance, when I ask him about the collision with Gordie Howe that sent the superstar to a Toronto hospital with a concussion and a 10-stitch cut, he says, "It was just one of the times we cracked heads. We were always whackin' each other. It was my job." Or when I show him photographs of himself stretched flat on his side in an already blood-spattered white jersey, or being led off the Montreal Forum ice, his arms over the shoulders of trainer Bobby Haggert and teammate Larry Hillman as Haggert presses a gauze pad to a cut over Shack's eye that would take 15 stitches to close, Eddie has no memory of the incidents that caused the injuries.

He can recite the events leading up to the Henri Richard coco-bonk, but only because they have become part of hockey history and because they are funny enough to work as a crowd pleaser on the banquet circuit. For the most part, though, he is vague and noncommittal and has to be prompted about his past. Any interviewer has to settle for either the established, repetitive lines and stories, or be patient, pressing forward gently, risking a shrug or a hand wave of dismissal. Eddie remembers what he wants to remember, and repudiates anything that in any way infringes on his understanding of the facts.

Shack has little conception of time or dates as they relate to his lifetime. Rare is the case when he states anything emphatically such as a season or a turning point in his life. When he is asked about particular events concerning the Stanley Cup-winning Maple Leaf teams, the subject seems to become a blur to him. So in order to get a better perspective on Shack at the crossroads of his professional hockey career, I went to the people who had played with him during those glory years.

Goaltender Johnny Bower remembers those years well: "Eddie was a big factor on those Leaf teams of the 1960s, much bigger than most people imagined. If you think about the six-team league, Punch Imlach sent Eddie out there to make sure the other club played honest. Look at those Montreal teams. John Ferguson always caused a lot of trouble, crashing the goal crease and harassing me, so Punch put Eddie on and things settled down. As far as I was concerned, Eddie was great. He was doing his job. Sure, I'd get mad when he'd get penalties at a bad time, because he had a mean streak when things perturbed him, but he was doing exactly what Punch told him to do.

"Take a look down our bench. There weren't too many who could handle that job, who could go out on the ice and do what Eddie did, because they just weren't cut out for it. He was big, as strong as an ox, and perfect for his role on those great Leafs teams. He was a leader, too, and not many people know that about Shackie. Sure he was a happy-go-lucky guy, but an absolute competitor. He'd get up in the dressing room in between periods, waddle around in his untied skates, stick in his bare hands, and growl, 'All right, you guys, we can beat these assholes. Let's get going. Let's get at it. Let's do it goddamn it.' Take another look down our bench. There were some pretty big-status boys there — Davey [Keon], Tim [Horton], big Frank [Mahovlich] — and Eddie would get them going. No, he wasn't just a cheerleader. He did it at the right time, to the right guys. He got involved in his own way.

"Take me. I was a loner, you know. I kept to myself. Hell, I had enough to worry about, but Eddie would get up and say what was on his mind and the boys would listen. He was a workhorse, tireless in practice, and while it seemed like Punch was always mad at him, I don't think that was the case. In fact, I thought it was an act, part of the Imlach show. Occasionally Punch blew the whistle on Eddie, telling him to stay on his own side of the rink, but I firmly believe they had a mutual respect for each other.

"At the start of the season Punch took Terry Sawchuk and me aside and spelled out how he was going to settle the issue of who was number one. He told us the training camp was where he'd make up his mind and the goaltender who won the battle would play until he was either injured or pulled, then the other guy would take over. I was lucky enough to start the season in goal, and we were going good, winning five of six games, but I was starting to tire, and Punch saw it. So next game he starts Ukey, who's goin' good, too. And I'm thinking, Geez, I'm gonna be sitting here for a dozen games, maybe more.

"Later, when we were playing gin rummy on the plane, I suggested to Shackie, since he had one of the heaviest shots in the NHL, that he should try to shoot at Sawchuk's catching hand in practice. Maybe, I thought, it'll get sore. But I cautioned him, telling him to be careful and not hit Sawchuk in the throat. Sure enough, Eddie went out in the next practice and fired a few bombs. Believe me, catching Eddie's wrist shot was like picking a brick out of the air, and you have to remember, Sawchuk was the worst practice goalie in the league. He'd just stand there and wave his arms from time to time. So, after a few of Shackie's bullets, out came Terry. He broke his little finger. I told Eddie I was gonna buy him the biggest steak dinner he'd ever had. Everywhere, anytime Shackie sees me, he always yells at me about owing him a steak.

"You know, Punch was a good coach, and he was smart, too," Bower observes cryptically, as if the two attributes were seldom seen together. "We'd be getting a whipping in the Gardens and he'd put Eddie out to rile up the crowd, get things going, but we'd still lose, oh, say, 5-3, and badly, too. I remember after one of those games when we stunk the joint out and I took the subway home. The fans were still talking about Shackie. 'Did you see Eddie this. Did you see Eddie that. Boy, whatta guy,' they'd be saying. He took the heat off us every time."

Suddenly he begins to chuckle, magnified peepers disappearing once again behind his thick glasses, no longer the eagle-sharp, unmasked eyes of a 40-plus hockey superstar. "We used to twist wrists every once in a while. I had big hands, but I could never beat Timmy Horton or Eddie. That's what I mean about being a real competitor. It didn't matter what it was. He and I sat together on the plane all the time, playing gin rummy. Eddie was a gambler, and at the end of the season we'd settle up. If I won, he'd say, 'Double or nothing.' If he won, he'd offer the same deal, double or nothing. He'd say he was giving me a chance to get my money back. Sure. He knew how to look after *his* money."

Perhaps, I think, Johnny Bower has hit on the definitive creed of Eddie Shack's life: double or nothing.

Among those, outside of the players, who had the second best position to "Shack-watch" were the beat writers who travelled with the team. One of these was George Gross of the Toronto *Telegram*, the man who had escaped from behind the Iron Curtain and carved himself out a spot on the Toronto hockey scene. He was known along press row as "The Baron," a title that had as much to do with his pronounced accent as it did with his fastidious and coordinated style of dress among a group who were, for the most part, renowned for their dishevelled and baggy, bargain-basement fashion statements. "The Baron" was as close to Imlach and the Leafs as it was possible to be, something his stories reveal.

"The team was in Peterborough for another training camp between Stanley Cups, as I recall, and Imlach and Shack were having contractual difficulties. They carried on their jockeying for position all over the hotel, and you could hear them in the corridors, in the lobby, out on the street. But Punch knew that both he and Eddie liked the sauna, and he arranged to meet him after a workout. So there they are, sitting in towels, getting on with their discussions, and Punch has his special pen, the one that writes in steam. Sure enough, when they came out, Imlach was carrying a damp but signed contract.

"I have to admit I was a fan of Shack. To me hockey is entertainment, and Eddie personified entertainment in every sense of the word. People pay good money to see the game, and Shack always gave his best, not as often or for as long as he may have liked, but in keeping with Punch's iron-fisted way of doing things, he got the greatest amount of playing time he could expect on a very, very good team.

"Shack was also a sensitive player, more so than he ever let on, and probably had a case for being the whipping boy, having to accept the slights that come in that position, centred out over his Leaf career simply because of his status as the extra forward. I don't think he was as disruptive to the Leafs as some would have us believe, but if that was the case, he was also good in the dressing room. And don't ever forget, he was good for hockey in Toronto. When the fans saw him coming out on the ice, you'd see their eyes light up."

But away from the glow of the fans there were moments when Imlach and Shack collided, and Gross recalls an unpublicized story when things came to a head. "I remember we took a charter to Boston and the team bused from Logan Airport to the Copley Plaza Hotel, pulling in at 2:00 a.m. Punch grudgingly agreed the players could go and get something to eat, saying, 'But you only have until 2:30 a.m. to do it.' There was a mad rush across the street to a place called Ken's Deli. Eddie was among a few stragglers who made it back with his bag of sandwiches at 2:35 to the waiting Imlach, standing in the lobby like a maître d'. Punch fined him on the spot, and they had a blowout right there.

"Eddie obviously hadn't slept on it, because the next morning he came to me and said, 'I'll tell you about that SOB Imlach, all you wanna hear about that bastard and more. I ain't gonna take this shit.' I remember explaining to him, 'You're angry now. I'd have to check all this stuff out, and I'm not going to write it, anyway, so take it easy.' Eddie cooled out, although he didn't like it.

"Deep down I know they always respected each other. Eddie knew Punch could make him a winner, and I believe Eddie realized Punch had given him an opportunity to play on a team that was head and shoulders above the Rangers. Hell, Punch bought all his hats from Eddie!"

Pierre Pilote, the three-time winner of the Norris Trophy as the NHL's best defenceman and a former captain of the Chicago Blackhawks, had his share of run-ins with Eddie and witnessed many of Eddie's altercations with other players. "Eddie got nailed, too, you know," he says, as if he wants me to understand that Shack wasn't the only one dishing out beatings.

"Talk about handfuls. We had Reggie Fleming and Howie Young on the same team at the same time. Reg was a tough guy and he also killed penalties, but the rest of the time he was our Eddie Shack. We were playing in Chicago, and Eddie picked up the loose puck behind his net, gave it the big windup, but forgot one thing. You don't come up-ice on your backhand side. And as he got by his own defenceman at the Toronto blueline, Reggie came across, jumped a bit, and splattered Eddie against the glass. Shackie was on the ice, blood from his nose, and 22,000 fans went nuts. Howie Young jumped off our bench, skated over, picked up Reggie, and carried him around the ice like he'd just won the heavyweight championship.

"Well, the Leafs came back a month later. Frank Udvari was the referee, and we were killing a penalty, working the four-man box. The play shifted to one side of the ice, and now we were missing a guy. When we got a whistle and I looked behind me, there was Reggie lying on the ice, bleeding. And Eddie was skating around with a big grin from ear to ear."

One night, Pilote says, Pat Stapleton thought he had Shack lined up for a hit. When the Blackhawk swerved to hip-check Eddie, the Leaf forward jumped and caught Stapleton with two knees in the back and his stick across the head. Stapleton was about 25 feet from the Chicago bench, but he might as well have been a mile away. He crawled across the ice, and his teammates yelled at him to get off. They might as well have thrown the unfortunate Stapleton a life preserver; he looked like a drowning man trying to reach a boat.

On another occasion the Blackhawks and Leafs were at a face-off in the Chicago end, with Pilote lined up against Shack. Pilote had broken his nose in the previous game and had Technicolor shiners. When the puck was dropped, Eddie turned, mashed Pilote's face with his glove, and asked, "How's she goin', Pete?" Other than that, Pilote claims, Shack never really bothered him. In retrospect Pilote's theory on playing against Eddie Shack was to "herd him into a corner and let him run around until he petered out."

Red Kelly claims he had a special interest in Shack, one that was quite personal early on: "Eddie and I 'met,' in the way players work against each other, as he came up to the Rangers and I was with Detroit. But in the 1959-60 season we really crossed paths. The Rangers were visiting Detroit, and after the game I was told to go to the office and see Jack Adams [Detroit's general manager] and owner Bruce Norris. They told me I was going to New York for Bill Gadsby and Shack. I was shocked, and I remember saying the first thing I could think of: 'I'll think about it.' And I also remember Bruce Norris saying, 'What do you mean, you'll think about it? You be ready to report to the Rangers tomorrow morning when they catch the train.' Again I said I'd think about it, and I did. Jack Adams had given Andrea away when we got married. Now he was giving me away. That's what I thought.

"The next morning I called the tool-refurbishing company I'd started working for that summer and asked if I could have my job back. They said sure and when. I said right now. And I took it. Meanwhile Shack heard the story after the game, like I did, but he's happier than all get out about leaving the Rangers and Phil Watson behind. and apparently told Watson as much. Of course, the deal fell through. Eddie told me many years later that he hated me worse for not reporting to the Rangers than he hated Watson."

While Shack suffered in New York, Kelly held out for 10 long days, making his sales calls but finding the only thing Detroit-area customers wanted to talk about was his Red Wing situation. But the gods of hockey work in strange ways and the path was set for Kelly and Shack to meet again.

The ever-watchful Imlach, sensing a deal, took up the pursuit of the Wings' all-star defenceman. "Punch wanted me to come to Toronto secretly to see if they could make an agreement," says Kelly. "So I drove to Windsor and took a plane to Toronto in disguise, wearing a homburg and a long coat and carrying a small bag and an umbrella. It must have been a good cover. I walked right past King Clancy, who was waiting at the terminal, and had to stop and tap him on the shoulder.

"We went to the Gardens, talked through most of the day, and Imlach made arrangements for a private dinner at Winston's. On the drive downtown we came to a stop, and suddenly Punch said, 'Get down, get down!' We had pulled up beside Jim Vipond of the *Globe and Mail*, and he missed the story of the day by a whisker." But the cover was unnecessary and blown, anyway. Walking into Winston's, they ran into the entire Montreal Canadiens team, also there for dinner, and were greeted by Maurice Richard, who asked, "'Ey, Red, what are you doing 'ere?" Later that night Kelly agreed to the Leafs' contract terms and was in Toronto when Shack eventually arrived from New York the next season.

"Eddie was a bit off-the-wall," Kelly says, "but he was rugged. He could skate and shoot and he was accurate. His passing wasn't up to par, but he could agitate, and that's a talent, as well. I've looked at Eddie from both sides, as a teammate and as his coach, twice. Under the right circumstances it's safe to say he could have scored 300 goals in the NHL. But a coach would have had to adapt the team's play to his style. Usually players like Eddie have to do it the other way around — adapt to the team's strength. But you have to consider another important aspect. Eddie was rarely on the power play in Toronto, because the Leafs had so many great passers and playmakers, plus most of the fellows were big, too. So Eddie's habit of taking penalties, instead of capitalizing on them, was a contributing factor in limiting his role. That's the risk he posed, especially at playoff time."

Defenceman Allan Stanley, Shack's centre on the "Crash" Line, remembers the good and bad about Eddie: "The Leafs back then played a simple style. Wingers went up and down the boards and centres had a bit of leeway. Yet some nights Eddie couldn't seem to follow even that simple system. But the fans and Eddie had a love affair, regardless of game plans, and he could do no wrong in Toronto. There were nights when he'd come out and do a stunt that landed us in hot water. For instance, we'd be leading 3-1 and Punch would send Eddie out to liven up the game, and damned if he wouldn't get a penalty instead. The next thing you'd know, it would be 3-2. Then we'd play tooth-and-nail to hang on. But when he came off the bench the next time the fans would bring the house down. They'd want more. He had a special thing with the people in the seats all right. But not with Punch."

Dave Keon, the Leafs' classy star centre in the 1960s, says, "When Eddie arrived in Toronto, he was good for us because of what he brought to the team. We all knew he was a personality, and he made a great contribution to the Leafs. Eddie had marvellous skills, especially a great wrist shot, and if you could get him on the right track, he was an asset. But in the six-team NHL you only got so many chances.

"In Toronto he was a star, a personality, and he certainly brought that little extra to the team, but then he'd goof off and take bad penalties. That was the main reason he was traded to Boston. You have to keep in mind, though, that Eddie was the Leafs' 10th forward. But for a while it was me, {Bert] Olmstead, and Shack, and we were successful. The first year Punch put us together, we did great. I think it might have had to do with the fact that Eddie was intimidated anytime Bert was around. Talk about big, tough players. Olmstead kept Eddie in line. Hell, Bert could keep anybody in line."

When it is suggested that Shack had his own agenda and couldn't follow a game plan, Keon replies, "Umm, yeah, he could stick to a game plan, but I don't think he could toe the line for 70 or 80 game plans. See, later in his career, Eddie became the same as he was in junior, the showman, the show, in fact. But when he arrived in Toronto, he knew he was with a potential winner. He was smart enough to know that Punch could get us there, and he instinctively realized there was a certain way you carried yourself. Shackie recognized and respected those things, and he changed and became one of those people who took enormous pride in the fact he was a Toronto Maple Leaf. He realized all he had to do was his part, because that team of the 1960s was the show. We didn't need anything else except a winning team."

Ron Ellis, the Leafs' top-notch right winger and one of the youngest players on the last Toronto team to win a Stanley Cup, says of those bygone days, "I was the first change they made to those three Stanley Cup winners. It was frightening to join that club, but true to the character of that team they made me welcome and part of it, which was likely due to the fact I had been a Marlie. We always practised before or after them, so they were familiar with me. And I'd say, more than Rochester, the Marlies were the Leafs' farm club.

"The first time I was on the ice with Eddie was at a practice, and I remember my initial impression was how big and how strong and most importantly how quick he moved with that unconventional style. He was a lot like Claude Provost in Montreal, with his choppy power stride. Back then he was fast for a big fellow.

"Eddie's record speaks for itself. I don't believe anyone else has ever done the 20-goal plateau for five different teams, but personally, I contend that Eddie was more effective as a role player rather than as a guy in the lineup shift after shift. I think Eddie relished the opportunity to be spotted, and he was always ready to go, but as a regular, I don't know that he would have been as effective. No disrespect to Eddie or his abilities, but I just think his best suit was his talent of coming off the bench and getting something going."

AND WHAT DOES EDDIE SHACK THINK ABOUT ALL THOSE STANLEY Cup–winning Maple Leafs? Just before Christmas, one afternoon, I arrange to meet Shackie at a bar near Toronto's Yorkdale Mall. Apparently Eddie has to deliver a Christmas tree to the place, so the spot was convenient.

After a bit of detective work because Eddie told me we were to meet at Clueless Joe's rather than Shoeless Joe's, I finally arrive and notice the young barmaid, Sabrina, has no idea who Eddie is or why he seems to have the run of the place. Acceding to a request by some barflies, Eddie says, "You guys wanna see a Stanley Cup ring?"

He passes it around the little clutch of mid-afternoon patrons. They all take turns looking at it and trying it on. One of the barflies notes that the ring fits his thumb, while his friend points out that it's nothing more than a pinkie ring for Shack. "What year is this?" another asks, looking at the engraving and not finding an answer.

Eddie names off the years, all four, and adds, "They never gave you a new ring every year, yuh know, just a bigger diamond. The cheap bastards."

As the lunch crowd thins down to those standing with us, Eddie returns to his van, wrestles a Christmas tree into the restaurant, and stands it in the corner near the front door. Placing heavy leather gloves on the bar, he grasps a full glass of draft beer that Sabrina has replaced on the instructions of the manager. Now she seems to remember Eddie's name vaguely, which is okay because she also barely remembers the Leafs. The regulars heckle her for her lack of hockey knowledge.

But Eddie is uninterested in the bar talk. He's intrigued by the tough-looking young waitress decorating the tree. She has randomly placed some baubles at strategic levels and is now trying to add lights. Eddie shakes his head and moves over to the corner, commenting that it does-n't look as if she knows much about brightening up a Christmas tree.

"You're doin' it backwards. Ever done one 'a these before?" he wonders out loud.

She nods and replies, "Lots of times."

Eddie, grunts, turns back to me, and says, "Bullshit. She musta deco-rated trees in the joint." This comment breaks up the bar crowd but only gains a sardonic grin from the waitress as she continues to butcher the decoration process. Eddie remains in place, draft in hand.

"Jeezuz, you don't even know the goddamn cords go under the branches? You gotta hide 'em," he roars. The waitress merely shrugs, stone-faced, and stands her ground, doing her best to ignore this big guy in the big hat. She continues to wrap up the tree in electrical cord like she was tying up a hostage.

Eddie shrugs and walks back to the bar. "Why the fuck did I go to the trouble of bringin' this guy a tree if she's gonna screw it up like that?" he asks in a stage whisper you can hear in the kitchen.

"What do you care?" I whisper for real. "Are you planning to open your presents here? Let it go."

But he only shakes his head again. Meanwhile the waitress has come to the end of the light cord and is now dragging the tree to the power outlet, which by visual estimate will put the tree in the front doorway. "I guess an extension cord is expensive," Eddie growls.

At that point I divert our conversation to the subject of our meeting. "Eddie, listen up, okay? I want to mention the names of the guys on those Maple Leaf Stanley Cup teams and I want you to say what comes into your head first."

"Okay," he says, suddenly interested and doing a passable version of The Twist in his excitement. "Like one of them tests they give nutcases?" he asks, laughing at the prospect of a game.

"Right," I say. Then I turn to the half-dozen customers and caution them on the ground rules. "You can listen but don't interrupt. I'm trying to make a living."

"Yeah, shuddup, this is my Arthur," Eddie bellows, attempting to appear stern. Then he places his elbows on the bar, intertwines his fingers, puts on an alert expression, like that of a typical grade 3 student, and peers intently at my notepad. "Shoot."

"Frank Mahovlich."

"He was a different bastard, eh? Smart, talented, but he never got along with Imlach. If the two of them could have quit the bullshit, they'd have gotten more out of each other. But Imlach wouldn't leave him alone, wouldn't let Frank play his own game. And Frank was always in good shape. He didn't need all that heavy practice and conditioning stuff. He was already in good shape. Maybe Bower and Stanley needed the work, but not Frank."

"Johnny Bower."

"When he played for the Rangers, do you know what Bower told me Phil Watson said to him?" Eddie wrinkles his nose, which is a heavy duty wrinkle. "Watson said he was a career minor-leaguer, eh, but like most other things Watson said, he didn't know shit from putty. John didn't even catch on in the NHL until he was 37, and I remember him telling me all he wanted was to play for 10 years. He got 15. Punch used to work his ass off, too, for no good reason, but John plugged every minute he was on the ice, game or practice, like it was gonna be his last, He wanted to play, and he didn't care how much as long as it was lots.

"Sawchuk was the worst I ever saw in practice. He didn't do shit, and [Gump] Worsley, the same thing in New York. Gump was a young guy then for Christ's sake and all he ever did was piss and moan. But John Bower, what an honest guy, one of them good ol' turkeys who always gave 100 percent. I used to kid him about being from Saskatchewan. Whisky-boo or Wass-kazoo, I used to call it. We'd play cards on the plane, and while he was dealing I'd say things like, 'John, I had a dream that I hit you in the head.' Then in practice I'd wire a few high ones and he'd come chargin' out of the net, wavin' that big goal stick, cursin', no teeth, spittin' and hootin', callin' me names."

Eddie lets loose with one of his trademark har-har-hars, then looks around at the grinning faces of the nearby eavesdroppers, who are caught in the act but don't care.

We press on. "Bob 'Boomer' Baun," I say.

"We'd go out to a restaurant and Bobby would order the wine, looking at the menu for half an hour. Then he'd ask about the Cabber-nay, Cabber-noo, Cabber-nut, like any of the rest of us winos gave a shit or knew the goddamn difference."

"Pete Stemkowski."

"Stemmer had that big stride, a big slapper, and a big ass. A nice Ukrainian boy from Veen-yo-peg," Eddie says, thumping the bar while the others laugh in approval.

"Marcel Pronovost."

"Those old Red Wings stuck together. Him and Ukey [Terry

Sawchuk] were drinkin' buddies, and Sawchuk lived in a goddamn hotel. When he went on the road, all he was doin' was changin' hotels."

"Ron Stewart."

"He was a loner. He lived in Barrie. Figure that out. That's a long goddamn way to come to practice."

"Mike 'Shakey' Walton."

"He was a good little player, but he could have been a lot better. Let's just say he was different. I think Shakey's problem at the time was that he was married to Conn Smythe's granddaughter, and he thought he was protected."

"Dave Keon."

"Bert Olmstead was the guy who first said to Punch Imlach, 'This little guy can make it happen.' I remember when he was startin' out. We'd go to the Isabella Hotel after practice, and Davey would order a Tom Collins or some chickenshit little drink. Hey, he was a different guy. You know, when he was captain, he was livin' in his own apartment and he didn't even have a goddamn phone. Didn't wanna hear any beefs from the boys. How d'ya like that? But he was a good little player."

"Red Kelly."

"He was so goddamn solid. You couldn't knock him off his feet, and he could skate. He musta been able to skate because he was a great defencemen, then he was a great centre, too. That should tell you something about how well he skated. But on top of that he was tough. Nobody ever screwed around with Red. I know 'cause I tried to run him a few times when I was in New York. Once I lined him up and, ba-da-boom, I bounced backward and he kept right on goin'. I'm just standin' there like a goddamn stupe, so I said to hell with it and gave up on that shit."

Just then, inside Shack's jacket, hanging over the back of the bar stool, his cell phone rings. Taking the phone out of the pocket, he wanders over to a window to get better reception. When he's finished, he returns and announces, "We're leavin'."

One of the men at the bar chirps up and says, "Nice hat, Eddie," for no particular reason, referring to the cowboy hat Eddie sports as usual.

"I'd jump in the car after practice and head her out to Guelph," Eddie comments out of the blue. "I'd go see Mickey McMillan, pick up a load of hats, and bring 'em back to Toronto to sell. I used to have lots of orders. Punch always wanted those white beaver jobs."

By this time the entire bar crew looks either confused or amused, depending on their age. And as Eddie visits the washroom, the Christmas tree waitress breezes by me while I wait at the front entrance.

"Your pal," she asks, as if I'm chumming around with a known serial killer. "Is that the shape of his hat, or is it just to cover his pointed head?" Then she flounces toward a staff table at the back of the room.

As Eddie makes his way to the front door, throwing an arm through his jacket, he takes one last disapproving look at the waitress's decorating. "Horseshit tree," he observes.

CHAPTER SEVEN

Boston

It was obvious to anyone who cared that the Maple Leafs were certain to lose Eddie Shack in the six-team NHL expansion explosion in Montreal on June 6, 1967. Each of the Original Six clubs was allowed to protect one goalie and 11 skaters going into the draft, and Shack had worn out Imlach's patience. Therefore, his chances of being one of those protected were either slim or none.

Although Shack remained the darling of the fans, his time in Toronto was at an end as he openly balked at the "old ways" of Imlach, a man living in the past, according to Eddie, who cites, by way of an example, Imlach's occasional stubborn clinging to train travel in a day and age of jet flights. While Eddie still couldn't read, even he could see the writing on the wall: "I asked Punch to get rid of me, trade me somewhere I could play."

Shack was itching to be on the ice and "doin' somethin'" instead of watching and waiting for that pat on the back. To Eddie, a "team" man in practice, the guy who livened up the drudgery of starts and stops, line rushes, and the "hard between the bluelines," the championships were secondary to playing as a regular. He had already climbed the mountain four times. Shooting for the top was old hat; playing as a regular was where he wanted to be.

It was apparent that the Boston Bruins, especially general manager Milt Schmidt, coveted the aggressive Shack, and had for many seasons. As far back as 1963, Schmidt was overheard in the press box saying, "I wish Shack was in Boston. Man, he'd pack them to the rafters in the Garden." It was a remark that found its way to Imlach, for even though Shack considered Punch a dodderer in terms of his travel skills, very little escaped the Leaf chief when it came to making deals.

It was also no secret to Imlach that Murray Oliver wanted out of

Boston and preferred Toronto. Equally obvious was that Boston coach Harry Sinden considered Oliver expendable in his desire to add bigger players to the Bruins. By 1967 Schmidt was given the finances and company credit card to construct a Stanley Cup winner, and in a single day of telephone calls five big bodies arrived that put the Bruins back on the hockey map.

On May 15, 1967, while playing in an Oshawa, Ontario, golf tournament, Shack was tracked down by a messenger from the Leafs. "I'll wait till I'm finished here to call," he told the others in his foursome. "I think I know what it's about." Later, after two quick calls from a pay phone at the club restaurant, Shack returned to his table and announced, "Boston got me for Murray Oliver and $100,000 U.S. Milt Schmidt said it was the best deal the Bruins have ever made."

There was talk about the "deal of the century," but it had nothing to do with Eddie Shack, even though the two deals were consummated on the same day. Hockey analysts were referring to the swap that sent goaltender Jack Norris, defenceman Gilles Marotte, and up-and-coming centre Pit Martin to Chicago for oversize centre Phil Esposito, garage-size winger Ken Hodge, and playmaker Fred Stanfield. True, it wasn't the only piece of the puzzle. Schmidt sent the polite Oliver (16 penalty minutes in 1966) to the Leafs with the bag of U.S. cash for the rambunctious Shack, and in doing so Schmidt cut space on the roster for one of the Bruins' prized juniors, a rookie named Derek Sanderson.

In one afternoon the Big Bad Bruins were born. If we leave goalie Norris out of the equation, since goaltenders are measured in their ability to stop the puck rather than height and weight, the Bruins netted an 11-foot gain vertically and added 500 pounds of beef. The Bruins were only two seasons away from their first Stanley Cup in 29 years.

For Shack it was a fresh start, a chance to be a regular. He was going to a place where he was wanted, and he was ecstatic, happy he was still with an Original Six team rather than one of the expansion clubs, which included the St. Louis Blues, Philadelphia Flyers, Oakland Seals, Minnesota North Stars, Pittsburgh Penguins, and Los Angeles Kings.

After training camp in London, Ontario, Shack headed for Boston with the air of a man who was completely confident in his popularity and his celebrity. In his first move in seven years it never occurred to him that this wasn't Toronto, one of the two hockey Meccas of the world, and that the Boston fans, although loyal and partisan, wouldn't have the same sense of proprietorship of their new player as the Toronto fans had always had. Of course, due to his demeanour and personality, Eddie didn't need to wear a Bruin jersey to identify himself.

Meanwhile, back in Canada, a cultural aftershock was beginning to build. To entire generations of kids across the country Saturday night was bath night, change-of-pajamas night, popcorn night, the evening when the entire family, including the dog, got together, with scrubbed faces and buttery fingers, to watch what became a legend. Hence, the name *Hockey Night in Canada*, our rite of winter. Part of the legend was Foster Hewitt, and another part was Eddie Shack and what he'd do next. Underlining Eddie's popularity in Canada, not only with the ticket holders at Maple Leaf Gardens but in an entire country, was the general dismay generated by the prospect of Eddie as a headliner in faraway Boston. The fact that Shack would only be available on occasion was reason enough for *The Canadian*, a full-colour weekend magazine supplement distributed through newspapers across Canada, to commission his good friend and former backyard rink rat compadre Paul Rimstead to write a lengthy article about him.

One of the leading feature writers of the day, Rimstead had a folksy, friendly, observational style, and his lifelong association with his subject allowed him to make his point about Shack's affinity for hockey fans, and people in general. The magazine's colour cover photo shows Shack in front of his new Saugus, Massachusetts, home, cigar clamped firmly in his big smile, holding a Stars and Stripes. That was just a teaser. The story lead said more about Eddie's unpretentious nature and everyday charm:

> The sweet young thing, her face set in a frozen smile, was perched demurely behind the cosmetic counter, the latest in French perfumes spread before her in sample atomizers.
>
> A large man strode up, a large man with a very large nose.

"Turpentine!" he said.

"I beg your pardon?" she replied, the smile vanishing and furrows breaking out on her forehead.

"Turpentine!" repeated Edward Shack. "Where is it? I gotta get some. And a rake."

With a look of relief, the young lady pointed across the open floor of the Boston department store to the hardware division.

"How are ya?" bellowed Shackie, slapping a wooden mannequin across the shoulder as he passed it.

To show his confidence in the marriage of team and player Eddie went out on his own and bought a house, demonstrating a certain disregard for the distinct direction of Norma who, with six-year-old Cathy and four-year-old Jimmy, soon joined him in New England.

Today, sitting in Shack's kitchen in Toronto, I ask him about the house in Massachusetts. He says, "Yep, I bought this place in little Saugus, about 20 minutes, half an hour to the Boston Garden."

While making a pot of coffee, Norma calls up the memory of what she told Eddie before he left for Boston. "'Whatever you do,' I said, 'don't buy a house.'" As she tells me this, her husband looks out the kitchen window over the garage, seemingly waiting, almost hoping, for some distraction to occur on the street outside.

"The one thing, no, the *only* thing I told him before he left was, 'Don't buy a house,'" she repeats needlessly. "I gave him explicit instructions. A week later he calls and says, 'I bought a house.'"

From his window lookout, Eddie merely grins and blinks, then nods as though someone has just rapped him on the head.

"Then," Norma continues, "when he started describing it, all I kept saying was, 'Oh, no, wood panelling in the living room! Oh, no, green wall-to-wall carpeting! Oh, God, no!' And I kept saying, 'I'm gonna hate this house.' Actually, though, it was a cute little place.

"I have to admit, aside from that little glitch, I was excited. I have a very positive outlook on life and I never took any of the trades hard, but I can recall when Ed was traded from Toronto to Boston. Even though he knew it was coming, he seemed despondent at first. He took it hard. Me, I was so happy. I loved the idea and I was excited to leave Toronto.

I found it hard to understand that Ed wasn't happy about the change. At the time I thought nothing could be better for Ed's career. I felt even more confident when we went to such a good team, especially since Boston made the playoffs and Toronto didn't. It was a great year."

On his first return trip with his new playmates to Maple Leaf Gardens, Shack made his entrance at the game-day practice wearing a ski mask, the now-famous nose a dead giveaway as he took a few laps around the ice to loosen himself up as well as the Toronto media. When Eddie returned to the bench to doff the temporary disguise, a newsie asked if he had knitted the head cover himself. "Yeah, remember, I had all kinds of time with the Leafs to knit, parked on the end of the bench," he groused with a touch of bitterness.

While he eventually put the dour mood of leaving Toronto behind him, it wasn't long before things returned to the status quo. Soon Shack and Sinden were crossing swords, or sticks, in this case, and the resulting fireworks made the newspapers. One reported that "Boston coach Harry Sinden has fought a losing battle in his efforts to convince Eddie Shack he cannot used the curved stick. At one point he forced Shack to use a straight blade, but Shack became so upset that the coach broke off the experiment."

But Shack was a different player. He took to positional play with a vengeance, so much so that Sinden later complained to reporters, saying, "I wish he'd bust out, take one of those wild flings up the ice and show us some of that flair we've come to expect. Playing by the book isn't Ed's strong suit."

In fact, the line of rookie Derek Sanderson at centre, with Shack and Ed Westfall on the wings, was proving to be a new threat opposing teams had to prepare for. In addition, Shack's exuberance and unique characteristics were helping on the ice and in the dressing room.

Back in his Toronto kitchen, Eddie says cryptically, "We had to dress at the Boston Garden." Then his attention is diverted by the awaited diversion outside. Before I know it he races, laughing, through the kitchen to the front door, and I follow him. From the top of the stone staircase leading to the driveway, he bellows, "Watch them goddamn cans!" as the garbage collectors make their way along the street. "They cost a lotta money. I'm a retired guy fer cripes sake." The workers look up and break into smiles. "Yeah, sure, laugh, you bastards. You got jobs. I'm stuck here in the house with the wife, and it's cleaning day." After the garbagemen point and chortle their sympathy, Eddie and I return to the kitchen. He's cackling now, happy that he's raised the spirits of "them litter bugs."

"Can you imagine gettin' up in the morning and pickin' up shit all day?" he asks. "That's why I go out there and shake them up a little. Jeezuz, it shouldn't be the worst goddamn thing in the world to have a job, yuh know."

"You were saying about the Bruins," I prompt, bringing him back to the conversation as he waves goodbye to the departing garbage crew through the kitchen window.

"What? Oh, yeah, we had to dress at the Garden, then bus somewhere else to practice, so we were in our equipment but wearing shoes. I had to wear my shower slippers 'cause the goddamn shin pads wouldn't fit into cowboy boots, but I put my skates over my stick, slung the stick over my shoulder, and went out of the dressing room, singing, 'Hi ho, hi ho, it's off to work we go.'" As he yodels, he marches out of the kitchen again, adding a couple of skipping steps to the routine. "That's Phil Esposito's favourite story," he says, almost out of breath from laughing.

But another story made headlines that first year in Boston: the stick fight he had with longtime adversary Larry Zeidel. Not only was the incident shocking, but it took place in an odd location. When I ask Eddie about the confrontation, he answers in a far more serious tone that changes the mood in the kitchen dramatically.

"When I was playing in Springfield, back in my Ranger days — I think it was an exhibition game or somethin' — we played against Hershey. Zeidel speared me and I told him if he did it once more I'd conk him. Next time we were on the ice he did it again, and bang, I whacked him right over the head. We were rejected [ejected], sent home to the dressing room, right? So I got changed and was standing by the seats, minding my own business and watching the game, when Zeidel came up from behind, yappin' and chirpin', gettin' after me again. We had a fight right there, boom. The cops came and we ended up in jail, me in one cell, him in another. I asked him, 'Are you nuts? What the fuck is the matter with you, anyway?' And the big stupe just sat there, glarin' at me.

"Well, about 10 years later [late in the 1967-68 season) the roof blew off the Philadelphia Spectrum, so we had to play against the Flyers at Maple Leaf Gardens. And Zeidel and me met again. What did the guy do? He speared me, and I figured that was it, and we got into a stick swinger. He got stitches, not me. At that time I was going good, but I got sat down, suspended, for almost two goddamn weeks. It really pissed me off."

For his part Shack was suspended for three games and was fined $300. Years later a retrospective Larry Zeidel passed the incident off as visually incorrect. "Ah, we just nicked each other. Hell, as a good stick fight it didn't even rate. Yet after, it was like I invented using the stick. I was a 40-year-old defenceman. I had wrinkles and the blood flowed into them. That's what made it look bad."

In reality it was a vicious, sickening, brutal scene: two hockey players, blood flowing from their faces, swordfighting on ice, given a wide berth by alarmed officials, fearful players, and 12,000 horrified fans transfixed at this bloody spectacle at Maple Leaf Gardens.

As Eddie gets ready to attend a business meeting in downtown Toronto, he decides to lighten the mood and reveals a fact that has often been rumoured — the nonaggression pact with "Mr. Hockey," Gordie Howe. It was a gentleman's agreement consummated in the summer of 1967 as Eddie prepared to move lock, stock, and family to Boston.

"We were at a golf tournament," he says, slipping into a Legends of Hockey jacket, "somewhere in Vermont, I think. We were havin' a beer, Tuborg, bullshittin', and we struck up the deal. I wasn't beyond acting up now and then, you know, and he knew I had no fear. Gordie says, 'How 'bout this, Shackie? You don't hit me, I don't hit you.' Shit, I gotta nose for value, eh? I took the deal and said, 'Put her there, big boy.'" Eddie sticks out his meat hook to clasp an imaginary hand. "We shook, and that's the way it stayed until I retired. Gordie never retired.

"Sinden used to warn me, 'Gordie's gonna get ya, Shack.' But I used to smile like a goddamn lunatic and say, 'No fuckin' way, Harry. That big bastard won't touch me. He's scared shitless. I'm too goddamn tough.' I'd piss my pants laughin' and Sinden figured I was nuts, but I knew Gordie and me had a deal." As Eddie finally leaves for his appointment, I find myself thinking that his trust in Gordie Howe says a greal deal about him, not to mention his unshakable faith in any man's handshake.

Shack has the kind of attitude that says, "If I said it, I mean it," as in the case of the Zeidel incident. People find this quality intriguing, and several of Eddie's teammates and opponents can vouch for his word being his bond. One is Fred Stanfield, who was another of the "new" Bruins in the Boston Garden in 1967.

Sitting in Stanfield's East Amherst, New York, kitchen overlooking the backyard patio deck, pool, and hot tub shrouded for winter, I notice the Stanley Cup ring on his finger, signifying the two Cups he won with Boston in the 1970s.

"When Eddie arrived in Boston," Stanfield says, "people made the mistake of taking him for a fool. Like I said, that was an error. They forgot Eddie was from a very good team [Leafs] and in that respect he was a leader. He was good for the team, and he was a good 'team' man, an excellent addition to a club that had some solid veterans like [John] Bucyk and [Ed] Westfall, the greatest up-and-coming player in the game in Bobby Orr, a collection of players from all over, including me, and a pretty good rookie in Derek [Turk] Sanderson. I also happen to think Eddie was a steadying influence on Turk that year because Derek was cocky and considered himself the king of the juniors."

At that moment Alice, the Stanfield dog, erupts into barking. Outside the pool gate a sign pictures Alice with a caption that says, "Beware, she's little, but she knows kung fu." Now we watch as the dog scampers across the deck in pursuit of a rabbit. "She's never caught one yet," Stanfield advises me as Alice hurls herself two inches off the floor with every little yipe.

"We made the playoffs both years Eddie was in Boston," Stanfield continues. "Before that the last time the Bruins made the playoffs was in 1959. Eddie was a character. He kept us loose and had a say when it was needed. Sometimes he was outspoken . . . for the times. But you always knew when Eddie was in the dressing room. For that reason he wasn't Sinden's type of guy, and they didn't hit it off. Eddie could skate and shoot holes in the net, but if I was only allowed to say one thing about Shackie, it'd have to be that he never backed down. From anybody.

"That night in Maple Leaf Gardens when he and Zeidel went at it was the scariest battle I'd ever seen. Man, they whacked each other with those sticks. In fact, they broke them and got other ones. Nobody, including the officials, would go near them.

"It wasn't the first time I heard about Eddie. The last Stanley Cup year he was with the Leafs I was trying to stick with the Blackhawks, and there was this story about Eddie being stopped by the police in my dad's jurisdiction." At the time Stanfield's father, Gord, was deputy chief of Toronto Township, a collection of small communities that soon became Mississauga, now a burgeoning city of more than a half-million people.

"Eddie was moving from one party to another, I guess, and he had some beer in the car when the officers stopped him for speeding. Of course, being a member of the Stanley Cup Leafs, he ended up in my father's office. Dad said to him, 'If you don't have a dozen autographed Leaf sticks in here by tomorrow afternoon, you're gonna be in deep trouble. Do we understand each other?' Eddie just nodded, and my dad slipped in another stipulation. 'And don't be running over my son next year, either.'

"Sure enough, Eddie showed up the following day with a load of lumber on his shoulder. I still have one of the sticks in my rec room, but my dad was a hero after that incident because he gave the other sticks to the officers on shift that night. For Eddie it was an even trade."

I ask if Eddie kept the other end of the bargain. When Stanfield looks at me with puzzlement, I add, "Did he ever try to bulldoze you?"

"No, but he came close," he remarks, with a knowing smile.

Dave Keon is another former teammate, albeit a Leaf, who can vouch for Shack's word and dispel any rumours that Shack was a backstabber on the ice. "No, I don't agree that Eddie was ever a backstabber, but if he got a chance to run you, it was lights out. When he left Toronto for Boston, he maintained any Leaf was fair game. He said he was gonna get us, and I sure as hell know he got me. When we went to the Boston Garden, I came face-to-face with Eddie breaking out of our end. I had this sneaky move, a tricky little sidestep, and I tried it on Shackie. I guess he'd seen it before, so it wasn't the big surprise I thought it was going to be, and he really took me into the boards. I was flat on the ice, trying to get some air, and Timmy [Horton] came roaring up, incensed, and tried to get hold of Eddie. 'What the fuck are you doing?' Timmy yelled at Eddie. Shackie just kept backing off, saying, 'I told him. I told everybody, Timmy. I told him when I left Toronto I was gonna get him,' as if that made it okay," Keon says, laughing.

One of the strangest pairings in all of hockey was the bond between Derek Sanderson and Ed Shack, two diametrically opposed personages who were thrown together in the right place at the right time, a hockey marriage that comes along all too infrequently.

Shack was the northern boy from a mining town, no pretences, no education. Sanderson was from the Honeymoon Capital, Niagara Falls, much more schooled, much of it in how to appear larger than life. Both of them had street smarts. While one was a heralded rookie, the other had already been there. Later in life both would be able to look back at their lives and be proud of what they had made out of the tools they'd been given. But Sanderson, in his own helter-skelter way, is the storyteller, and among his other accomplishments he knows how to spin a tale.

"I loved playing with Eddie. I really did. I was a rookie, hadn't been anywhere in the States except Boston, or Buffalo and across the river to Niagara Falls, New York, if you wanna count those places. And on my first ever road trip to California, Eddie was really good to me. What the hell, I'm a kid, and when you get to play with Eddie Shack your first year out of junior, it's a big deal.

"We get to Oakland and naturally I've never been to San Fran, so Eddie says, 'C'mon kid, we're gonna rent a car.' Geez, I'm sayin' to myself, Eddie Shack wants to go out with me, this is great. We rent a car, I gotta go through all the paperwork and shit, but Eddie says I'll drive and you ride, and pay attention rookie because we're looking for downtown, Broadway exit, okay? So we're zipping along, up comes a sign, Broadway . . . one mile. Next it's Broadway, a half mile. Everything is goin' good. Next, Broadway quarter mile, and we're still bombin' along with a three length lead in the race, and here comes Broadway, next right, and zing, we blow by the exit. I said, 'Eddie, what the fuck you doin', we missed the turn!' And he looks at me all pissed off and says, 'You dumb bastard, why didn't you tell me? I can't read, I need somebody along to get us home, ya goddamn dope. You think I brought you along 'cause I like ya?'"

In Boston, Sanderson says, people listened when Eddie arrived. "We went to training camp in London [Ontario], had a team meeting, and Eddie was the first choice for captain. What? you say. He was senior man, right? The Bruins were losers, and Eddie was the only winner. There was myself, Bobby [Orr], Phil [Esposito], Freddie [Stanfield], Kenny [Hodge], Ed [Westfall], and John [McKenzie], so there were no winners. I think it was Phil who said, 'Eddie, you be captain.' And Eddie said, 'Nope, the captain has to be able to read.' Funny, nobody became captain. All we had were A's that season.

"Our line's job was to create havoc. I thought it was an honour to play with Ed Shack. He was a veteran. When I was a kid, I'd watched him on *Hockey Night in Canada* when he was a Maple Leaf. Hey, everybody grew up watching the Leafs. So what if he was shuffling through by the time he got to Boston, kinda playing it out. He got 21 goals that year." The truth was Eddie scored 23 goals, Sanderson 24, and Westfall 14 in the 1967-68 season.

"One night," Sanderson continues, "we were playing in Detroit and Eddie was in the slot. I got it out to him and he knuckle-balled it at Roger Crozier, who I think was the 'dodger' that night. Anyway, the pass was on end and the top of Eddie's blade caught the bottom of the puck. It flipped and fluttered toward Crozier. Maybe it was going in, maybe it was gonna miss. Who the hell knows? I deflected it, and Eddie came up to me and said, 'Jeezuz, Turk, I needed that one for 20 and my bonus.' So I said, 'Go ahead, take it. I don't give a shit. Take the fuckin' goal.' Then I went over to John Ashley, the ref, and said the goal was Eddie's. Ashley shot back, 'What are you talking about? I saw you touch it. You think I'm blind?' I explained it was Eddie's bonus, and John said, 'Okay, what's the difference?' So Eddie got the goal. Next night Eddie got two and said to me, laughing his ass off, 'See, shithead, I didn't need your goddamn goal, anyway.' Now I needed that one for 25 and a bonus for the big payday, and there it was, sittin' in Eddie's column."

Sanderson shakes his head and laughs quickly, relishing the memory, then he launches himself into another story. "You know how most teams have the goaltenders come out first for the warm-up? Not with Eddie. In Boston he'd be the first one out, burning rubber all the way from the dressing room, jumping on the ice, doing a pirouette, dropping a puck, and slapping it. Just like clockwork. Never a variation.

"Another night we were in the Olympia in Detroit and Eddie came galloping out, but this time he took a full-tilt twirl around the ice first, then wired one from the goddamn red line. By this time I was out there, too, skating along, and I said, 'Oh-oh, it's goin' high. Oh, shit, it's over the glass. Oh, my Gawd!' In the Olympia they had a concrete wall at the top of the first tier, and there were two guys, sorta turned in their seats, gabbin' about a foot apart, and I figured the puck was gonna kill one, maybe both of them if he gets a good bounce. Whack, it hit right between their faces. All Eddie said to me was, 'I almost drilled one of those assholes, eh?' I mean, nothin' ever bothered him, but man, I was freaked for the whole goddamn warm-up."

Turk lets out one of his snuffling chuckles, takes a drag on his cigarette, and plunges ahead. "Nobody thinks the old-school guys were good to rookies, right, but Eddie was great with me. You know, if you weren't goin' good, gettin' down on yourself and your game, Eddie'd come over and say, 'Hey, buddy. Hey! None of that. We don't need that shit around here.' He always picked me up. He was always fun to play with, and believe me, he came to play every night with all kinds of energy.

"In fact, that goddamn energy was the one thing that caused me to get really pissed off at Eddie. I think we had come close to losing to one of the expansion teams, and Sinden was aggravated. He had us skating blueline to blueline, redline to the blueline, to the far blueline and back again over and over. Shackie and Don Awrey were having a great old time and got into harpin' on Sinden, because those two bastards could skate all day. They didn't give a shit. Now Harry was really pissed off, and it was more skating, no pucks, nothin' but groin strain and snot.

"Eddie'd come barrelling down the ice, stop, and blow snow over the glass from beside the net for cripes sake. I never saw anyone who could throw as much snow as high as Eddie could. Hell, in practice he'd come off the wing and absolutely bury E. J. or Cheesy [goalies Ed Johnston and Gerry Cheevers]. They used to hate it. They'd look like they just came in from a goddamn blizzard. I never saw anyone who could accumulate that much snow, and I never figured out how he did it, but it was just Eddie's way of enjoying life at practice. So him and Awrey get goin' on Sinden's torture test — two big, strong, powerful skaters — and they just covered the glass. Man, I'm pukin' my guts out as Eddie skates by Sinden and roars, 'Yah think this bothers us, Harry? Donald and I can do this fuckin' shit all day.' And they could, too. Man, Eddie could skate. Him and that goddamn Awrey. They really pissed me off."

I ask if it was true that Sinden and Shack never got along.

"Nah, but Eddie wasn't a fan of Harry, because Sinden was so young. I was oblivious to all that shit. I had enough to worry about just mindin' my own business. I never heard any insults or knocks from Sinden, but Eddie would rag on Harry all the time. That's the nature of the game. The coach is a prick and the players all band together against him, yet Harry was a fabulous coach, a terrific motivator, and the best I ever played for, bar none. Hey, look at Team Canada '72. Anybody who played in Russia will tell you that. Mind you, Shackie was a loose cannon out there, and I'd have to watch out for him, but Harry would let him roam, telling *me* to watch *his* wing, to back him up if he was goin', and you gotta know he'd go.

"But in my opinion Eddie handled the puck better than people give him credit for. He set me up for a good dozen goals, absolute gifts. He made nice plays. He could hit, skate, was a great shooter, and he was a big man who created a lot of trouble, which buys you a lot of space.

"Two years later, when he went to L.A., he jumped me. Yep. I hit him along the boards, dinged him on the beak — how could I miss — and he jumped me. He'd told me before, said he was gonna get me, and sure enough — bang. I said, 'What are you hittin' me for, you big jerk?' He just laughed like a goddamn hyena. Still, Shackie had a lot to do with pulling that Boston team together before he left, and I know that I really hated to see him go."

Sometime later Eddie and I are driving down the Queen Elizabeth Way in Toronto and I mention my talk with Derek Sanderson. Of course, Shackie has to get his two bits in about Turk: "All that piss and vinegar, and he was a cocky son of a bitch, too. Always bullshittin'. He was way underpaid at the time, but when he eventually started gettin' some money, he couldn't handle it."

Then, before I know it, Eddie throws himself into yet another humorous anecdote. "Ah, shit, the reason Turk liked me was because he did somethin' to Timmy [Horton] in Toronto. He jabbed him or somethin', and Timmy grabbed him, so I stepped in and grabbed Horton. It was no big deal. Timmy couldn't fight worth a shit, and I just got in there and wrassled him a bit, you know, protectin' the rookie 'cause Horton was tossin' Turk around like an old pair of pants. Next thing I know, Turk let 'em fly, punchin' the shit out of Timmy. And here was me, a big stupe, holdin' him. How do ya like that? I saved that goddamn Sanderson's ass, and now Timmy was pissed at me! Holy sheepshit, I thought, how the hell did I get mixed up in this crap?"

But Eddie's time in Boston was appreciated, and when the party was over, he moved on, as always, with great memories. "Wayne Cashman and me used to ride together, because we lived pretty close, and one night when we went in for a game, I asked the trainer for a benny [benzedrine tablet]. That was in the days when everybody was takin' 'em, right? And he also gave me a sleepin' pill for later. So I took a pill, and man, nothin'. It didn't even faze me. On the way home Cash said his foot was achin' from a shot he'd taken, so I said, 'Here, take the sleeping pill. You need your rest, big boy.' Next day he told me he was up all goddamn night. Oh, my achin' ass!" Shack suddenly exclaims in the car. "I figured out why I had no energy, why I was almost noddin' on the goddamn bench and dozin' off between periods. I'd taken the wrong pill.

"Geez," he suddenly says in a more serious vein, "when you think about people like [Red] Kelly, Big Frank [Mahovlich], [Bobby] Hull, [Phil] Esposito, and [Bobby] Orr, I can say I played on teams with the best players in the world. I remember I ran Bobby Orr a couple of times, yuh know. But he was classy, and I can honestly say a real gentleman. When I was with the Bruins, he always told us to 'look after the trainers,' reminders like that, because he was doing it all the time. He'd look after guys on the team, pick up tabs in restaurants, talk to the rookies. He did everything. Hell of a man.

"Esposito was a pretty good player, eh? But he needed a guy like Cashman, because Phil could get the shit kicked out of him. The Bruins were a good team. We always had laughs on the train or on the plane. All those guys felt lucky to be in the NHL, to have a job. Know what I mean? Hockey players tend to trust other players, you know. Then when Espo got to be management he tried to be a good guy, one of the boys. But hockey players get fucked by hockey people. So Phil looked after Phil. Nothin' wrong with that. Hey, he played good hockey."

By the 1968-69 season some said the Boston fans started to dislike Shack when he seemingly backed off from a fight that erupted in front of the Bruin bench. Truth was, he had just returned from a bicep injury, the result of a early-season fight with Chicago's Gilles Marotte, a guy with a grudge. Marotte was the player the revamped Bruins had traded to get Esposito, Hodge, and Stanfield. By taking it up with Shack, he took the opportunity to prove that shoving him out the door to Chicago was a mistake.

More important than the misconception of the fans, the Boston brass soured at the thought of Shack sitting in the penalty box at the wrong time, and once again Shack's penalties were "stupid" rather than the by-product of his boisterous play. Eddie felt he was made the goat by management, and he lumped coach Harry Sinden in with the suits upstairs.

For Eddie it was business as usual in the playoffs. He was benched for his penalties in the Boston series with Montreal. Late in two different games he was penalized; both times the Canadiens scored, once to tie it up in a game the Habs went on to win in overtime. Publicly, in a backhanded way, Harry Sinden sided with his player and took it out on the referee. "We may have to bench Shack. It seems Eddie's barred from playing in the NHL. The officials are out there looking for him every time he gets on the ice."

The usually mild-mannered Ed Westfall was seething after that game, as well, and took his own backhanded rap at "them." He was quoted as saying, "It gets me angry when I hear somebody rap Eddie Shack for supposedly taking 'silly penalties.' That's a lot of BS. Shackie's hitting helps us tremendously, even when he's called for it. It lifts us mentally. Besides shaking up the player he hit, it usually shakes up the guy's teammates, too. So I'll happily kill all the penalties Eddie draws. And I've told him that."

But by now the Bruins knew they were going off in another direction, up, and the decision was made to bolster their lineup with future picks while they could. They found a willing accomplice in the Los Angeles Kings. On May 14, 1970, one day short of exactly two years from when they acquired Eddie, the Bruins traded him and Ross Lonsberry for Ken Turlik and two first-round picks in 1971 and 1973.

Eddie remembers that well: "Boston was goin' places at the time, and Sinden said, 'We got you here to play. We don't need any entertaining in Boston.' Yeah, right. They wanted me to hit, be aggressive, use my size, and when I did, they benched me. So I yapped about it and said, 'Why don't you get rid of me?' So they did. I shoulda shut my mouth.

"But d'ya know why I really got traded? I made fun of [Bruins owner] Weston Adams's hats. I used to sell Biltmore hats all over the league, but bein' a millionaire and a real cheap son of a bitch, he wouldn't buy any. Remember them beauties Imlach used to wear? They all came through me. Well, Adams used to wear the oldest, dirtiest, crappiest, horseshit hats in the world. And I'd let him know about it, too."

When Shack finally left Boston, he was heard to wonder aloud: "I was hurt a lot last season, and I missed too many games. But I got 11 goals, and seven of them were game winners."

He also missed his fifth Stanley cup by one season.

CHAPTER EIGHT

Los Angeles

IT ONLY TOOK A WEEK FOR ED SHACK TO MAKE NEWS IN CALIFORNIA.
Speaking to a reporter in Long Beach from Saugus on May 25, 1969, he
took on the mantle of the reluctant missionary coming to spread the
gospel of hockey. In addition he allowed that Toronto was his first
choice of destination.

"My wife is more enthused about going to Los Angeles than I am,"
he told the reporter. "I wanted to go back to Toronto, maybe get a business started. In Toronto the fans understand hockey. In California
there's a few things they don't get."

Not to worry. There were plans and people in place, waiting for
Shack to arrive. It was no secret that Jack Kent Cooke, the expatriate
Canadian wheeler-dealer and king of the Kings, heartily endorsed the
acquisition of Eddie to boost attendance and put the game at the front
of the newspaper sports section.

It is a line of thinking that Milt Dunnell, a qualified hockey watcher,
sees as being flawed. "Cooke realized he could sell tickets with Shack in
the lineup, but he overestimated Shack's draw. Up here we Canadians
had some history. We knew about Sudbury. We knew about Eddie's
junior career, his trials and tribulations with Imlach. The fans up here
had background, chapter and verse, on Shack. I don't think he had the
same appeal for Hollywood."

Dunnell, as usual, is bang on. In Canada Shack had reached folk-
hero status. He was a Robin Hood on skates, one of those rare public
figures who was never begrudged his celebrity by the regular people.
Then there was the Shack & Imlach Show, the Leafs' Frick & Frack com-
edy team, a cranky straight man and his happy-go-lucky foil.

The Los Angeles Kings' newly installed coach, Hal Laycoe, was
almost as buoyant as his boss, indicating as much in a summer inter-

view that he had great things in store for Eddie. "Shack is a whirling worker, and he's been too restricted in the past. I'm thinking of moving him from the wing to centre to let him have more room." And a bit later the coach let it be known that the feedback from other Kings contacted was positive. "Shack has put new spirit into the whole team," Laycoe enthused.

But when Shack became a training camp holdout, the lyrics to the sing-along changed. Strategic leaks said Shack was going for the moon and fixed the two stumbling blocks in the contract as his insistence for no trades without his consent and the use of the Kings' colours and their logo in his business endeavours without compensation to the team. As the date for the opening day neared, Shack put on a happy face about the negotiations with reporters.

"Mr. Cooke has plenty of money," Eddie mused expansively. "And I'm sure he wants to share it with us younger guys." When Eddie was told the fans in L.A. were going to love his brand of hockey, he har-harred and said, "Yeah, and Cookie loves me, too. He's always sayin', 'Hello, Mr. Shack, how are you today?'"

Jiggs McDonald, the longtime play-by-play man and Kings broadcaster of the day, remembers the excitement surrounding the subterfuge and murky goings-on in the Shack contract signing, all of it orchestrated by Cooke. "He had arranged to have Shackie flown in by helicopter the first day of the Barrie, Ontario, training camp, which was a staged, last-minute, out-and-out publicity stunt."

Photos show the stylishly dressed Shack being strapped into a dinky two-seat helicopter, nothing more than a glass bubble attached to a rotor, while the pilot, as expected, is stern-faced and wears the prerequisite aviation glasses and baseball hat. The chopper landed in the parking lot of the Continental Hotel, just off the bend of Highway 400, where Shack changed into his uniform for the waiting photo opportunity being set up at the Barrie arena, which was the next short hop for the helicopter. Once there, Shack stepped out in his full Kings uniform, barefoot, walked to the dressing room, put on his skates, and made his way into the arena for video footage of himself, an ex-holdout, now a member of the fold, actually skating around at training camp.

But Laycoe, already running drills for the Kings, was furious and ordered Eddie off the ice. "Where were you when camp opened?" the coach roared. "Get off the ice and wait. Come back at 3:00 p.m. and skate with the rookies." Shack, after a few vain attempts to make a spin around the ice for the cameras, which only made the situation worse, succumbed to the bristling Laycoe's shouted demands and waited in the dressing room for another 65 minutes.

"Although it was falling apart in chunks," Jiggs McDonald continues, "Cooke had a method to his madness. In 1969 there were no satellite feeds, no instant sharing of video. Everything had to be processed and done by the TV station. Cooke knew if he got film of Eddie, the big-name star arriving and skating, the same helicopter could fly the cassette back to the Toronto airport, get it on an L.A. flight, and have it as the headline on the six o'clock news in California."

But Cooke's elaborate scheme had fallen prey to a simple lack of communication. The only guy he didn't let in on the cagey scheme was Laycoe. All the same, back in Los Angeles, Cooke was furious, and the whole affair didn't bode well for Laycoe's future prospects.

The Kings jumped out of training camp in 1969-70 as a club with some promise and with a new coach who was determined to mould the team into his model of what a hockey club should be.

The honeymoon period didn't last long, though. The Kings held their own in October, going 4-4-0, then fell to a 4-7-1 record in November, a speed limit the Kings would stick to till the end of the season. With that tempo came many problems, which fell, rightly or wrongly, squarely on Laycoe's shoulders.

Today, sitting in my Mississauga office, Ed Shack peers at the pictures on the wall, completely disinterested. "How come you got a picture of Spinner [Brian] Spencer up there?" he asks, stifling a laugh.

"Because I'm in the picture, I guess" is all I can come up with on short notice.

"Yeah," Eddie says quietly, as if he understands. Then, the moment gone, he sits down, all warmed up to go over his days in Los Angeles. "Al

Laycoe. That's what I used to call him. 'Hey, Al.' Really pissed him off. Who cares? I used to call Imlach, George. I used to call Sinden, Harry. I used to call Watson, Shithead." At that Eddie stomps both cowboy boots on the rug in a fit of laughter.

"We were on a bus somewhere, and I had an unlit cigar when Laycoe got on. He went apeshit, yelling, 'No cigars on the goddamn bus! None! Understand? No cigars!' I said, 'Okay, okay, maybe I can't read, but I can fuckin' hear, yuh know.' Next day we're goin' to the airport, and I had a pipe, so he went ballistic again. I said, 'Settle down, big boy. Has the plate in your head shifted?' Yeah, that's when I started callin' him Platehead. Maybe he's why I look back on coaches and I gotta wonder. Laycoe was a beaut, yuh know? Another goddamn dictator. He had a lot of winners in the minors, in the WHL, but he was the kind of guy who liked trainers. Screw the players. He'd help the trainers carry bags 'n shit. Nothin' wrong with helpin' a trainer, but it's real bush league, right? The goddamn trainers have money and gofers for all that shit. His first job was — what do you call that thing? — pridery."

"Priority?" I offer.

"His first priority was to the players. That was his job, not luggin' equipment bags and helpin' pack the sticks. My first game in the L.A. Forum, when I get a hat trick, we were really goin', and I said, 'Let's work as a team. Let's get the guys together.' But no, here we go again. Laycoe had his old ways. Those guys always have their old ways. They think they can do it all through coaching, but it's the players who put the puck in the net, it's the players who do the skating, the players who get hurt." Eddie gets out of the chair and begins to circle the office, obviously agitated, the bone of contention still there after all these years.

"I never saw a coach get hurt all the time I was playin'. Laycoe had a lot to work with. It wasn't like somebody stuck him with a bag of doorknobs. Take the defence, which you know is important, right? We had Gerry Desjardins in goal, Dale Rolfe, Bill White, Bob Wall, Dale Hoganson — not exactly mashed potatoes. And we had Eddie Joyal up front, with Ted Irvine, Ross Lonsberry, Bill Flett, guys you gotta work with, eh? You had some talent there, and we could have fun together out on the ice, but Laycoe had to have his own stupid ways. Even so we did all right. We beat Montreal . . . in Montreal," he adds cryptically. Then, as an afterthought, he says, "There's no goddamn way we shoulda finished last. But we did. Yeah, coaching got us into the lead for last."

It was thought that Los Angeles was tailor-made for Eddie Shack, a marriage made in Tinseltown. But according to Shack's friend Paul Rimstead, who was once again assigned to track down his buddy for an article, although Eddie had everything to do with show business, he could never lose sight of the fact that he was a hockey player first, and as such had to stay within his own field. At the suggestion he could conceivably become a movie star, Shack reminded Rimstead, "Naw, them bastards go in to work early in the morning. It's still dark for Christ's sake, and they gotta remember all those lines. If I can't read, how the hell am I gonna remember lines?"

But that was the least of Eddie's concerns. Hal Laycoe was fast taking the place of Phil Watson on "Sweet Daddy Shackie's all-time shit list," which was the way Eddie put it to Rimstead back then. "They got rules here. I can't smoke a pipe or a cigar on the bus. I can't have a beer in my hotel room at trainin' camp. I've never seen anythin' like this before. You know, Rimmer, it bothers me so much I don't fell like playin'."

The Shacks purchased a house in Encino, and even that mundane event was grist for the media mill. Much was made of the fact that the house hadn't sold because it was on a cliff. The house next door, it was said, had problems with its pool sinking, and everyone was wary of the place relocating itself to the nearby freeway.

Hearing Eddie mention the Encino house, I recall a conversation I had with his wife, Norma, some time ago at the current Shack residence in Toronto: "It sure wasn't on any cliff. The grade wasn't any more than our street," she said, pointing toward the great outdoors. "It wasn't as sloped as our driveway. In fact, it was flat, all the way down beyond the property line. The only danger there was bramble bushes gradually dropping away to scrubby brush. Later one of the neighbours said there might be snakes out there. And that," she whispered, shivering, "was scarier than any danger we might be in from a landslide."

Still, Norma carefully checked the house room by room for cracks or hairline marks in the ceilings and over door frames, not an uncommon blight in "Shakeytown." She also checked the pool, but found nothing and concluded the house was in no danger. So the Shacks bought the property for a song.

"It was the year after the big rains," she told me. "There were no roots there, no trees, it was basically desert, and a couple of homes in this subdivision had had 'a displacement of earth,' which was the way Californians described it. We looked in Sherman Oaks and Bel Air and finally settled on this place in Encino, 3358 Red Rose Drive," she said, flashing a smile for being able to remember the address. "The savings and loan company owned it because the previous owners had just walked away from it. The conclusion was that they must have been Californians, familiar with next-door dwellings disappearing overnight into the gulches and arroyos Los Angelinos call valleys. But because the two houses farther to the right were condemned, no one would touch this piece of property. But there was never anything wrong with the house. Never. It was just sitting there empty, by association. Nothing ever happened to the pool, and sure, we were taking a bit of a chance, but we certainly weren't afraid.

"It was a fabulous bargain in a upscale area, a gorgeous house with a typically large pool. It also had an extra bedroom, which the salesman always called the maid's quarters, and it had three more bedrooms, all kinds of closet space, everything. We bought it at about half of what prices were in the area for something comparable. It had been lived in by hippies, squatters, I guess you'd call them, but all it required was a clean up.

"Those other two homes stayed there, boarded up behind high fences, empty all the time we were there, and when I went back in 1980 for a visit, I passed by and they were still there. But just recently, when we returned to L.A., they were gone and two brand-new magnificent homes were built on the same properties. Those original houses stood there, boarded up on solid ground, for almost 20 years. Isn't that something?

"You have to remember getting a house there was easy. The down payment in L.A. was about eight percent, and the payments were reasonable. But our water bill was higher than the mortgage payment. First month there, I didn't realize you had to pay so dearly for water, and I wanted a nice green lawn. Well, I got it. We had the most beautiful, luscious property on the street, with the greenest lawn. Everybody else had this Arizona desert look to their place, but ours looked like a golf course. When the bill came, my eyes got real big and I said, 'What's this? There's gotta be a mistake.' It was astronomical. I let the lawn dry out a bit after that.

"But it was a beautiful place, and when we sold it a couple of years later, we made lots of money." She laughed. "Real estate has made a lot of stupid people a lot of money." The Shacks, it was said at the time, were one of two things: too dumb to be let out alone in the afternoon or as cagey as foxes.

After a bit of silence between Eddie and me in my office, I realize he's losing focus on our topic for the day: his days in Los Angeles. So I search my memory for inspiration, then recall that Eddie once told me how aware Jack Kent Cooke was about having the people on the Kings have appropriate nicknames. Then I play my card when Eddie asks, "Who's that?" about a picture in a book lying on a side table next to my desk.

"Tickets," I answer. "Danny Gare. They call him Tickets."

"Stupid nickname," Eddie snorts.

"Good story, though," I reply, and wait.

"In L.A. they spent most of their time jerkin' around with crap like that, makin' a big deal out of makin' up names for the players. Eddie 'Jet' Joyal, Real 'Frenchy' Lemieux, Bill 'Cowboy' Flett. I always called him 'Platehead,' too. I'd skate around at practice and say, 'Platehead,' and both Laycoe and Flett would turn around. Neither one was ever sure who I was talkin' to. Even their broadcaster, Jiggs McDonald, had a nickname. Jack Kent Cooke said to him, 'Your name is John, ain't it? What the hell kind of a catchy name is that — John McDonald? What do your pals call you? Jiggs? Now we're gettin' someplace.' And that's how he got the nickname known around the NHL.

"But you know how players are," Shack says, sighing, tilting the high-backed office chair, and giving it a little spin. "We had some fun, anyway. In St Louis curfew was at 11:00, and we were in a bar down the street from the hotel. At about 10:55 every one of us downed our last beer and started running like goddamn thieves, tryin' to beat the deadline. Them other bastards that got back earlier were waitin'. Dale Rolfe was up above on the balcony or leaning out a window, whatever, with a waste basket full of water and, spa-loosh, they got me. Almost knocked me on my can, water down my boots, up my ass, in my eyes, but I didn't give a shit. I just kept runnin'. There was money at stake, eh? When I got inside, the desk clerk looked really surprised and asked me, 'Is it raining out there?' The boys in the lobby were just pissin' themselves laughing.

"Hockey players do funny things. One time I came into the gym and there's one of the boys — a rookie, one of them French kids, I think — pedallin' on the goddamn bike. Laycoe told him to do five miles forward and five more backward. So when I come in he's sittin' on the handlebars, a couple of folded-up towels under his ass for a cushion, pedallin' away, sweatin' like a pig. I said, 'What the hell are yuh doing?' And he said, 'What's it look like, asshole. I'm pedallin' backward.' There's a switch, eh? You can reverse the pedallin'. Dumb shit. Yeah, and this was a guy who could read."

When I talked to Bill White, one of those big defencemen who had received his grounding in the basics of hockey from the master defenceman, Eddie Shore, he told me he had been just as confused about Hal Laycoe as Shack was. "I found it hard to read Laycoe. It was like he was above you. Eddie and me bought these phony moustaches, stick-ons, in Montreal, and we went on the bus like a couple of Zorros. You know those straight-line moustaches? Laycoe blew his cork over that one, too. He didn't like it one bit."

Skip Krake, who had played with Shack in Boston and had moved to the Kings the year before, remembered those mini-Laycoe confrontations in a detached light. "Laycoe was two things — a very successful guy in Portland [WHL] and very set in his ways. Yes, he was a good hockey man. You don't have the success he did without having something going for you somewhere along the line. But then he came to the Kings in the NHL and had a whole different ball of wax, a whole lot of guys he couldn't get to, according to him. Let's face it. He was from the old school, the kind of coach who'd skate you, stops and starts all day, just to make a point and show you who was the boss. Eddie didn't like all the rules and he didn't much like slave drivers, either. I'll always remember Eddie telling me one morning, 'Take it easy, kid. This guy will kill you.'"

Krake also remembered being the tour guide at the start of the season for two projects. The first one was house hunting. "I used to ride with Eddie when he was looking for houses, because I could read street signs." Later it was for a new car, as Shack turned his attention to a fad he had observed on the West Coast: dune buggies. Krake was there to read the street signs again. "There was a dealer who did custom building, and Eddie was fascinated by them and decided to get one. For a while we were going out there regularly, every other day when we were in town, while it was being made. It was top-of-the-line with everything, and as I recall, all the models came with two sizes of engines. When the time came for the guy to ask Eddie for his preference, Sweet Daddy didn't hesitate. 'Gimme the big one' was all he said.

Within two weeks Shack was cruising the streets and San Diego Freeway from his house to the Forum in a one-vehicle billboard decked out in metallic gold and purple (Forum Blue, as Jack Kent Cooke steadfastly referred to the colour), with a big "23" and Kings crown emblazoned on the finish. The Kings paid for the paint job.

Just after New Year's Day 1970 Cooke and the Kings struck it rich on the gossip column circuit when Eddie cracked the Hollywood lineup. Newspapers reported: "Yesterday afternoon Los Angeles Kings star Eddie Shack was seen on Sunset Strip cruising past the Playboy Club." In Los Angeles that was big news.

By mid-season, though, it wasn't all fun and games, as evidenced when Laycoe snapped at a hallway-cruising reporter near the dressing room after practice. The man innocently asked, "How's Shack playing these days?"

The bespectacled coach fixed the reporter with an icy glare and said, "Exactly the way I thought he'd play. Erratic."

For his part Shack was eventually threatened with the bench by Laycoe. Eddie was told, "The only reason we didn't trade you is because nobody wants you." But Shack felt he was playing well, banging in goals and playing with his old zip. And he told all the newsies who were listening that the transformation was due to a change of scenery and equipment.

"It got together when they put me back on right wing and let me use the curved stick again," he tells me now in my office, no doubt wondering why Laycoe had insisted on changes in the first place. "I've always been better on the right side. And I had my best years when I used a hook."

Shack went on a bit of a tear, scoring 10 goals in nine games, upping his total to 20. This was the third team he accomplished that number with, but it came too late to save Hal Laycoe's job, if it was ever meant to. Johnny Wilson took over as coach, the same Wilson who had been traded by Imlach to the Rangers for Shack. To reporters Wilson contended that Shack, under his tutelage, was "thinking now" and was therefore "in the right place to get better shots."

"I played in 73 games out of 76, and we finished out of the playoffs, dead last in the 12-team league. Great coaching, eh?" Shack says, shrugging. "Twenty points, count 'em, twenty points behind Philly and Oakland. Now that's pretty goddamn low. But I had a good year [22 goals, 113 minutes in penalties], one that wasn't bad for a guy in the coach's doghouse. If one player scores 14 percent of the entire team's goals, I think that's pretty good.

"It was the last game of the year in L.A. and we lost 6-4. After the game we were in the Forum lounge when [L.A. general manager] Larry Regan started on me. We used to call him "Pig Eyes." He was half pissed and started yappin', 'You didn't do nothing, Shack.' Then he got on my education. I said, 'Yeah, well, the only reason you got me in L.A. was because of Weston Adams and his horseshit hats.' I was tryin' to lighten it up, make a joke, but Regan didn't take the hint. So he started spittin' and sputterin' and said he was gonna kick the shit out of me.

"It got settled down, but I left mad as hell, and I called Larry Mann, the Canadian actor down in L.A. He was a big hockey fan who was also a good pal of Jack Kent Cooke. 'Course the Kings were afraid I was gonna sue. When we got back to L.A., a meeting was called in Cooke's office and things were smoothed over. The next season [1970-71] Regan took over as coach and benched me. I only played 11 games for the Kings that year. Then the genius traded me to Buffalo. I got 25 goals for the Sabres. So much for 'Pig Eyes' Regan."

Listening to Eddie took me back to a winter visit to the Beef & Bird, Jerry Toppazzini's Sudbury watering hole and home of the porcetta sandwich. I walked in one afternoon, fashionably late, navigated the three steps to the elevated bar area, and selected a spot near the corner cash register. A bleary-eyed customer glanced up, looked me over, and then studied the draft beer in front of him. It wasn't until then that I noticed we were the only two at the bar while a few people sat at the tables spread throughout the room.

"You got a hangover?" the man at the bar asked without looking at me, but I gathered the remark was directed my way.

"I just walked in. Give me a little time," I answered, turning toward the kitchen and trying to spot Jerry. It was 2:45 in the afternoon.

The man looked up and challenged me through secondhand-smoke-burned eyes, cupping the draft glass in his hand. "Well, you can't stand there, pal. This is a hangover corner. You gotta stand somewhere else." He blinked, painfully it seemed.

"I'm looking for Topper," I offered lamely as a defence for my trespassing.

"The Beef & Bird Bulletman?" Mr. Bleary grunted.

Just in time Topper emerged from the kitchen, apron on and baseball cap in place, and waved me over to a table. "I'll be back," I said, doing my best Arnold Schwarzenegger impression.

"Anytime," he said to his draft.

After Jerry and I did a bit of preliminary kibitzing, I brought up the subject of Eddie Shack. Topper removed his cap and ran a large hand over his gleaming shaved head, then launched himself into an assessment. "Like I've said many times before, Shackie had tremendous ability, but just never knew how to apply himself, which is a damn shame because look at him. He had all of the six S's," he rasped, leaning forward to check S's off on the fingers of one hand, "size, strength, speed, stamina, skill, and maybe the most important, soul. Some people call it heart, but that don't start with an S," he relays for my benefit, counting his thumb twice. "Look at Gordie Howe, Bobby Hull, Orr, the really great players, they had the six S's.

"But you know, Eddie wasn't that physical, at least not in my opinion. They say he'd really bang people. Maybe so, but I think it was a matter of him barrelling around the ice and not being able to get out of other people's way. I think Eddie could have scored 500 goals if he'd applied himself, tried to be a better player, you know, adhered to the coach's plan. Hey, that doesn't mean he wasn't a hell of a hockey player.

"Goddammit, I was a player, I was a coach, I admired Hal Laycoe, and I remember him saying Eddie was uncoachable. Laycoe said he'd ruin a team meeting, speaking up in front of the players and saying, 'Ah, to hell with that shit. We'll just dump it in and chase it. Screw this [plan].' By the time Eddie hit L.A. he was getting that kind of reputation, see, and I was hearing things from my friends in Boston, so it's not hard to understand the disruptions in Los Angeles. But I also remember his first game at home in the L.A. Forum. He was a star, came out and did that, you know, twirl-a-rama routine. The fans went bananas. They absolutely loved him."

By the fall of 1970, a year after that first game, Hal Laycoe was gone. So was Johnny Wilson. Larry Regan had assumed both jobs as GM and coach, and although the problems from the previous spring were supposed to be behind the Kings, Regan was determined to get rid of Shack. According to Eddie's critics, the big winger was doing what he was known best for: languishing on the end of the bench, this time for a team that had broken the tape finishing dead last in its division. To Eddie's detractors, the L.A. debacle was Sweet Daddy Shackie's swan song. There would be no encores for "The Entertainer."

Then there was the rumour floating around certain circles, attributed erroneously to Norma, that suggested the Shacks wanted to move on.

"Yeah, I told people that Norma said real estate was going up," Eddie says in my office. "I told them she said, 'We can make some good money, Eddie, so act up, get traded, and let's get outta here.'" Shack smothers a laugh into his moustache with his hand. "It was just a bullshit rumour I started."

Eddie played one last time for Los Angeles on November 21, 1970, a Saturday game at home against the Vancouver Canucks. It was the 11th game he had dressed for out of 16. Dick Duff had played in only seven, scoring one goal. Between the two of them the former Maple Leaf teammates had five points, counting Shack's two goals and two assists.

In Buffalo Punch Imlach was reaching out for bodies and felt there was some life left in Duff and Shack, who had both been part of those glorious Leaf Stanley Cup winners when Imlach was a high flyer. The truth was the Sabres' first coach and general manager had nothing to lose. The only player Regan could pry from Imlach for taking two of Hollywood's "over-the-hill gang" off his hands was defenceman Mike McMahon, who would never play for the Kings. In fact, McMahon only played one more career game in the NHL and that was with the New York Rangers. At the time it was an ignominious trade for all concerned, a trade that only made the newspapers in Buffalo. No one knew then, but Shack would make Imlach look like a genius all over again.

Eddie left Los Angeles with sidekick Dick Duff for the shores of Lake Erie and Buffalo's Memorial Auditorium, two old teammates going back to play in an old building for their old nemesis, an old tyrant and dictator, for one of the newest doormats in the league. As Eddie says, "I put my stick over my shoulder, hung my skates off the end, and marched down the hall, singin', 'To Buff with Duff, to Buff with Duff.'" And as in every other city he'd played in, and left, Shack's irrepressible spirit, his gallant enthusiasm for the game, and his rapport with the people in the seats would be sorely missed in Los Angeles, and fondly taken to heart by the paying customers in Buffalo.

Shortly after New Year's Day 1971 a picture arrived in Shack's Auditorium mail slot, showing the outside of a restaurant and bar Eddie used to frequent. It had a large painted sign hanging prominently in the window beside the front entrance: "Coming Wednesday, January

27 — Eddie Shack & Dick Duff vs. L.A. Kings. Bus leaves at 6:00 p.m."

For Norma the Los Angeles experience had been anything but happy. After the initial thrill of the house-hunting safari, the main item of note in California was a TV spot for the folks back in Canada. As Norma herself told me, "Ralph Mellanby was supposed to do a piece on us for *Hockey Night in Canada*, about moving, setting up and living in Los Angeles, that kind of thing, but it rained. When it rains in L.A., it's like standing under a waterfall, so they had to cancel. Eventually the Disney people shot the piece for them, and all I can remember was take after take, coming through a tunnel about 10 times in a little boat with the kids, because there was no way they could get Eddie into this little boat with us. And that dumb song was playing, 'It's a Small World,' over and over. God, I heard that tune in my head for three months after. It drove me nuts, and I'll never forget it."

By the time Eddie went to Buffalo, his fifth team, the changes in uniforms were becoming routine, and for some people it was a sign of the end. To a hockey player there are only two ways to look at such a situation, and Leo Labine, a Boston Bruin and Detroit Red Wing back in the 1950s and early 1960s, spelled it out best for me. "It's like this. You're either so good everybody wants you or you're horseshit. When Eddie went to L.A., he was all antics, made his mark on antics. It may have been because Jack Kent Cooke wanted it that way. I don't know. But in a lot of ways, at the time, Eddie reminded me of [Harold] Ballard and Imlach. Just like them, it seemed Shackie had to be the show, the main attraction. It's too bad. He was a hell of a player. He could have done it by just playing hockey."

Now, in my Mississauga office, I look at the floor where, sandwiched between a half-dozen thick scrapbooks, a 1969-70 Los Angeles Kings program stands out. The cover has a close-up photo of Eddie, pregame face smeared with Vaseline, the better to avoid razor burn from sweating. For once there is no wild-eyed happy face, no leg-in-the-air cavorting, no exaggerated hockey pose. Instead he appears pensive and serious, an unfamiliar look for the man known as "The Entertainer."

"What's this?" I ask, pointing at the cover. "Somebody beat you at bullshit poker? Bad day at the golf course?"

"Nah, that's my Laycoe look," Eddie grunts. "The No-Fun Zone look."

I point out how times have changed, noting the 50-cent price of the magazine.

"Yeah, them bastards. They'd rip you off any way they could." In a twinkling the braying har-har-har rings through my office, as if to say, "Case closed. Who's next?"

As someone once said, "That's Eddie."

CHAPTER NINE

Buffalo

IN HIS 1969 TORONTO *TELEGRAM* COLUMN PUNCH IMLACH HAD THIS to say about Eddie Shack:

> Everything Shack does is done to extremes. His skating style is exaggerated, his arms, his legs, his stick. Eddie is where the action is, and he was in more trouble on the ice than any other player I ever had anything to do with.
>
> Eddie certainly has something to offer the hockey business, and now that I look back, I really think I enjoyed having him around. It was never dull.

A year later Imlach would have to suck it up and refute all the nice things he'd said. Shack was back, and Punch had no one to blame but himself.

Imlach was a man with an agenda that drove the former Leaf five-star general with a purpose that was blatantly obvious. A sign stood out starkly in foot-high letters against the office wall behind his desk, addressing each visitor, friend or foe, "Beat Toronto." This quest was worth any sacrifice, including reaching out and plucking Shack and another former Leaf, Dick Duff, from the Los Angeles Kings.

The Buffalo that welcomed Eddie when he arrived on November 25, 1970, from Los Angeles had changed very little from its American Hockey League roots when the Bisons were the big hockey game in town. The Sabres were one of the two new teams (along with the Vancouver Canucks) in the breakneck expansion that saw the NHL go from six to 14 teams in the space of only four years. Although the dressing room door made reference to the NHL, there was little to distinguish between minor-league and big-league status except a fresh paint job and a new home team dressing room complete with real carpeting. That, and Punch Imlach.

Candid as always, Shack torched a few more bridges: "I was happy to get out of L.A.," he openly admitted to the clamouring media in Buffalo, and much was made of the fact that the two ex-Leafs were rejoining their former mentor. Certainly it was Shack who had the most appeal for Imlach, whose job was to put hockey on the map in Buffalo. All Punch had to work with was a budding superstar in the much-heralded Gil Perreault, and Roger Crozier in goal. Perreault, a young man who had proved nothing so far, could barely converse in English. Therefore, his value as a media personality was limited, as was Crozier's. The former Red Wing goalie let his goaltending do the talking on the ice. If Punch desired nothing more than respectable and professional play from the slowing Duff, he wanted and desperately needed flamboyance from the ever-youthful Shack. And he got both. In effect, Punch needed Shack as much as a hungover cowboy needs a hot taco to put some colour in his face.

Allan Stanley, another of the 1960s Leafs fraternity, was in Buffalo helping Imlach assemble a semblance of a team. Today he says, "I went to help Punch with the Sabres for a while and was there when Dick Duff and Eddie arrived from Los Angeles. It was just before practice, and Punch was in the dressing room. In walked Shackie, cowboy boots, huge coat, long hair, equipment bag, and a taped bundle of sticks under his arm, which he dropped on the floor. 'Punch, your troubles are over,' Eddie announced with that goofy grin. 'Here I am.' Then he let go with that big laugh of his. Imlach just looked at him, glanced around the room at all the players getting dressed, and walked out."

While it was the first time Imlach would leave before getting into it with Shack, it wasn't the last. The cranky GM and coach required veterans to steady the play of his rookies and a supporting cast of green minor-leaguers and NHL journeymen. In that regard he had veterans with Stanley Cups to their credit spliced into the lineup, people like Jean-Guy Talbot, Phil Goyette, Donny Marshall, and even Reggie Fleming. In addition he was looking for compliance in a regimen that featured himself as the all-seeing, all-knowing, steely-eyed captain of the Sabre ship. To a certain degree the idea was feasible.

Imlach confided to Shack that if the coach was to ream him in front of the team for various transgressions like penalties, or not staying on his wing, Shack would be doing a great service to the team if he were to take it with a sense of sincere regret and remorse. This, Imlach reasoned, would show the young and inexperienced players that you were never too old or had too much silverware to learn, and that if a veteran like Shack wasn't safe from the slings and arrows of the coach's criticisms, then neither were they. The net result, Imlach suggested, would be better team discipline.

What took place for the next 111 games that Shack was a Sabre was somewhat removed from Punch's idea of contrition. Example: One of the recognized no-no's in hockey is taking a penalty in the first or last minute of play. Shack took a no-no with only 20 seconds remaining in the second period of a game, and as the Sabres trooped into their dressing room, Imlach scurried in behind, red-faced and seething. He blasted Eddie, who was sitting down and eating an orange section, calmly taking everything in, no doubt considering Punch's ranting as nothing more than a lesson for the others, part of the coach's instruction to the "kids on the team."

"When the goddamn penalty is over, Shack," Imlach roared, "I want your ass straight to the bench. Don't even look anywhere else. Just get to the goddamn bench."

Shack's face took on the glow of an idea. "But, George, what if I get a breakaway?"

Imlach lost it. "I don't give a shit if you get six breakaways, goddamn it! I want your sorry ass on the bench." Then, after sputtering various obscenities, he stormed out of the room.

Shack looked around at his subdued teammates and nodded, as if to say, "Now there's a great coach, eh?"

As the last five seconds of Shack's penalty wound down, he began pawing the floor of the box with his skate, making whinnying noises. Then, when the door was yanked open, he came out of the chute like a rodeo bronc. "Yaaahhhhhhhh!" he bellowed, barrelling across the ice in a beeline as no one else in hockey could. Finally, with warp speed, he dived headfirst over the boards, taking out the stick rack, Gatorade canister, medical kits, and trainer Frankie Christie, who later admitted he would have ducked if he'd thought Shack wasn't going to stop.

"Fast enough for you, Punch?" Eddie asked as Christie cursed and tried to find his glasses. Imlach, fedora pushed back, hands on hips, walked toward the rubble, took one look at the giggling Shack and, steam coming out of his ears, walked back down to the other end of the bench while the Sabre players guffawed and pounded the boards for relief. To Eddie it was just another day at the office.

"Yeah," says Shack now, "when I got to Buffalo in 1970, you could tell Punch had changed. He knew why he was there, and what we had to do. Just play exciting hockey. It didn't mean we were goin' to win, but we had to be exciting. We started to fill the building, and that was all they wanted at the time. Hell, he wasn't under pressure to make the playoffs, but we almost did. It was close. Shit, we were only 19 points behind the Leafs, snappin' at Ballard's big ass."

In their first season the Sabres finished in a tie for ninth place with Shack's former team, Los Angeles. They managed to get 63 points, ending up ahead of Pittsburgh (62), Vancouver (56), Detroit (55), and California (45). "Punch was a little more relaxed," Eddie says, "but not enough to let you relax. Know what I'm sayin'? Yeah, Buffalo was a great place to play, really good fans, and on that little patch of ice we didn't have to run so far to catch those other bastards, eh?

"Most of us — Jean-Guy Talbot, Tracy Pratt, Kevin O'Shea, Gil Perreault, Billy Inglis, Al Hamilton — stayed in Fort Erie. I had a beautiful place on Lake Erie for $250 a month. I could run the snowmobile up and down the beach. The games started at 7:00 p.m., and we'd be back at the bar, or in the house, by 11:00. The customs guys knew us, the cops knew us, and we'd be hootin' and hollerin'. Like I said, it was a goddamn great place to play hockey.

"I remember a party we had at my place — card games, a couple of beers, Floyd Smith was the captain that first year, and he bet me he'd outscore me, said he always got hot toward the end of the season. I got 25 goals in 56 games and Smitty got six in 77, but he never paid the bet."

Skip Krake was in Buffalo when Shack arrived, just as he had been in

Boston and Los Angeles before. "Diane and I lived just around the corner from Shack's place in Ridgeway, if I remember correctly. Near the Waverly Hotel, that's all I know. I think I had to walk home from there once or twice," he says ruefully.

Often referred to as one of those "tough grinders" by television colour commentators, Krake wasn't particularly big, but his reputation was such that opponents rarely mixed with him. His 74 games with the first-year Sabres turned out to be his last in the NHL, and for that reason his memories are uncluttered and focused on the 1970-71 season. Although Krake was familiar with Shack, Imlach was new, but it didn't take him long to get a feel for the boss.

"I don't think you're gonna play for Punch and not have some pressure to win," he says, "and Imlach was always serious about winning, not like going to the Stanley Cup serious, but he wanted every damn point he could get that first year. Well, I'll tell you how desperate he became. He had Eddie on the power play. You can see that Imlach was clutching at straws. That's when they first had films. The boys didn't like that."

As Shack tells it, "We were playin' pretty good, but losin' a lot, yuh know, and Punch called a meeting. Oh, God, not another meeting. Like he could figure out what was wrong with us by holdin' another goddamn meeting. So I waited until the films started, put a glove behind my head, and went to sleep. Next thing I knew the lights were on, the boys were laughin', and Imlach was goin' nuts about me dozin' off during the movie."

On another occasion the team meeting was held in what became the Aud Club, nothing more than an empty cavern that first season. But with space at a premium in the ongoing refurbishing of the old Memorial Auditorium, chairs were arranged theatre fashion and the team trooped in for a "discussion" about "team destiny." Shack, spotting some two-story scaffolding on wheels, climbed to the top platform while the boys below pushed the scaffolding around at full speed, giving Shack a new midway ride. However, they left him stranded in the farthest corner at the back of the room as Imlach swept in. Eddie, a schoolboy caught in an irreversible prank, stayed on his perch rather than reveal his presence, occasionally waving and grinning at his snickering teammates until Imlach, in the midst of giving a severe tongue lashing, finally noticed his prize student missing and wanted to know where Shack was. Eddie, his feet hanging over the platform, piped up happily, saying, "I'm right here, George. And I think you should know you can get more bees with honey than you can with shit." For Punch the moment was broken and the meeting was over.

After I tell Krake this story, he grins, nods, and relates another view of The Entertainer. This one concerns the rumour that the two had fought toe-to-toe at a practice. "Naw, never," he says, dismissing the idea as a smile creeps back into his eyes. "But you can tell him if we did, he'd have absolutely no problem remembering it. I'd lay a whuppin' on him. Four stitches here, six stitches there . . . No, we never fought. I know Shackie gets boisterous and that he pissed off some of the guys from time to time. But he was really good to me, and I love him for it."

Shack had performed above expectations, a new legion of fans were flocking to the Auditorium, and Norma and the children joined him in Fort Erie for the 1971-72 season. For a hockey player life doesn't get much better, and the kids felt the difference between life in Tinseltown and Canada, as daughter Cathy remembers: "Jimmy and I were seven and eight when we moved to Fort Erie and started the school year. They had an assembly where we were 'welcomed,' probably not a good idea for kids that age, but we took it well. In Fort Erie I used to write stories, little things about what was happening at school, at the games, and I saved them to read to Gil Perreault every time he came over to the house. And I remember it as a time when Dad used to bring something home for us, every road trip. See, we had what kids consider the good, and the bad, from the same source."

As for Norma, she says, "When Ed was with the Sabres, the kids got a new taste of notoriety. Living in Fort Erie, they attended school on the Canadian side. Cathy came home one day and asked, 'Is Daddy famous or something?' Norma admitted that he was, but asked why she wanted to know. 'Because all the kids at school want his autograph,' she said. The children turned out to be the two little heroes at school and they ate it up."

One of the Sabre defencemen who was there for Shack's entire tour of duty was Tracy Pratt, the son of Hall of Famer Babe Pratt. Although not up to his father's speed as a player, Tracy can tell a story to match "the Babe" any day. After labelling Shack "a tad irreverent," Pratt reminds me and himself of those heady days in Buffalo.

"One morning before practice we were sitting around in our long johns and I asked Eddie to hand me some of his fan mail from a growing pile so I could help him go through it. So I knocked off a couple, the usual stuff about wanting pictures and how good he was, how much they liked him. Then I read one silently, raised my eyebrows, and said, 'Oh-oh.' Eddie was getting concerned. 'What?' he wanted to know. I said, 'Holy shit, this one says you're no entertainer and that you sure as hell ain't a hockey player because you can't fight, you never pass, you shoot like a girl, your nose is too big. Plain and simple, you're an asshole.' We looked at each other and then I said, 'It's signed, love, Mom.' Eddie laughed the loudest.

"Another time Eddie was showing us the latest, top-of-the-line, silver-coloured, insulated snowmobile suit he'd bought, about $150 back in those days. He put it on at practice before we got into our equipment, and he had everybody rolling on the floor laughing while he modelled the suit.

"Most of us lived in Fort Erie and a lot of the players had snowmobiles. Around lunchtime that day Eddie called and asked me to come out on the snowmobile. I guess he couldn't find anybody else, 'cause most of us just wanted to take it easy after working out. I begged off and said I had enough lumps on me from hockey. I didn't need more from driving around the countryside in snow that was crotch-deep. So Eddie said, 'Well, I'm comin' over. Have some hot toddies on when I get there.' At that point I suggested some Chinese food, which he agreed was a good idea.

"I jumped in the car and headed down Highway 3 in a swirling snow squall off Lake Erie. I spotted this machine, front runners sticking straight up in the air on the other side of a culvert, and there was Eddie in his new snowsuit hung up in a barbed wire fence. When I got out of my car, it was blowing and snowing, and all I had on were jeans, a jacket, and sneakers. I was out there freezing my ass off on the shoulder of the road, and Eddie was upside down, giggling and howling at me to get over and help him.

"I took two steps and the snow was over my knees. By that time a couple of other cars had stopped, both guys better dressed for winter than me. So I said, 'Screw you and the snowmobile, too.' Then I told him I'd meet him at the house when he got untangled, and I took off to pick up the food. When Eddie finally came roaring up the driveway in a cloud of snow, I was looking out the living room window. His snowmobile suit was in tatters, and I told him he looked like a frozen block of shredded wheat. He just stood there, moustache dripping, laughing like a goddamn loon.

"That first season with Buffalo Eddie had a clause in his contract that gave him a bonus for 25 goals. And when he got to 24, Punch sat him out, with only four games left. But there was a change on the go in our second-last game and Eddie jumped on and scored. Imlach was so pissed off that he yanked his hat down with both hands and buried his eyebrows under his fedora."

Billy Inglis is another of the original Sabres with fond memories of his time in Buffalo with Shack. "Any time I'm asked about players who made an impression, Shackie always comes to mind. When we were in Buffalo that first year, I had a knee injury right off the bat and spent the better part of the season in rehab. Those of us who lived in Fort Erie on the Canadian side used to have our *own* team meetings at a local bar, just like back in the American Hockey League days.

"At one of the meetings it was decided we'd get into snowmobiling, which seemed like a good idea at the time. See, sometimes when you spend all afternoon in a critical meeting like that you get very creative, and since I wasn't playing, I was assigned to go out and get a deal on a dozen snowmobiles. Twelve machines! I remember walking into this dealer and him blinking at me. That's it. He just blinked and eventually said he didn't think there were 12 snow machines in all of Fort Erie, let alone could I get a deal if we bought a dozen.

"Needless to say, most of the boys eventually got those snowmobiles on their own and I had to avoid riding them like the plague, but I recall Shackie's. He got his through a trumped-up promotion with a local dealer, and it was the biggest, baddest, fastest. He'd be out there bellowing like a rhino in shin pads, whizzing around the lake like a bat out of hell, terrorizing the local wildlife.

"The other thing I recall about Shackie has nothing to do with his talent, or his antics, but it said a lot about his sticking to a deal once it was made. It was back in the summer of '67 after the last Toronto Stanley Cup. I needed a job and Harry Watson asked me to work the hockey school at Tam O'Shanter in Toronto. As I recall, there was Frank Mahovlich and his kid brother Pete, plus a few other guys, including Eddie. I remember him as never being late, always on the ice when he was supposed to be, and very much into coaching the kids. Remember, Big M and Eddie had just won a Stanley Cup. You don't often see people that conscientious when they're sitting on top of their own little world. Later, being a coach and a GM, I often remembered that about Eddie, and I've passed it along many times. He was a hell of a man."

Rick Martin was typical of the young Sabres back then because he represented a glimpse of the possible, the culmination of a dream, a combination of success and the never-ending good life the team always heard about but never experienced. A player like Shack held a profound attraction for the new and inexperienced NHLers, players like Gil Perreault, Kevin O'Shea, Paul Terbenche, and Dave Dryden, because he was a relief from the relentless, insistent Imlach. And to the newest of the future Sabres, Rick Martin, an out-of-the-box freshman carrying a superstar label, Shack was a revelation.

"Eddie," Martin says, "would come through the dressing room door for practice in this ankle-length, fire-engine red coat, bigger than a house, like one of those dusters the cowboy bank robbers used to wear. It had huge inside pockets, all kinds of pockets, and he'd bring Foo-Foo, his little dog, with him. Coat closed, no dog. Open it up like a flasher, and there was the damn dog in one of the pockets. Eddie would do it about four or five times to the boys as he was coming into the dressing room, like he was selling watches, laughing like hell. He'd have everybody in there busting up with him, even trainer Frankie Christie, who was in charge of Foo-Foo when Eddie was on the ice.

"We had a team barbecue in October, early in that first season I arrived, and Eddie said to me, 'You wanna go out on the snowmobile?' We were standing outside having a beer, and I looked around as if he was kidding. Hell, I looked at him, then up at the sky. It was as clear as a bell, golfing weather for Christ's sake, a beautiful day, about 70 degrees. But he said, 'Lemme fire this sumbitch up and you get on the back.' Then me, him, and the machine went roaring down the beach, sand and shit flying, about 100 yards toward this pier where a bunch of people were casting and fishing.

"Man, I thought we were going to hit that pile of rocks until Eddie let out this war whoop, turned on a dime, and sprayed all those people with the seaweed and crap piled along the shoreline. Then we tear-assed back down the beach, bounding across the lawn to the backyard of the house. You know, those things heat up in winter weather, never mind summer conditions. Well, now the goddamn thing was smoking, my pant legs were almost on fire, my ass was burning, and Shackie asked, 'Howja like the little ride, kid?'"

Aside from the thrill of snowmobile racing, the 1971-72 season was mundane and predictable. The Sabres settled into playing at sea level rather than over their heads, eventually finishing 12th overall, with only two other teams (Vancouver and Los Angeles) doing worse. Shack contributed only 11 goals, less than half of his first-year output in almost the same number of games, and his antics had worn thin on the highstrung Imlach, the kind of hockey man who took things personally and figured he could be A-one if he only had a better steering wheel. Punch was inexorably falling victim to the stress factor, some of it brought on by the pressures of doing two jobs, part self-inflicted through his competitive nature. On January 4 Imlach had a heart attack that put him in a Buffalo hospital. He replaced himself as coach with Joe Crozier, one of his longtime cronies, who was handling the AHL Americans in Rochester.

The coaching theories of Imlach and his protégé Crozier were a mirror image, a continuous thread, and the change in coaches did nothing to improve Shack's playing time or his statistics. As Imlach recovered, he put the stamp of approval on a trade with Pittsburgh for a former farmhand he had first seen in his final season in Toronto. On March 4, 1972, Imlach, now a man with only one job, sent Shack to Pittsburgh for Rene Robert.

Like all the other trades, the one to Pittsburgh had a lot to do with putting people into seats, and necessity. Shack had served his purpose in Buffalo, being part of the Sabres success story, filling the little building in the inaugural season, and contributing scoring punch to a team that overachieved in its debut.

Rene Robert put up impressive numbers in each of the Leaf minor-league cities he visited in five years, and now he was unhappy in Pittsburgh. In 49 games he had seven goals, anemic production given Robert's considerable talent, but Imlach saw in him a puck handler with a good shot who could complement the power play. Besides, he was looking for a right winger to play with Gil Perreault and rookie Rick Martin. Red Kelly, now the coach in Pittsburgh, convinced his replacement as GM, Jack Riley, that Ed Shack could put people into seats and bring some experience and goal scoring to the Penguins. Robert was happy to get out of Pittsburgh. Shack was happy to get away from Imlach, even though he liked Buffalo. As a page in the Sabres' history, it was the beginning of the French Connection, another "deal of the century." But no one knew that at the time.

Former Maple Leaf Billy Harris puts a final perspective on Shack's time as a Sabre: "Expansion didn't bother Eddie. It bothered Punch. When he arrived in Buffalo, Imlach never learned to live with Eddie's maturity, if such a word can be used with Shackie."

CHAPTER TEN

Pittsburgh

WHEN SHACK ARRIVED FOR THE LAST 13 GAMES OF THE 1971-72 regular season, the Pittsburgh Penguins won five games, lost three, and tied five. At home in the Igloo they earned four wins and two ties.

As an immediate return on a trade, Robert suited up and did his thing for the Sabres, scoring six goals and three assists in 12 games. Shack did better with five goals and nine assists in 13 games. The following season Robert scored 40 goals in 75 games, and Shack, 11 years older, put in 25 goals for the Penguins over 74 games. It was the last time he would have a 20-plus season in the NHL.

"When I got traded to Pittsburgh," Eddie says today, "I flew into Detroit to join the team, but I eventually had to go back and get the car. Can you imagine me drivin' from Buffalo to Pittsburgh by myself? I had to stop at a hundred gas stations to make sure I was headin' in the right direction."

Pittsburgh coach Red Kelly found himself in much the same situation with the Penguin fans. It wasn't the first time a trade was unpopular. Kelly says, "Glen Sather for Syl Apps, Jr., the year before Shack arrived was a very upsetting trade for the fans. They liked Sather, and rightfully so. He was a good team man, worked hard, and was a very effective penalty killer. I was aware the Rangers needed penalty-killing help, so I already knew they'd be interested. What I needed was an offensive centreman, and New York had brought Apps up, but he was sitting and not playing. Just because it made complete sense to both teams didn't mean it flew with the fans. When the deal went through, what few fans we had in the arena were up in arms, demonstrating outside and waving signs — 'Why Sather?' — inside. If I'm not mistaken, in Apps's first home game for us he came in and deked the goalie out of his shorts and scored. We never saw the signs again.

"As for the Shack-Robert swap, Rene had ability, but he wasn't producing, he wasn't happy, and he was pouting. If he wasn't going to be helpful to us, if he was going to sulk, we had to do something, because despite our attendance, we had a pretty good team spirit and his attitude wasn't helping.

"The reason I got Eddie was that the team was dead. We needed some life, some zip. I felt we had a good team, but we were missing that one special ingredient. More important, you can have a good team, but the fans won't come, and it was absolutely necessary to turn that part of the franchise around. We had Bugsy Watson and guys who gave you everything, but they weren't the spark we needed. And I knew Eddie could give the fans that light. The bonus was I knew he could play, that he wasn't just a one-dimensional guy. I knew they'd love him in Pittsburgh, and they did. The fans started coming back. We turned the crowd situation around, and in doing so the team came alive, too."

Shack, as he had in every other venue, seemed to thrive in his new environment: "Red said we made the playoffs because of me. He said I did exactly what he figured I'd do — get the guys goin', get them fired up. We had a good team in Pittsburgh, played some good hockey, and had a lot of fun. Our line was Schinkel, Schock, and Shack."

It was mid- to late summer of 1972, give or take a few days, and the Vaughan Valley Golf Club was about to open. Eddie had invited a lengthy list of associates and old pals to help him celebrate what was the realization of a dream: owning a golf course in Toronto. True, he had partners, another ex-NHLer in Dave Creighton, and lawyers Bob Watson and Gerry Ublanski, but he had a 25 percent share and he had green grass, rolling hills, sand traps, and water.

He was also the subject for Milt Dunnell in a *Toronto Star* column that indicated fame was fleeting:

> I was there, to do a column, the day he opened his golf course, Vaughan Valley. He'd invited all these players, who were friends, teammates, ex-teammates, and hardly any of them showed up. I recall feeling sorry for him, listening to him bemoan the fact that he'd been there for them on this occasion and that occasion. It may have taught Eddie a lesson about

loyalty, a quality he sometimes lavished on others to no avail.

It was also the summer of the Soviet Union–Canada hockey summit series which, surprisingly, was taken lightly in Canada at its onset. There was no pressure, according to the experts, merely the chore of taming the Soviets while trying not to patronize them. The idea was to show the Russian bear how the game was really played, then get on with a new NHL season. We were the best, and certainly no one on the left side of the Atlantic questioned our copyright.

The thought of that series always reminds me how cocky we were as a country, led down the garden path by our spoon-fed belief in the NHL. In an early 1990s interview I did with Bill White, the Chicago Blackhawk all-star defenceman who was chosen for Team Canada and quietly became one of its best blueliners, he recalled for me the distinct lack of urgency before the eight-game series began. "A writer asked me if I thought we could take the Russians, and I remember saying if we do, who'll know? We never thought it would even be close, so who'd care?"

Given that scenario, many people in the media made extravagant and farfetched predictions, smug with inside-trader knowledge about how good we were and the fact that the poor Soviets had never played our big boys. But one of the finest columns of the day, which took a humorous look at ourselves and the upcoming series, was a *Globe and Mail* piece written by Scott Young, who wondered aloud about the flawed selection of the home team. The article appeared on August 8, 1972, and was headlined: "What, No Shack?":

> What have the ordinary Russian people ever done to us that we should deny them the sight of Eddie Shack in full flight?
>
> By leaving Ed Shack off the Team Canada squad, coach Harry Sinden has been guilty of the most serious oversight in international affairs since Napoleon departed for Moscow without his overshoes.
>
> This Canadian team, even with its exclusions, will be billed as the world's best. Would any collection of the world's best long-distance walkers be complete without Charlie Chaplin? Would any aggregation purporting to represent this planet's womanhood be acceptable without Cupcakes Cassidy? . . . To make the point in reverse, if Team Canada were made up of Shack, Derek Sanderson, Larry Cahan, Reggie Fleming . . .

would there also not be a place for Dave Keon, or Stan Mikita, just to show how the other half lives?

But they have no Eddie Shack. . . .

Shack would learn the language. Make himself beloved of children by showing them how to go up and down escalators the hard way (against the current) start a snowmobile agency in the Kremlin, and generally become the Pied Piper of old Arbat Street.

While the statement was true, Young went on to finish, as all good columnists do, with the best point of all — his considered opinion on the value of Ed Shack to the Canadian fabric:

He is always at his best in new surroundings, and no surroundings have ever been as new for a pro hockey player as Moscow will be. Shack is a part of Canadian hockey culture. We do not see ourselves clearly, if we allow any hockey team to be called representative when it does not include Eddie Shack.

Keith McCreary was a five-year man with the Penguins when Shack arrived. They were only together until the end of the season when McCreary was selected by the Atlanta Flames in the 1972 expansion draft. "Eddie," says McCreary, "always came to the rink ready to play, because he knew that was his strongest card. I knew from playing against him that he was a formidable player, and ruthless. He'd run right over you if you got in the way, do what he had to do to play the game. And as the standard went in those days, he was a big forward.

"He played tough, and the one thing that's continually overlooked in that vein is that he had very impressive stats. Yet it's always amazed me how other people continue to think of him as nothing more than a roughhouse entertainer. To me it was a case of the people in hockey not knowing how to handle him, and the people who were coaching then answered to no one but themselves. However, they fell a long way short of being psychologists, and as a consequence of that Eddie was the one who suffered, because he didn't have the formal education to deal with it.

"There are people I know in the NHL, administrative types, people who've never put on a pair of skates, who consider Eddie little less than a clown. I've gotten into some heated discussions with at least one of them, saying, 'Take a look at his stats and compare them to some people in your Hall of Fame.' But even with black-and-white numbers staring them in the face they'd never admit they were wrong.

"I remember when we'd go into Vancouver. Whoever distributed *The Hockey News* out there always put a copy of the latest paper out for each player, and being in Pittsburgh, we were starved for information about the rest of the league. We'd all sit in our stalls, happier than clams, reading, while Shackie would bounce around the room like a goddamn pinball, hanging off the pipes on the ceiling, talking to guys who weren't listening, making jokes, heckling, being a general pain in the ass in the 'library.' When someone would say, 'Bugger off!' Eddie would laugh and come back with, 'What the hell do you expect me to do while you brain surgeons are reading?' And maybe that's the key. Maybe that's why nobody took Eddie's play seriously despite what he brought to the game. It had to do with his illiteracy.

"Quite frankly, when I have bad days, I remind myself that if Eddie can function the way he does without being able to read, then what the hell do I have to worry about? For instance, pick a spot, give Eddie directions, and say you'll see him in Kitchener at 8:00 a.m. or whatever. You'd toss that off as nothing, no big deal, 'cause we can read. If Eddie hasn't been there before, it sure as hell is a big deal to him. But it's guaranteed that he'll be there, and in good humour. That sure says a lot for his disposition."

Darryl Edestrand was a defenceman with the Penguins who has two sides of Shack to comment on: "I was already in Pittsburgh when Eddie arrived. Playing there was great. The Steelers were into their dynasty, the Pirates were on a roll, and the hockey team was nowhere, which was good because I finally got a chance to play after kicking around in spot jobs for so long. But it was hard on your ego, too. You could stand outside the arena for hours and nobody would recognize you.

"When Eddie arrived for the last month of that 1971-72 season, we were looking for help, more specifically we needed leadership on the team, and I looked up to Shackie. In fact, being a junior from the London Nationals, a Toronto-sponsored club with guys like

Gary Smith, Gerry Desjardins, and Walt McKechnie, I worshipped those Toronto Stanley Cup winners. And at first that's the way it went. He showed respect for Red Kelly, then the second year he seemed to have his own game plan.

"Was he smart enough to know he was marketing himself? I don't know, because on the bottom line he was having a good year, over 20 goals [25], but he wasn't a team player. He was into doing his own thing. I told him to his face one day at practice, 'You're playing for yourself.' All he said was 'Yeah, yeah,' and brushed it off the way he does. In many respects Eddie was another Turk Sanderson. Or maybe it should be said that Turk was another Eddie, since Shackie was there first, you know, creating an image, more into preparing for an opportunity he saw down the road. Most hockey players at this level have used their talent to excel, and though they are very involved, they know instinctively the correct balance between on-ice and off-ice. They know what's right and when it's right. But others begin to feed off themselves instead of the team, and that was Eddie toward the end of his career.

"But after Kelly things in Pittsburgh fell apart, plain and simple. Hey, you can look it up. They got rid of Red, they sold Shackie, didn't even get a warm body in return, and they dealt me at the start of the '73-74 season, too. We'd finished three points out of a playoff spot, but I'm thinkin', How the hell could they trade us? The year before [1971-72] I'd played 77 games with 10 goals and 23 assists. In 1972-73 I played in 78 games with 15 goals and 24 assists. Meanwhile Eddie played 74 games and scored 25 goals and got 20 assists. That's 16 percent of the team's goals from two guys, a winger and a goddamn *defenceman*, and we were both gone for '73-74, Shackie back to Toronto and me to Boston. Think about it. How the hell could they trade us?"

Kelly took the heat in that 1972-73 season when the Penguins slipped to fifth place in their division. He was replaced by Ken Schinkel, the other winger on Shack's line, which was centred by Ron Schock. There were rumours that the dismissal was because Kelly had ignored general manager Jack Riley's instructions to play "kids" more often and to leave Shack on the bench. But with 25 goals, Eddie was one of Kelly's most productive forwards, and the coach could afford to dismiss management's suggestion. There were those who said playing Shack as much as Kelly did cost him his job.

"That's BS," Kelly himself says, using language that's very strong for the former Leaf and Red Wing great. "If I thought the team would have been better without Shack, I'd have sat him."

Eddie, when reminded of the situation that saw Kelly leave the Penguins, simply says, "Smart move, eh? That's what happens when you let owners call the shots. They take a great coach from behind the bench, take an active player off our line, put him behind the bench where all he can do is play pocket pool, and expect us to do better."

But if there were many bad memories about the Pittsburgh years there was a good one in Red Kelly's eyes. "One night the team was having a barbecue toward the end of the first season Eddie was there, and naturally I wasn't invited. It's a fact that coaching is a lonely life, in that respect. But it's one of the rules you accept when you cease being one of the players.

"About the time I was getting ready to go to bed, there was a knock at the door. When I opened the door, there was Eddie, a drink in his hand, Foo-Foo standing at his feet. One of the NHL's security guys from the arena who had been invited to the dinner was also there. 'Eddie wants to see you,' the man informed me, so I invited them in, but the guard declined, saying Eddie was all mine. He was just the delivery boy. When Eddie got into the house, we sat down for a moment. It was plain he was into his cups, but suddenly he dropped down on his knees like he was in church and said, 'Red, there's something you've got to know. Remember when we were in Toronto and you shot the puck and I raised my stick and the ref gave me credit for the goal? Red, I wasn't even near the shot.'

"Next thing I know Eddie was stretched out on the floor, out like a light. He was too big to drag, too heavy to lift, so I went and got a blanket and a pillow. When I returned, Eddie was sound asleep, and so was Foo-Foo, with his feet in the air. As I tried to get the pillow under Eddie's head, the dog growled, so I said to heck with that and left the two of them right there. In the morning they were gone, and I've often thought about that incident over the goal and how it must have bothered him for all those years."

Kelly didn't have long to wait for a new job to come along. Surprisingly he first found out about it through a telephone call from columnist and broadcaster Dick Beddoes. "The first call I received was from Beddoes, asking if I was interested in the coaching job with Toronto. I said to myself, What's this guy know about the Leaf job? Is it a story he's working on? And since I couldn't figure it out right then and there, I asked him.

" 'Because Harold wants to know,' Beddoes said. Next day there was a call from Ballard from Millhaven Penitentiary. It was pretty abrupt. Ballard asked me if I'd take the job. I told him yes, and the rest was history, as they say."

On July 3, 1973, the Pittsburgh Penguins sold Ed Shack outright to Toronto.

CHAPTER ELEVEN

Toronto Again

Once more Ed Shack was happy to be leaving a town for the next roundup. He was returning to the scene of his greatest years as a player, the place where his legend was without limits. His harmony with the fans had continued, if subdued, as a Bruin, King, Sabre, and Penguin. But Toronto has always coveted its heroes with a certain possessiveness and maternalism. And now that this favourite son was returning he was expected to do his usual thing. After all, he was still The Entertainer.

When Shack arrived in Toronto, he wore a moustache for the first time as a Leaf. Why not? The Toronto uniform had changed and so had the team. Aside from Harold Ballard and King Clancy in the ivory tower, only three teammates from those crowning moments of the 1960s remained: Ron Ellis, Dave Keon, now the captain, and the new Leaf coach, Red Kelly.

Still, the Leafs of 1973-74 at least had the look of a team going places. The defence was starting to show signs of coming together after the disruption of the WHA raids that saw three promising blueliners, including Brad Selwood and Rick Ley, leave. Jim Dorey, although traded away to New York, only worked one game for the Rangers before taking his equipment bag and heading for the upstart league, too.

Coming off a 25-goal year with the Penguins, Shack, as a veteran and a player who was still capable of delivering, was welcomed back to Maple Leaf Gardens with open arms by the fans. But the fans, and management, expected more than just his marquee value. They wanted Eddie to deliver and that didn't happen.

"We got Eddie back in the summer of '73," Jim Gregory, the general manager at the time, remembers. "We had just lost more players to the WHA and Eddie was available. Our organization was one of the hardest hit by the WHA. We lost 14 or 15 players from the entire system, so we were vulnerable, we were in need, and Eddie was a legitimate player. We spoke to Red [Kelly] about it. I always checked with the coach about any deal bringing guys in, and he was all for it. Shack had 45 points for Pittsburgh the year before and we figured with his ability, and his rapport with the fans, he couldn't do anything but help.

"Well, he did, in a lot of ways, but unfortunately not on the ice. It wasn't his fault, and though he was injured, he did everything we asked of him. He played and worked hard, but he had an injury to his arm. He even went to Oke City [Oklahoma City] but, quite frankly, we had a struggling team. In fact, the year before he arrived was the first time I'd missed the playoffs either in the NHL or junior. Eddie was never a problem, and I can't recall any difficulties with him, including contract talks.

"When Eddie and his lawyer [Bob Watson] weren't completely happy with the deal, I offered to flip Eddie for the difference, which was a small amount. Shack agreed. We flipped and I won, so Eddie asked for the best of three. We did it, and I won again. Then he wanted to cut cards for the money. We did, and I won yet again. By this time we were having a good laugh, and I gave him the money."

Coach Red Kelly backed up his GM's little gamble. "Yep, I was in on the approval to get Eddie back in Toronto," he recalls. "Look what we got — a guy who could score, obviously a player who could help the team. That's what it came down to. Could he help the team? The answer based on his past performance was yes."

For Shack the problem was that the game didn't look that entertaining anymore. After Boston, which was a team of destiny, his career seemed to take a swing in another direction, his role changed subtly from veteran to nothing more than one of the acts in the Kings' circus. Now on his way back to Toronto, his team and location of choice, it seemed he had come full circle, a player ready to play out his days in the place where his greatest light as a star had been generated. But behind him was the production he used to enjoy in Buffalo and Pittsburgh, even Los Angeles, and all that was left were the antics, the gyrations, the irreverence, and the clowning.

As for being The Entertainer, the problem there was less playing time. That meant he had little opportunity to strut his stuff, fewer chances to be selected one of the stars. With all that came something new that hadn't been there before: resentment. Not from the loyal fans, but from his teammates. Some of them, intent on carving out their own careers, saw Shack as little more than one of those players Shack himself referred to as "old turkeys."

He was now a diversion, an interruptive force at practice who had suddenly taken on the personal role of telling them how to play hockey. They said he was critical; Eddie thought he was helping. Using 16 years in the league as a platform, he assumed the self-anointed role of assistant coach, perhaps with reason. As a veteran, he was often accorded the responsibility by Kelly, his old-time linemate and link to the Stanley Cups, of handling drills, such as working the second-team power play.

I recall a particular December morning at Maple Leaf Gardens when Kelly did just that. He took the bulk of the team to one end and assigned the frisky Shack, bouncing along and crowing in his full gear, to work with nine players and a goaltender on figuring out the complexities of having more people on the ice than the other team. Kelly's instructions to the second-in-command were explicit and clear: "Only high-percentage shots, fellas, and move the puck around. Eddie, make sure they keep the dang passes crisp." Shack's eyes lit up, and he went about the business of positioning his team, skating from spot to spot like a dog herding sheep, pushing, shoving, turning bodies, placing sticks on the ice in certain positions, lining up angles like a pool player setting up a three-cushion carom shot.

Norm Ullman, Errol Thompson, Lanny McDonald, Jim McKenny, Doug Favell, and others of the day stood in their assigned spots, welcoming this relief from the usual practice fare.

"All right," Shack bellowed, taking his prerogative and placing himself on the blueline, the point man on this drill. "I'm gonna start 'er up, and you guys on the A team, if you don't like the guy that's checkin' ya, let's do what we always do — spear him in the balls, take a penalty, and get rid of the man advantage. It fucks up the coach's line combinations, anyway." The penalty killers and power play experts dissolved to the ice in giggling. "Okay, goddamn it, I'm gonna give a crisp pass to BJ [Borje Salming]. Here we go." And with that he fired a lethal cross-ice wrist shot that sent the star defenceman to the mat in order to avoid a puck that clanged off the glass behind him like a church bell. The other players just regaining their feet collapsed to the ice once more, and Shack, turning to look up the ice, caught Kelly glaring at him. The boss was unhappy with the assistant boss.

"Passes crisp enough for ya, Leonard?" Shack asked Kelly as the players behind him, again just recovering, broke down into human puddles of laughter, while an ashen-faced Salming skated in little circles, unnerved and shaken.

The above story always precipitates gales of laughter at any gathering of hockey players of any era. As a classic example of "the inmates running the asylum," of students taking over from the teachers, it gives genuine joy to tough and skilled athletes. But Eddie thought he was contributing more than just hockey knowledge and experience. He believed practices should be fun. To Eddie, who cavorted to a different drummer, having fun was paramount, and he never believed his actions undermined or disrupted other players.

"See," Eddie says today, "Red was a decent man, a smart man. I always thought if the Leafs had made me an assistant coach, we could have done something together. The guys laughed at Red, yuh know. He scratched his head, didn't swear, said shoot, hang, and dang. He never raised his voice, never got mad. And you know, he was one of the best players ever in the game, but the guys figured 'cause he didn't get his ass outta gear that he was soft.

"Red's mistake was that we should have worked together, like I'd get the guys in shape and let him do the coaching. If he could have realized that, instead of going on the ice, but he wanted to play. He loved it. I coulda got the guys to yahoo, skate good, and everything. Instead he'd be out there scratchin' and blinkin', gettin' the pyramids out, shit like that.

"Look at the good tips about fightin' I gave to Borje Salming. He was a great player, an excellent player, but everybody was always after his ass. I told him all you gotta do is have one good fight, even if you just get the other dummy tired, just one good fight and they won't bother you no more. I told him he'd feel and play a lot better. Nobody's a good fighter on skates. You just gotta get lucky. When you're fightin', you gotta grab their shoulders. They can't do fuck all to you. And I told Hammerhead [Inge Hammarstrom], too. I said he'd just have to get into it once and they'd give him some room. Jeez, don't worry. Neither one of you is that good lookin', you know."

The fact that Shack's theories fell on deaf ears was a mystery to him. After all, it was only seven short seasons since Eddie and Red had played together on that last Maple Leaf Stanley Cup–winning team. To the new generation of aspiring Leafs, and their ornery owner, it might as well have been 70. And in one respect Eddie was right: his playmates saw him as relief, comic relief, a means to cover the drudgery of daily workouts and long plane rides, someone to look to when the heat from management and fans became intense. In that respect he was acceptable. The problem was that some of the players didn't see him as a contributor when the game was on the line, and they brought those very concerns to Kelly.

If the players' patience was wearing thin on the ice, Shack never let it hamper his idea of togetherness, or his appreciation for snowmobiling, nurtured in Buffalo, as a kind of therapy perfect for hockey players. "We'd go up to my golf course and snowmobile," Eddie says. "The boys could store their machines in my barn where we kept the golf carts. I'd get a little pig, cook it up on an outdoor barbecue, and we'd have a hell of a time. Once I decided I was gonna climb this hill, the one leading up to the 12th hole, with [Darryl] Sittler on the back. I had one of those fast machines, and I figured if we got a good run at it, we'd make it over the top of the ridge. We went zoomin' up the hill and almost to the top before we went flyin' ass over teakettle. Didn't matter to me, but holy sheepshit, Sit was gonna be the goddamn captain someday."

Darryl Edestrand, Shack's former Penguin teammate who was

traded to Boston shortly after Eddie was dealt to Toronto, says of The Entertainer's reunion with the Leafs: "Eddie and I had a falling out. In fact, there was a time when I went looking for Eddie, back when I was playing for the Bruins. I was already in Boston when my father passed away and I flew to Ottawa. Harry Sinden called, said that Bobby Orr was hurt, and asked if I could get back and play in Toronto. I figured that was what my dad would want. They buried my father in the morning, and immediately after I caught the first plane to Toronto and took a cab to the Gardens, just making the opening whistle. On the first shift I was fumbling with a bouncing puck behind our net and Eddie came around the goal, jumped, and parked his big ass on me. I went down in severe pain, but you know us hockey players, I got up and waved off the stretcher. Later I found out the check had broken my shoulder and that I needed surgery to remove a piece of bone.

"For a lot of years I blamed Eddie for that interruption in my career, and although I only played against him a few times after that, I've got to admit I was gunning for him. Pure and simple, I blamed him for the injury, figured it was his fault, and I wanted to get even. But looking back, I never should have played that night. I should have told Sinden no, that my mind wasn't in it. I was preoccupied, and in retrospect I realized Shack wasn't specifically trying to hurt me at all. It was just Eddie being Eddie. When he put it together, he was as good as anybody, and if you were playing against him, you had to watch out. He could hurt you. Believe me, I know."

At the end of that "one more last chance" 1973-74 season Shack had seven goals and eight assists in 59 games plus 74 minutes in penalties, which his critics said were the result of hanging on to catch up. Finishing fourth in the East Division, the Leafs didn't embarrass Jim Gregory by not making the playoffs, but it took only four games for the powerful Bruins to eliminate them in the first round.

Early in the 1974-75 season Kelly received a number of messages from the players who complained that they couldn't play with Shack, that he was creating problems. Some said he was simply making the most out of finishing his career so he could set himself up for life after hockey. Kelly had heard all that before in Pittsburgh. "I knew Eddie might irritate some teammates," he says now. "He's direct and calls them as he sees them, but I knew that under all the rasping he had a heart as big as a house." And Shack proved him right.

In the early part of the schedule Eddie suffered another arm injury similar to the one he got in Boston, forcing him out of any contention as a potential regular. But Eddie still wanted to play and get himself in to game shape, so he offered to report to the Leafs' farm club in Oklahoma City.

The trip was a rousing success and was covered by the Toronto media. In his first game on January 11, 1975, Eddie scored a goal, and when he was picked as one of the stars, he took off on his usual postgame pirouette just as two rink rats were venturing out onto the ice to take off the net. Eddie, being nothing more than Eddie, buried them both with snow in a 60 mile-per-hour skate-up and stop. At the time the Blazers were averaging 2,900 fans per game, but that night when they played league-leading Denver, and fuelled by pregame publicity on the arrival from on high of Eddie Shack, they brought in 6,100.

Sportswriter Trent Frayne described the game's excitement in the *Toronto Sun*, January 12, 1975:

> They clapped their hands and yelled Shackie's name, and you could sense the lift the goal gave the Blazers, who patted Shackie on the rear with their sticks and yelled, "Way to go, Eddie."
>
> They scored three more and went ahead 5-3, and though they got a little sloppy with 22 seconds left when Denver slipped a fourth goal past the clever Pierre Hamel, they won it 5-4.
>
> The announcer said Eddie had earned one of the stars. Claire Alexander, who had three assists, and Shack's nifty centre, Pat Boutette, got the others. And Eddie did his pirouette, laughing under that Salvador Dali on his upper lip, and then a radio guy stepped onto the ice for an interview carried on the rink's PA system.
>
> People stood to watch and to smile from their seats, and Eddie said, "I'm here to bring in more fans. You've got the next six games at home and I'm here for the whole six games!" (Great cheers and more clapping.) "I think it's good hockey here, and now we're in first place in our division, and when you're in first place, that helps a hell of a lot, eh? So let's get this

thing under control here right now."

And everybody laughed and cheered as they headed for the exit.

And when it was all over, eight or ten players and their wives or girl-friends all piled into cars and went to a place called the Silver Helmet and danced to a loud band and drank draft beer, and who do you think picked up the check?

Of course. Eddie the Entertainer.

Today Pat Boutette, a soon-to-be-Leaf and a member of the Oklahoma City crew back then, recalls Shack's visit to the minor-league team quite clearly: "He was big and strong and had a great shot, and I don't think he knew what a great skater he was, at least to the rest of us down there. Here was a guy who had played in the NHL, and you could just tell right away. But, most of all, he was fun on the ice all the time and especially in the dressing room. Shackie stressed from day one that hockey was fun, and he showed a lot of rookies, and some guys who had been around for a while and had never made it, how you could play the game and still have a good time."

Another new Maple Leaf in that second "first" year for Eddie was goalie Doug Favell, who was snatched from the Philadelphia Flyers in time to make him miss the Broad Street Bullies' first Stanley Cup. "In Toronto," Favell says, "I saw Eddie as more of a distraction, just a guy having fun, putting in time. I think the players would have looked up to him as a leader, as a guy who had done all these things, including the Stanley Cups. But Eddie seemed to be more interested in promoting himself, establishing his business interests, and as a result he turned out to be the one totally distracted while distracting others. I know I was looking for somebody to lead the team, but I don't think Eddie wanted any part of that. Coming from Philly, I had seen firsthand what it took to build a winner, and Toronto was in the position to take advantage of some leadership. But it never came.

"As a goalie, you were aware when he was on the ice. Once again he was a worry, and you'd find yourself watching instead of concentrating on the puck. You'd get caught up on Shackie. What the hell was he gonna do next? But I'll tell you. He'd pump up the fans and his team.

His role wasn't any different than that of an enforcer. But he had a shot that could hurt you."

Ron Hewat was the Leafs' play-by-play radio man during Shack's second time around with Toronto, and on road trips it was the players who didn't dress who were the best friends of a lone-wolf broadcaster. Hewat was always looking for a sidekick to while away between-periods airtime, and Eddie fell into that category. "Back then his role had changed," Hewat observes. "They threw him out there mostly as an agitator. In my opinion he was always miscast."

With his career winding down, Shack found himself relegated to the press or broadcast boxes more and more. And it was there that Hewat became acutely aware of Shack's lack of reverence for the basic rules of the microphone. "We always had a lot of fun on the air, but sometimes we got carried away, and I was warned about it more than once. One night in Oakland I shanghaied Eddie as a guest and colour commentator, and in a break in the play for a penalty, after a player either tripped or was hit, Eddie pointed and started laughing. 'Oh-oh, look at that,' he said. 'He went right on his ass.' We were helpless for about two minutes. I heard about that one.

"About a month later there we were again. Ed came on, and during the break I told him, 'No fooling around. Let's keep it serious and to the point. Don't act foolish.' While we waited out the commercials I cautioned him three more times, and everything was fine. We had our game faces on. In fact, we looked so serious that I should have known we couldn't keep it together much longer. The first question I asked concerned a move made by the visiting coach. Eddie got that look and said, 'Oh, my Gawd, isn't that awful? I think the plate in his head musta shifted.' Well, that was it. We laughed through the whole damn intermission. Same thing all over again. Every time they came back to us we'd either still be laughing or couldn't get started. It was bad, real bad. I heard about that one, too. A lot."

But while they had their fun there was still a serious side, and that's where Ron Hewat saw another aspect of Shack: "Our daughter Katy was in Sick Kids Hospital in Toronto following a serious and painful kidney operation. Because Eddie and I had been on a broadcast, he knew all about her and came to the hospital."

At this point Hewat's wife, Jane, takes over: "I heard this commotion in the hall and a change in the noise level outside her room. Suddenly there was Eddie. He had come to visit and he stayed for quite a while, acting like only Eddie can. Later he went around to the other children in the ward, handing out some kind of little memento from the Leafs. I'll never forget it. Neither will Katy."

George Gross was still patrolling the NHL arenas for the *Toronto Sun*, and although the times had changed, Eddie had remained the same. "I'm reminded about the time, 1973, I think," Gross says, "when Eddie caused a 90-minute delay at the Peace Bridge in Buffalo. The Leafs had lost by five goals to the Sabres, and when the customs officer came on the bus, asking, as usual, if we had anything to declare, the next thing we knew they told everyone to get off the bus. They checked the overhead racks, the luggage, the storage bins underneath, the works. Apparently Eddie, who was sitting in the back playing cards, had said, 'We got a bag full of pucks in our own net to declare.' The officer must have been one of the cheesed-off Leaf fans that night. No sense of humour, I suppose."

To Eddie the incident was a case of "shit happens," a source of amusement, another story in the legend, but to some players the delay at the border was one more in a series of continual irritations, and if there was one player in the cast of square pegs in round holes the Leafs had sprinkled through their lineup who was a kindred spirit for Shack, it was Jim McKenny.

"When I was with the [Toronto] Marlies," McKenny says, a laugh in his voice, "we'd practise on Saturday mornings before the Leafs' game skate, take a quick shower, then sit and watch. There would be Eddie in his track suit, cigars in his pockets, and I always thought Punch must have used Eddie to get the Leafs out of their military boot camp mode. Remember, Imlach was the guy who brought in a couple of jarhead PT instructors from the goddamn army and a lot of other regimented shit.

"There's the great story about Imlach painting lines on the ice. They ran about 15 feet from the boards between the two bluelines, then angled into the net. The wingers weren't allowed to go anywhere else but between the boards and the line. The Leafs practised for several days like that, and things were going along smoothly. At the next game in the Gardens, without the lines, as soon as Eddie was on the ice for the first shift, he was off and running into the opposite corner. When he got back to the bench, Punch screamed, 'Jesus H. Christ, Shack, why do you think we practised all week with those goddamn lines?' Eddie turned with that surprised look on his face and answered, 'What fuckin' lines, George?'

"Eddie is one of the most sensitive guys I've ever met in the game. One time we were speaking at a dinner in Orillia [Ontario]. I got up, and as usual, cut up the head table and said something like, 'What do I know about what's going on with Eddie Shack? Do I look like I'm from the Clarke Institute [a major Toronto psychiatric facility]?' Eddie didn't speak to me for about two years after that. You know, I said later in my speech that Eddie couldn't read or write, but he could count with the best of them and could probably buy and sell the entire head table. But Eddie still kept his distance. I suppose if I thought for a moment he was *that* sensitive, I could have gone down the table right after I finished and apologized or something. But what the hell? It never occurred to me that this guy who'd cut you a new asshole as fast as anybody was gonna take offence.

"Hell, I admired him. I always have. He had more things going on than anybody. He worked his ass off at the golf course. He was there from the crack of dawn, unlike other guys who put their names to projects and then showed up on a semiannual basis. He'd be out there loading up the beer cart, driving around, bullshittin' the golfers, keepin' it movin', and the people at the course loved him for it. He didn't remember names, probably not one, but shit, the course was always packed."

Many Shack watchers felt that, in his second time around with the Leafs, Eddie was more interested in promoting himself, setting himself up for business. Not everyone felt that way, or cared. On that point McKenny says, "I don't think too many hockey players really give a shit what the other guy is doing after work. Hockey players are into their own thing. It's a non-interest business. Look at what happens when a guy gets traded. It's so long, goodbye, happy trails, and the player in question has to look at the trade as an indication that at least somebody wants him. You never read anything into what another guy is doing with his off-ice life. That's his business, his problem.

"Eddie had difficulty realizing he didn't have to entertain all the time. You know, I've often said that prior to Don Cherry, Eddie was probably the most popular Canadian figure. He'd get on a plane, and before you knew it he'd be carrying on and have 100 people laughing, but he'd notice the four or five who weren't. Remember what I said before? Deep at heart he was sensitive, so even though he usually said he didn't care if a few people were pissed off, I think he was kidding himself. I believe it bothered him a lot.

"With most other players there's always something to shoot the shit about. If you wanna talk, you can always get going about what the papers said, or the latest stats, or something in a column. Eddie didn't seem to have any interest in what the rest of hockey was doing on a given day. Why? He can't read. He didn't go over the games like the rest of us. He just played, got on the bus, got on the plane, and went to the next game. Someone was always there to tell him if there was anything important for him to know."

McKenny feels that one of Eddie's chief concerns is money, that, in fact, he's almost paranoid about it. Because Eddie doesn't have an education, money serves as a security blanket. To Eddie other people are rich because they can read and write, so making money is The Entertainer's way of keeping up with the rest of the population. As far as McKenny is concerned, Shack's way with money is brilliant.

Lingering over that thought, McKenny then says, with more than a trace of mirth in his face, "In a lot of ways we're the same kind of guy." He then proceeds to count off the similarities on his fingers. "First, I'm brilliant, too. Two, I'm every bit as goofy as he is. Three, both of us could bring a hockey crowd to its feet, even though it was for different reasons." After rolling his eyes, McKenny's voice becomes more serious. "And four, like it or not, when the time came to take a lesser role, we began blaming other people instead of ourselves. I know I did toward the end when I wasn't playing, when I couldn't cut it. Eddie was the same way when he wasn't dressing. Night after night sitting in the press box, he'd get pissed off with himself but take it out on other people. Maybe he had a reason to, because let's be fair, the Leafs were a boring team to watch in those days. Then, too, whatever reasons they gave for sitting him out, Eddie wasn't buying into the bullshit the club was serving up.

"In the dressing room he was great, stirring things up, but the problem was, that's okay when you're winning. But if you're not winning, the question becomes, Who needs it? It was easy to turn on Eddie. He always took that chance, and that's a great quality. But we weren't exactly burning up the league, and some players wanted to know what this guy was yapping about.

"While most players were into what they had to do, Eddie was from the old school. He was very aware about his responsibility to the other players and how they were feeling about themselves. Hey, some guys didn't take to his pep talks. They got pissed off if you got on them too often, and they'd say, 'Get the fuck outta my face.' Then Eddie would do a 180 and consider them total assholes if they didn't want to go along with his way of thinking. Yet, as a person, if the chips were down, Eddie would go to bat for you, or anybody on the team, anytime."

Unlike Jim McKenny, Ron Ellis was one of the designated round pegs on the Leafs of the mid-1970s. "When Eddie came back," Ellis relates, "he was more the entertainer. He was a valuable player when he was first with the Leafs. He was an important part of the machine with his toughness and aggressiveness. But, hey, we all get long in the tooth eventually."

If there was resentment among the Leafs in the era of Shack's reappearance on the Toronto scene, it may well have been due to his popularity, which went well beyond his playing time or effort. Ellis says, "Eddie still held a 'sweet spot' in the hearts of Leaf fans who have always welcomed their favourites back to the fold even if their skills have diminished. Although he had returned to the Gardens on a regular basis with four other teams, it had been six years since Eddie had worn the

Maple Leaf and still the crowd roared, 'We want Shack.' Meanwhile the rest of us were out there playing shift after shift, playing hurt, playing when we weren't 100 percent, and the crowd would still be yelling for Eddie. Nobody blamed Eddie, but I can see where it was a source of resentment, especially with some of the younger Leaf players.

"In our own way we have a good relationship. One on one I find him a lot deeper than people like to think, and compassionate, but as soon as other people come around, the entertainment mode clicks in and it's usually at someone else's expense. I've been ridden by Eddie a lot, and that's the unfortunate part. I wish Eddie didn't feel he has to get into that attitude, because it isn't necessary. But he's got himself convinced it's the way he has to be. It's what people expect.

"He gets away with saying things that would land the rest of us in court. Yet I give him a lot of credit for being able to read the situation on each of the teams he played for. To me that shows intelligence, and even today, if you polled people on the streets of Toronto and asked who the most popular Leaf player ever was, Eddie's name would come up in a very high percentage."

Norm Ullman, easily one of the greatest hockey players ever to put on shin pads, was also in Toronto when Shack returned. "When he first came back," Ullman recalls, "I suppose he was pretty enthused, figured he could still play, and when they didn't play him much, he got disillusioned. Was he disruptive? He's not the kind of guy who's going to give you leadership in the traditional sense. Not like a [Darryl] Sittler or [Alex] Delvecchio. He's not that type of person. He's just going to be Eddie looking around the room, browbeating guys with some kidding and a laugh, loosen the boys up.

"He's got so much energy, it's amazing. When he was on the ice, you had to be aware of where he was at all times, because he was a big, strong guy and he'd run right over you, or through you. It always amazed me when I was in Detroit all those years how he'd take a run at Gordie [Howe]. Eddie would run him all the time. Of course, he also knew how to get out of there quick, so he'd start all kinds of things and be gone, just like that. Not too many guys gave Gordie a tough time, and

Eddie was probably the only player who never got it back.

"I played with Eddie for two seasons, but they weren't really indicative of how he could play. I remember we were in St. Louis and he got into it with the Plager brothers. He started with one of them, aggravated another, and pretty soon everybody on the Blues was chasing him around the ice. He could really get the other team upset."

That Toronto meant a lot to Eddie Shack doesn't really need saying. But after that last season with the Leafs, retirement certainly loomed in Eddie's future. When asked about his decision to retire, he says, "I was really unhappy. Yeah, I was injured, all right. They ripped the goddamn heart out of me. I even okayed the deal to go to Oklahoma City in the Central Hockey League. I didn't even know where it was. I figured it was south and that I'd get some good weather, play a little golf. Bullshit. But I put on a hell of a show. When I hit town, I made those clowns in Oklahoma a lot of money.

"All my career I got along with all the players and the people. Coaches and managers maybe not, but sometimes that's the way it is. But even when I played shitty, even when I knew it, I never got booed by the fans. At the end the Leafs pushed the panic button. They wanted me outta there." Couldn't he have gone to the WHA? I ask. "The [Toronto] Toros' offer wasn't even worth considering. There was also St. Louis, but I didn't want to leave Toronto."

After the 1974-75 season when Eddie finally finished with the Maple Leafs, it would be the first time since the Rangers he hadn't scored 20 goals for a team.

CHAPTER TWELVE

Business

"WHEN IT BECAME OBVIOUS THAT RETIREMENT FROM HOCKEY WAS here, I became very apprehensive," Norma Shack recalls. "I thought, My God, he'll be around here all the time and he'll drive me crazy. Then I began worrying about the serious stuff, the security of a cheque coming in every two weeks. We had some investments, on paper, the golf course, sure, but in that situation there were also a lot of risks and most of the investments were supposed to be for later. We didn't have any idea about what he'd be doing, or for that matter, even what he could do. There were no endorsements or commercials on the horizon then, and it was a tense time.

"In fact, the Blues called and asked if they could work out a deal and was Ed interested in coming to St. Louis? I'll always remember Ed giving an emphatic 'No!' to whoever was on the phone. He wasn't even curious enough to listen to what the deal might be. Ed didn't like hockey anymore. Maybe he even hated it by then, and he's the kind that when he loses interest, that's it. I've always thought that when he came back to Toronto he had made up his mind that it was over. Jim Gregory, Red Kelly, whoever worked the deal to get him back here, did him a favour because Ed wanted to return, to end his career in this city. But he didn't like hockey anymore, and it may have happened in Pittsburgh. Maybe when they fired Red."

Eddie Shack was never out of the spotlight, although he had to "boogie," as he says, to stay front and centre. Retirement suited him immediately, much to his surprise, but although he had the golf course to keep him busy, and entertained, it didn't even come close to soaking up all his energy.

Instead he threw himself into doing things and seeing people. He drove the dune buggy, he showed up at openings, pursued speaking dates, appearances, and television opportunities. He never waited for anyone to come to him; he landed on their doorsteps.

Teaching Foo-Foo to sneeze every time he said, "Scott," as in Scott Tissue, was a project he took to the company's ad agency offices. The executives there turned the idea down, but eventually Eddie's effervescent personality and bull's-eye sense of timing would seduce Canada's version of Madison Avenue. Over the next few years a series of appearances on commercial television nailed his place in Canadian culture as a "face," someone who rivalled any and all comers.

It is said his television career started with the Esso garbage bag commercial. If that's accurate, it was a Hall of Fame beginning. As the story goes, Imperial Oil had a line of green plastic bags which, according to the company's spiel, were tougher and less likely to break. Eddie's role, as a recognized and certifiable tough guy in boxing gloves, was to punch an Esso bag, then the competitor's. When the inferior bag broke, Eddie was to stand, hands on hips, and smile, a satisfied customer.

By take 50 the director was almost in tears, Eddie was sweating, and the competitor's bag was still suspended, undamaged, alongside the Esso sack. Eddie had already told the crew, "This is it. Either the bag or me is going." They did take 51, and Eddie gave it two of his best punches, then hoofed the bag with a major-league kick. The bag burst, Eddie turned toward the camera, wide-eyed, his big moustache twitching, and guffawed. The freeze-frame that ended the commercial was the "kicker" in an award-winning commercial.

Sitting in Eddie's living room, I ask him to play the "word association" game we used when we talked about his Maple Leaf teammates. Only this time the subject is his off-ice entertainment and business gigs. "Ronnie Hawkins," I throw out.

"I was the bartender on the Hawk's TV show, kept the place buzzin' and the crew full of beer. Rimmer [Paul Rimstead] and I would travel with him sometimes, and he'd do a show in places like Sudbury. Some kid banjo player would come up to him and say, 'Will you listen to me play, or listen to this song?' Shit like that. And Ronnie always saw them after the show. Oh, my God, he'd sit there with these guys, and I'd be askin', What the fuck is he doin' that for? C'mon, let's get outta here. But he'd listen to all the songs and guitar players. Once I asked him why and he said, 'You know, there's so much talent in this country and we haven't even scratched the surface.' He was absolutely terrific that way."

"Mark's Work Wearhouse."

"Every month I'd go out to Edmonton to do commercials, and I'd see Rimmer. He was there working for the *Toronto Sun*. I suppose they shipped him out there either to get straightened out or find a new set of clowns to hang with. I did everything with those Wearhouse guys. Mud wrestling, for one thing. I even went parasitin'. What d'ya call that, you know, hangin' from the thing?"

"Para-sailing?" I suggest.

"Naw, me and this other little dope, Pete, in a basket."

"Ballooning?"

"Yeah. Jeezuz, we went up and it was freezin', and the wind was strong. Holy sheepshit, we landed in a goddamn lake six miles away. Another one had me and Pete at a construction site, eatin' our lunch, sittin' on a steel girder, hangin' from a crane. When we got to the punch line, they took the goddamn beam up in the air. That 'Whooooaaaaa' you hear is for real. I almost pissed myself. It scared the hell out of me."

There was another classic in the Mark's Work Wearhouse commercial series, which usually featured Eddie and little Pete. In this one they enter a western saloon through swinging doors, looking absolutely ridiculous. Pete is in sheepskin chaps, while Eddie sports a 15-gallon hat. They're challenged by a rough-looking sheriff who asks, "What do you tender-foots want?" Eventually they wind up onstage, and when ordered to dance for the outlaws in attendance, Eddie delivers his line: "But, Sheriff, we don't dance." Several shots are fired at their feet while Eddie and his sidekick, tap dancing furiously, exit stage left singing "I Got Rhythm."

"Facelle," I say, continuing the game.

"I was at this shoot, tryin' to get myself cranked up for my lines, and they had an actress in the scene with me who was really well built. Well, I guess I was starin' at her boobs and she got all huffy and upset, called me names and walked off the set. One of the suits started on me, and I

Shack and author Ross Brewitt at Toronto's Exhibition Stadium in 1978, on opposing teams in the annual Prostars Fastball Game. DENNIS MILES

Shack at a practice as a member of the Boston Bruins, after being traded from the Maple Leaf Stanley Cup team in 1967. JEFF GOODE, TORONTO STAR

Shack corrals Gerry Ehman in Bob Shaver's famous photo: "I saw that look in Eddie's face and I knew he was going to do something unusual." The picture is considered one of the top three hockey photos, the other two being Bobby Orr's and Paul Henderson's winning goals.

ROBER B. SHAVER

Bill Shack (left) and Paul Rimstead regale Eddie at a Guelph roast. Former New York Ranger teammate Lou Fontinato is beside Shack. JOHN MacDONALD

Sabre rookie Gilbert Perrault with Shack on his wing against the Los Angeles Kings in Buffalo, 1971. ROBERT B. SHAVER

Shack and his mother Lena in his backyard garden, 1989.

Former teammates Shack and Johnny Bower at a Leaf practice in 1984. Bower was goaltender coach for the Leafs. JEFF GOODE, TORONTO STAR

A night on the town: Eddie and Norma.

Eddie and his travelling partner Twiggy, in one of the many cars in Eddie's life, 1997.

tried to tell him, 'Now hold on, big boy, all I was tryin' to do was get pumped for the scene.' But they kept raggin' on me, so I got pissed off and said, 'Fuck it!' and left. Show business is great, eh? That's when I got a reputation for being temperamental. They called me back and I did the commercial, but with a different girl."

"Miller Lite."

"Even when I did the commercials with Bob Nevin, Pierre Pilote, Billy Harris, Boomer Baun, and Bill White, they had it all written out. Can you imagine all them guys capable of reading and they pick me? Nevvie helped read it to me, then I told him to write the three key words, BOBBY — GORDIE — NOSE, real big on a cue card and we went from there." After a few run-throughs, Eddie was able to recognize the words.

"Quality Inn."

"Those commercials where I come out of the suitcase? Well, we were up to our asses in executives and all kinds of people around saying this was good, that was good, this wasn't good, all that kind of shit. I tell them right off the bat, 'Look it, give me one person who will relate to me and tell me what to say and how to say it, then you guys can yap all day, go for lunch, phone Hong Kong, do whatever the fuck you want.' So I'd learn my lines, know my lines, and they'd say, 'Okay, practice run.' I'd say, 'Bullshit, no practice run, please trust me, shitheads. Put some film in that camera. Every one 'a these could be a keeper.'"

"The golf course," I say, changing direction.

"I met Norma at a golf course, so later I bought her one." Eddie laughs at his own standard line about the golf course. "Sure, I wanted to run my own course. I also wanted to get my sister Mary in to run the kitchen, but Gerry Ublanski and Bob Watson said no family members in the business. Eventually Watson and I busted up when I had to have Jim Garvey intervene [Shack's personal lawyer] because they didn't come up with answers to questions."

Norma jumps in and tries to explain the golf course venture that carried Ed Shack's name for so long, then disappeared with little or no fanfare. "At one point we got so frustrated at their refusal to deal with us, to get any information out of them, that we got our lawyer,

Jim Garvey, after them. After all, we were partners in the business. Finally we said we were coming in with Garvey, and Watson said if you come into our offices with a lawyer, then our friendship is over. I said, 'This isn't about friendship, Bob. This is business.'

Later, after I leave the Shacks' house, I meet up with Jim Patry, a good friend of Eddie's, at the Chick 'n Deli restaurant in Toronto. A light snow falls outside as Patry and I discuss the first business venture he and Shack were involved in.

"When Eddie came to Toronto in 1960, I got hold of his bio, which mentioned he was into meat cutting, butchering, something like that. I had a meat-processing plant called Horn Provisioners, so I wrote a letter about the possibility of Eddie doing some advertising for us. That shows you how much I knew about Eddie. I don't know who read my letter for him, but we got together at the Ports of Call on Yonge Street. I explained we'd want him to be our quality control inspector. The ads would read: 'I personally inspect our beef for tenderness and quality — it's great.'

"We worked out a verbal arrangement and went up to the office of his lawyer [Bob Watson], who eventually came up with a 20-page agreement. I took a quick read-through and said to Ed, 'I'm not signing this. You have the right to do everything except rent my kids for the weekend.' You know what Eddie did? He picked up the contract, tore it in half, and said, 'You're right.' We talked over the deal, shook hands, and that's the only agreement we've ever had.

"We gave away little hockey sticks with his autograph. I must have bought a million of them. It got to be such a problem with Ed on the road that I'd do the signatures. It took some practice, but I bet I could write a cheque for Eddie right now.

"We kept that ad campaign for about five years and it was getting a bit tired, so we switched to Norma, Cathy, and Jimmy in the picture, saying how hard it was to fix a nutritious meal for a hockey player, stuff like that, and it worked great for two years until Eddie was traded to Boston. That's when we decided to branch out. I said, 'Let's get a meat-packing company in Boston. I'll bring down samples of our beef patties to Boston, and we'll do a tour of the restaurants and suppliers.'

"Eddie thought the idea was great and said, 'If you're coming to Boston, why don't you bring the stuff down in my Cougar? That way I'll have the car.' It was training camp at that time, September, October, so I shipped the frozen patties to Buffalo, then me and this salesman of mine picked up Ed's car and drove to the Peace Bridge. The customs officer asked where we thought we were going, and I explained I was driving my hockey player friend's car to Boston and that I was picking up the meat at the depot and that the customs papers were already there. He said that was all very interesting but wanted to know if I was aware I didn't have any licence plates. Goddamn Eddie.

"Me and the salesman, who by this time was thinking in terms of a jail sentence, waited and waited. About two hours went by and still nothing. I figured they'd forgotten about us and I thought about the car sitting right outside. It seemed to me that if we walked out the door and just drove away nobody was going to notice. Although it took me a while to convince my salesman, I finally got him to agree to walk out to the Cougar with me. We started the car, went to the depot, picked up the meat, and headed for Boston. With no plates. Never even got so much as a parking ticket.

"When we arrived in Boston, Bobby Orr loaned us his car, and as we began looking around, we discovered our meat patties were the best. Nothing could touch them in Boston. Most of the stuff down there was pork-blended. Everything was going great, calls were made, samples tasted, interest was high, and after one of the Bruin games, we were invited to a party with some of the players. At the party I ran into a guy who asked what us Canadians were doing in Boston. I told him, and he just listened. A little later Johnny Bucyk came up to me and said, 'Do you know who that fellow is?' I just shrugged. Bucyk said, 'Well, he imports all the olive oil for the East Coast and he doesn't think your idea is very good.' I said, 'Shit, it's going great.' Bucyk said something like, 'Olive oil. Think about it.' It took a few seconds, then it dawned on me. I think we took off the next morning, left the balance of the samples somewhere in a cold locker, and forgot about doing a meat-packing operation in Boston.

"Later I got into a company called Chambers Meats and developed Eddie Shack's Top Secret Steak Sauce. Still later I helped him with his Christmas trees, running a couple of the lots. The deal was I could use him in any way I wanted if I worked the lots. All this from a 'contractual' handshake back in 1960. That ought to tell you something about Eddie Shack."

Without question The Pop Shoppe was the crowning achievement in Ed Shack's posthockey world. It was a perfect vehicle, in fact, a marriage made in heaven for the soda pop maker and Edward Phillip Steven Shack, one that put them both on the corporate map. It's rare when the business and its identifiable spokesman take on the real-life mantle of the old puzzle, What came first? The chicken or the egg?

Although The Pop Shoppe wanted everyone to believe it was taste and variety, a franchise was nothing more than a beverage dispenser and an area depot for bottles along with their sturdy cases that remain footstools in garages and workshops all over the country even today. Taste is in the buds of a consumer, and for a time the product was an acceptable and inexpensive substitute for the major players, a creative logistic edge that made the big boys compete. And the company's success had a lot to do with Eddie Shack being the leader of the parade. But The Pop Shoppe went against the grain of our throwaway society. It was an idea that came and went when the multinationals brought their money to the fight.

Sitting behind a bigger-than-life desk in Burlington, Ontario, is bigger-than-life Al Biggs, and in a voice he himself describes as "loud" the stories roll by like floats in a parade. They run the gamut from classmates in primary school, which in Shack's case are early and not that many, to the streets of Sudbury, to the streets of Vienna, Austria, to the halls of The Pop Shoppe.

"In one of those ongoing meetings," Biggs says, "when the subject of a spokesperson came up. I was asked by my boss, Wilmot Tennyson, 'Like who?' Fumbling around for an example, I used the name Carroll O'Connor, who played the Archie Bunker character in *All in the Family*, probably the most watched program on TV at the time. Off the top of my head I expanded the idea, saying, 'Archie hands a Pop Shoppe cola to the Meathead [Rob Reiner] and goes on about drinking a beverage with some quality.' Tennyson said, 'Call him,' just like that, and we did. Wow! O'Connor wanted a half million for something like 14 hours of time and a dressing room with this and that. Hell, the demands were so prohibitive that the project was cancelled right away."

At this point the story takes several divergent routes, concerning where the name of Eddie Shack came up. It's safe to say, though, there was some knowledge in the business world of the waves being made by Ed Shack, a recent retiree from the Leafs who had made points with a television ad for Esso, as well as with a survey conducted by yet another advertiser. Obviously Shack's name was in the air; it's not clear who suggested him, or when. but what is clear is that when O'Connor didn't work out, Shack was next on the list. "Somebody, maybe Tennyson," Biggs says, "suggested we get a guy like Eddie Shack, 'a Canadian who could do equally as well.' No one realized I had gone to school with Eddie in Sudbury."

Bill May, another friend of Shack's, can shed some light on the whole Pop Shoppe question. With the exception of seeing Eddie on television as a hockey player, May didn't know the Leaf winger at the time of The Pop Shoppe venture back in the mid-1970s. May was a businessman who worked with big corporate flyers in the retail trade. He knew about promotions and selling inside out and was the man who was eventually saddled with the task of implementing the marriage of Shack and The Pop Shoppe.

We meet in the offices of Brick Brewing in downtown Toronto, where May directs traffic in sales. Dressed in a club jacket, jeans, and a "Salary Cap" hat, he looks much the same as he did when I first met him in 1975. I'm happy to see his old habits remain constant as he begins pacing his office while he talks, occasionally stoking a pipe. I sit at a second desk with a blotter irritatingly curled beyond repair at both bottom corners. It looks like a tattooed man's back: a tangle of doodles, arrows, happy faces, boxed-in phone numbers, and scribbling. May is pacing because he's taken me literally and has started at the beginning, rattling through a list of corporate names — Imasco, Shoppers Drug Mart,

Peter Jackson — until I finally wave a white piece of paper in surrender just as he gets to the good part.

"By 1975 I had a job with The Pop Shoppe, then moved to the head office at the corner of Yorkville and Avenue Road [in Toronto]. One morning Biggs told me he'd met with Alan Eagleson and the Team Canada people and that Pop Shoppe had bought a $100,000 section of board advertising in the tournament being held in Vienna, Austria. That was the first I'd heard about it and I was supposed to be the marketing manager. Biggs was excited and asked what I thought. I said it was the stupidest thing I'd ever heard. You have to remember, looking back to those days, the world championships weren't a big deal, and here we were, this fledgling company, buying a sign in Europe for a hundred grand.

"Biggs, as you know, is a large, heavy man, and he pounded his desk and demanded, 'Well, what would you do?' I said I'd rather get a personality. He said, 'Like who?' 'Hell,' I said, 'I don't know, but I'd make sure he was bubbly and fizzy like our pop. Like Eddie Shack.' Biggs said, 'Yeah, I like that. Get hold of him.' I lied and said, 'Sure, no problem,' but I didn't have a damn clue how to reach him."

As it turned out, May says it wasn't that hard to find Eddie. He took out his Toronto telephone book, found "E. Shack," and simply dialled. Eddie answered gruffly, and May explained. Shack told him he'd heard grand schemes before and suggested May leave his number and he'd get right back to him.

May was surprised at Shack's abrupt behaviour over what May thought was a pretty good idea. It seemed to May that Shack was treating the offer as if he were a pizza delivery store checking to see if May were some kind of prank-pulling kid ordering a bogus pie. But Eddie did call back quickly and said he'd meet May and that he would be bringing Paul Rimstead along, too. He also made it very plain that May was picking up the tab.

"During my presentation," May says, "neither of them interrupted. I told them all about the company, that we were the little guys, underdogs, taking on the big bullies. I underlined our belief in the product, our stress on quality, value, and variety, that this was a good thing for the consumer, the environment. Just about every conceivable feel-good angle was covered. I finished with the fact we were participating in the world hockey championship to underline our commitment to bringing the message to all Canadians. The only thing missing was a pulpit and some gospel music. When I was done, all Paul Rimstead said was 'So you want Eddie to go to Vienna?' The negotiations were about to begin."

Back in Al Biggs's office in Burlington, I'm joined by Eddie himself as Biggs continues The Pop Shoppe saga. "We got Eddie to Vienna. He wore a red blazer with a goddamn crest — Pop Shoppe on red and white stripes, the size of a turkey platter, the whole ball of wax. He went on TV for an interview and knocked them on their ears he was so good. Someone from Al Eagleson's group called Tennyson at the hotel and said that Eddie wasn't going to be on TV anymore, certainly not wearing that coat. He went on to say the other major sponsors were complaining about the size of the signage on Eddie's jacket and the amount of exposure given to a company that had only paid a fraction of what they had laid out for publicity.

"Sure enough, they made Eddie take the blazer off and he never got to wear it on TV again over there. But we did real well with our board advertising, and Eddie, too. I think it had a lot to do with Tennyson saying he needed this much advertising budget for the boards and that much money for the cameramen. Our Pop Shoppe advertising panels were on more than any others. You figure it out.

"The year before we got Eddie the recognition factor for The Pop Shoppe in the Toronto area was 23 percent. A year after sending him and Tennyson to Vienna, and after the 'I got a nose for value' promotion was launched, it was over 70 percent. The Pop Shoppe resurrected Eddie. It was the best deal he ever had. It was good for us, good for him, and it proved just how popular he really was across the country. It didn't matter where we went. East or west they knew Shack. He filled a room with his presence, and sometimes he made it noisy, but you have to realize the reverse was true, too. There were times the *room* made it noisy for him. But what a shit disturber. We went to do a promotion for The Pop Shoppe, the grand opening of the Thunder Bay franchise, and we were in a hall with about 500 people — "

At this point Shack pipes up, "More than that."

Exasperated, Biggs waves a large hand attached to an arm that resembles a two-by-six piece of lumber, and continues. "I don't know. What the hell's the difference? There was a pile of people. Bruce Westwood was the president then, and I guess he felt things weren't going good enough, so he suggested I get Eddie 'to cause some excitement.' And I did.

"Eddie got on the mike and started doing his thing, cutting up the head table, Westwood, me included, saying, 'My friend Tiny [Biggs] here was a star in the World Wrestling Federation. Tiny may look fat, but it's all steel and muscle. This guy was a pro wrestler, and he can take anybody here.' With that he took a money clip out of his pocket, waved it around, and banged it on the table, saying, 'I got $1,000 says he can beat any of you bastards.' Well, you know Thunder Bay. Everybody's got biceps out to here, and I was in a goddamn roomful of them. Shit, by the time we got ready to leave, I was walking through the crowd and guys were coming up, giving me a slap in the chops, and saying, 'You don't look so goddamn tough to me, pal.' Thank God none of them had any money to cover the bet."

Eddie, standing on one side of Biggs's desk, mops a hand over his face, chuckles, and adds, "Oh, my God," as if the very idea of creating such a tense situation was misconstrued.

"I must have been whacked 15 times on my way to the front door when the cab came to take us back to the hotel," says Biggs, looking up at the ceiling and shaking his head. "Eddie didn't drink as much as Rimstead and I did then," he admits out of the blue, not mentioning that he's a practising teetotaller now. "So he was the best behaved in our group of three little boys from Sudbury."

Shack groans, turns his face to the wall, and says once more, "Oh, my God," as he leaves the room.

"Eddie was the Don Cherry of the 1970s," Biggs continues in a more serious vein. "People, ordinary people, gravitated to him because he related to them so well. And though he might appear to be a buffoon, every time he went into a plant he'd touch all the right buttons instinctively. He stressed cleanliness, keeping the place looking shipshape, having pride in your job. He told the workers that he spoke from his own experience as a butcher, from the early days in Sudbury and as a hockey player. Everywhere he went his talks had a tremendous effect on the staff, their morale and productivity, stuff you could actually measure before and after he made an appearance.

"See, making soft drinks is a tough business — steam, heat, humidity, particularly in the summer. More than a motivational person, Eddie was an inspiration to the people on the toughest job of all, the bottling line. Eddie may be impulsive, but he's instinctive, as well, and like any of the great entertainers, he can read a crowd. He knew exactly what to say and when to say it. You know, Eddie's always been shrewd, yet he basically trusts people, and he's been burnt in some deals by those very same people he put trust in. It's too goddamn bad."

BACK IN BILL MAY'S BRICK BREWING OFFICE, THE FORMER POP SHOPPE marketing manager says, "The deal we worked out for Eddie was for $60,000 a year plus expenses, of course. It included the commercials and 24 appearances per year, which immediately became an issue with Eddie. There was a constant battle for what constituted an 'appearance.'"

According to May, in the eyes of Pop Shoppe an appearance was the entire city of Kitchener, and the company charged the franchisee for Shack's appearance in the locale. "For instance," he explains, pointing the gnawed stem of his pipe at me for emphasis, "if we went to Kitchener-Waterloo, I didn't care if it was three radio stations, a television interview, a banquet, two franchises, and the local bridge club, all of that was one appearance. Eddie didn't see it that way, but as I explained to him, if we used his interpretation of the term *appearance*, we'd be out of 'contractual appearances' the first place we went to."

"Did Shackie ever agree?" I ask, knowing the answer already.

May just snorts and laughs. "Not once. I had him do what he considered an extra in Thunder Bay, a radio spot or a store visit. The next morning he announced, 'I gotta get some shoes.' He looked at my footwear underneath the bed and said I should, as well. 'C'mon,' he barked, 'we're goin' t'get shoes.' So away we went to some plaza and he picked out a pair, ordered me to do the same, and then said, 'Put it on that expense paper of yours.'

"In the world of franchising it's usually a nightmare between the franchisee and the franchiser, so you have to have some glue. Eddie became the glue. The dealers loved him and what he brought to the marketplace. We developed a whole style, and although Ed had worn hats since his days in Guelph and the Biltmore thing, his cowboy hat and moustache became a trademark, not to mention his nose. 'I got a nose for value' became a catch phrase. Shackie delivered the line not unlike the way Jimmy Durante would have. The whole concept was tied in with the Pop Shoppe product statement of value plus variety.

"Take the day we insured his nose with Lloyds of London for a million dollars. It was a big licensee meeting at the Hyatt [now the Four Seasons] right across the street from our offices in Yorkville. We held it in the SRO bar, invited the media, and signed the deal with the insurance reps, Eddie, and Biggs. I had two pairs of boxing gloves on hand with Pop Shoppe logos, and every licensee in the place, and more than a few media guys, had their picture taken in a fighting pose with Eddie and his million-dollar nose. As usual Eddie took to the spirit of the gig and kept saying things like 'Go ahead, big boy, poke me. Pop me a good one. I'll take the million and run.' It was a riot. Years after, every franchise we visited across the country we'd see an enlarged photo of the store owner with Eddie hanging on the shop wall. Like I said, the franchise owners loved him.

"As for the radio commercials, they were always 30-second spots. We'd get together with Eddie and Rimstead, talk about what we needed for about 20 minutes, then Paul would sit down and write the dialogue. Eddie would say, 'Don't make them too long, okay,' and for the most part they were four or five words at a time. When Paul tried to sneak in, say, seven, Eddie would always screw it up, and back we'd go to five, maximum. For instance, we wanted to get our variety of flavours across to the public and Ed would say, 'This one's lime. It's green.' And the second part went 'And I love my lime.' We had another catch phrase — cola — and I told Eddie never to say coke, because it was our competition. I can't tell you how many big shots, executives, and celebrities he told, 'It's cola, big boy, rum and cola.'

"Rimstead had a great deal to do with the Shack mystique. He had this genius for knowing just when we had what we wanted in a straight line. He'd jump in and say, 'That's it,' and they'd laugh at each other all through the taping. They were magic, they respected each other, and they were true friends. All I did at those sessions was hang on and steer.

"When we travelled, Eddie knew I liked the aisle seat and he would sit by the window and sleep. What the hell? He doesn't read, right? But often he'd look over and I'd read magazines or the newspapers to him. He'd often ask, 'What does that say?' and point at a picture. I'd give him a synopsis, but he'd say, 'No, read me all the words.'

"And I'll never forget the time we flew to Vancouver, where Eddie was supposed to go out in this salmon tournament and do radio updates on the contest from a yacht in the Strait of Georgia. Well, we went out farther and farther. Honest, you couldn't see land, and suddenly I couldn't find Eddie. I went downstairs, and there he was sitting on the bed, green, and a look on his face like I'd never seen before. 'Bill, you gotta get me off this boat now.' I said, 'Eddie, we're out to sea.'

"But that didn't make things any better. I could tell it was serious, so I went to the captain and asked what he could do, you know, a helicopter, hovercraft, beam him up, anything. The captain got on the radio, and we put Ed on a returning fishing boat. You could see the relief on his face as he took off. I did the remotes, and by the time we got back Eddie had the shore party all arranged, band playing, barbecue going. He was a completely changed man. A little later he put his arm around me and said, 'Billy, you saved my life.' It was so unlike him, that kind of a gesture, and it was only then that I began to realize how desperate he was to get off that boat."

Like Al Biggs, May mentions Eddie's ability to connect with people, then says, "I remember the time he was asked to do a banquet 'motivational speech' for city garbage collectors. He was really pumped up for the dinner, telling them every morning they got up something really good would happen just by being out there. When it was over, he was even higher, saying he should do more of this 'motivator stuff.' I believe Eddie could easily empathize with these people, not because they were garbage workers but because they were working people."

There were two other people heavily involved in the day-to-day workings of the magic between The Pop Shoppe and Eddie Shack. The first was Frank Mayne, a personable young man looking for his place in business, trying to gain that intangible called experience. "When I first met Eddie," Mayne says, "I was working for Heise Corporation, which was simply Pop Shoppe Toronto. Eddie had just been signed up as the spokesman, ambassador, pied piper, whatever his title was. The company told me to make sure he got from place to place, attended events on time, said the right things, and kept out of any trouble that might come up. They told me it was no big deal, nothing to worry about, that basically all I had to do was stick with him.

"You have to remember I'd heard about Eddie — everyone had — but I'd never met him. The first date on the calendar was the CHIN Radio picnic, a big event on Toronto Island. I had to pick him up at his house at 8:00 a.m., so I got into the driveway a bit early and rang the bell. I must have caught Norma coming out of the shower because she came to the door wearing a big towel. She caught me unaware, and honest, I was looking everywhere but at her. She asked if I wanted to come in and wait because Eddie was just getting into the shower. I said no and told her I'd sit outside in the car.

"Eventually Eddie came out and got into the car. He was very quiet, kind of grumpy, and I figured maybe he wasn't a morning person. But from the minute we started downtown he was distant, and it went like that until we arrived at a tent where The Pop Shoppe had a big pop cooler ready. By this time Ed was a little more animated because there was a bunch of people around. Suddenly he decided he was going to run a taste test and everybody should try the product. I must have made the mistake of asking, 'Do you want a coke?' Eddie got on me right away.

"He fired back, 'Cola, not coke.' Then he went into the cooler, yanked out a bottle, and said, 'This is *cola*. Coke is somebody else's shit.'

He ate my ass out in front of all these people standing behind the main stage. Then he took me aside and said, 'If you're gonna travel with me, here are the ground rules.' And he proceeded to give me a list of do's and don't's. By this time I was really pissed off with this big clown, but we got through the day. He did a good job, loosened up a little, and we made it back to his house without another problem.

"About three or four days later we had to go to London, Ontario, and while we weren't on good terms and we were still feeling each other out, we were at least getting along. We got to the hotel and the clerk pushed two registration slips across the counter. I started doing mine, and when I finished, Eddie told me to fill his out. Well, I gotta admit I bristled. He rhymed of his address and all that stuff, then said, 'You better remember this shit because I'm not sayin' it again.' I was about to tell him to fill out his own goddamn forms when I suddenly remembered something the Pop Shoppe office had alluded to, about Eddie not being able to read and write. No one at The Pop Shoppe, as far I knew, had actually asked him about it. So I could see that filling out forms for Eddie would have to be part of my job, too. Still, I was dumbfounded by it all. From that point on, though, once I was aware of the situation, Eddie and I got along great.

"We were in Timmins on another occasion, scheduled to do a morning talk show or some sort of giveaway on radio. On the way there I told Eddie about one of the trends I was noticing in his interviews. 'All these guys,' I said, 'want to talk hockey, nothing but hockey. I understand that, having a star like you in town but, Eddie, you gotta talk about The Pop Shoppe. You gotta remember the reason why we're here. So why don't we make a little rule? Remember to get The Pop Shoppe name into the conversation at least three times. How about that?' He agreed.

"Well, we arrived at the radio station. I stood outside the studio and watched the show through the glass with headsets on. The host opened with, 'Welcome to Timmins, Eddie. How do you think the Leafs are going to do this year?' Eddie looked over at me, pointed, and said to the host, 'See that guy there? Well, that's my boss. POP SHOPPE, POP SHOPPE, POP SHOPPE. How's that, Frankie? Okay, pal, now what did you wanna know about the Leafs?'

"There was an ongoing battle with Eddie about what constituted an appearance, but in all the years we went around the country I can't ever remember him not doing a show, a drop-in, or showing up for something that was going to publicize or move the product. In fact, we were in Vancouver once, going from one booked 'appearance' to another, when I spotted one of those little radio station trailers doing a remote broadcast in a plaza parking lot. So I pulled in, got out, and said to the announcer through the back door, 'I've got Eddie Shack in the car. Do you want an interview?' The guy waved us on, happier than a pig in shit. But Eddie wouldn't get out of the car, claiming that this was an extra appearance. I said, 'C'mon, you're on the air.' And at the last moment, just before the announcer was going to scrap the spot, Eddie went on, did a great job, got Pop Shoppe in three times, and we headed on up the road. He was tough, but he was never afraid to work.

"On another trip we boarded a plane up in Northern Ontario somewhere, maybe Sudbury, when the pilot came out and said there was a technical difficulty with the plane and we'd be delayed 90 minutes. Eddie just looked at me and said, 'Are you shittin' me? I don't like this. I'm gettin' off.' But I shot back, 'What do you want us to do? Switch airlines? This is it, pal. This is the last and only plane outta here.'

"He sat down and was quiet for a while. Then, I suppose, as he came to grips with the fact we weren't going anywhere without the plane, he warmed up and started into his regular act. Soon he had the passengers in a pool about the time of actual takeoff and got them to vote on things to eat. Next, he decided since we were all in this together that the pilot should at least buy a round of cocktails. Of course, the vote was in favour of that, so Eddie had a great time getting the flight attendants to relay the results of the vote to the flight deck.

"All through this exhibition an older couple was sitting across from us, and Eddie said to them, 'You married, or are you just fooling around? Oh-oh, look, they're grinnin'. Son of a gun, they *are* foolin' around.' Eddie had the whole plane looking and laughing, but all I could think of was that we were screwed. Eddie was out of control. Worse, it turned out the older man was the vice president of Venture-

Tec, which was the outfit that funded Pop Shoppe. I mean, what were the odds of that happening? By then I was certain that when we touched down in Toronto the guy would make one phone call and I'd be out of a goddamn job. But by the time we took off, the VP and his wife were having a hell of a time. The guy even remarked, 'Well, at least everybody knows about Pop Shoppe and how good it is.'

"Then the captain came back and bought the entire plane a round of drinks. With that Eddie said, "Let's hear it for the pilot,' and everybody gave the captain a standing ovation. At that point Eddie said to me, 'Okay, big boy, now we'll sit down and be real good.' Can you believe such bullshit luck? But that's Eddie."

The second individual who came into contact regularly with Shack on The Pop Shoppe project was Terry Trainor, a bilingual Montrealer who ran the Quebec operation. He was also the man responsible for bringing Henri Richard into the fold as Shack's counterpart in Quebec.

"Eddie was great for Pop Shoppe," says Trainor, "and the deal worked both ways. He'd bitch about all the radio stations and locations he had to visit, but he'd go all day and work his ass off nonstop. And though he was usually on time for everything, he'd always hold up his hand and say, 'Slow down, big boy. You gotta wait for the talent.' Meaning him, of course.

"It worked so smoothly when I brought in Henri to be Pop Shoppe's spokesman for Quebec. They were both famous hockey personalities, but we didn't need another Eddie. In fact, it worked out as well as it did because when they were together Eddie got Henri into the spirit of things and Henri brought Eddie back to earth. It was a nice balance.

"Eddie and Henri were in Shack's dune buggy, representing Pop Shoppe in the Grey Cup Parade, stopping and starting up University Avenue in Toronto, with me standing on the back holding on to the roll bar, dressed in this goofy Peter Puck outfit. Every time we stopped I was supposed to wave to the crowd, hold on to the roll bar again, and give Eddie the okay. Then we'd move on. Just finding the damn bar was a chore. The puck costume was the most ridiculous outfit I'd ever worn, and believe me, Pop Shoppe dressed me up in some beauts. Well, I guess the parade moved ahead while I was waving my ass off, because Eddie jammed the buggy into gear and away we went. I did a back flip, a one-and-a-half gainer, with a twist. The only thing that kept it from being a double was the size of the suit, and the only thing that kept me from a skull fracture was the goddamn puck head.

"The other quality I admired about Eddie was that he wasn't afraid to get his hands dirty. Any time we went to a franchise he'd look around, pick up stray bottle caps, tidy up, talk to the guys on the bottling line, check out the plant, and inspect the store, the office, and the washrooms to make sure everything was clean and presentable to the customers. I gotta give him credit. He was a legend just being a regular businessman, and very genuine in his concern for the company and the dealers. The people who worked in the stores, from one end of the country to the other, just loved him. He was never too busy to sign an autograph, pose for a snapshot, get everybody involved in some kind of memento of his visit. He was one of them."

Although The Pop Shoppe enterprise was perhaps Eddie's biggest business concern back in the 1970s, he always had other commercial gigs on the go, both during and after his hockey career. One of the most amusing and perhaps frustrating was the pop song "Clear the Track, Here Comes Shack", his very own Top 40 ditty.

One thing that isn't generally known about the song is that longtime hockey commentator and bestselling author Brian McFarlane wrote it. McFarlane himself tells the tale best: "I already had the idea when I approached Shackie, and I remember stopping him near the visiting team bench at Maple Leaf Gardens after a practice. I told him I was thinking about writing this little song and asked if he had any problem with that. He said he didn't and that I should go ahead and do it. So my brother-in-law, Bill McCauley, who had a doctorate in music, wrote the music, I wrote the words, and in about 20 minutes we had the thing done. It certainly wasn't Eddie's idea. He did give me sanction to do it, but maybe I should have gotten him to sign a release. Still, I've been told by people who know the business that you can write a song about anybody as long as you don't slam them.

"Well, the song went to number one on CHUM Radio for six weeks, ahead of the Beatles, the Stones, Elvis, all the rest of them. Was it popular across the country? I don't know. See, RCA distributed the record, and I don't think there was much play outside the Toronto area."

Reports indicate otherwise, and one music writer of the day used an influenza analogy to explain the song's spread: "A man has the flu, gets on a plane in Toronto, and arrives in Vancouver. Two days later he's in Winnipeg. Everywhere he goes there are people fanning out across the country carrying the bug. The same thing is happened to 'Clear the Track.'"

Continuing the novelty song's saga, McFarlane says, "It was later when the problem started with Eddie. He was upset because we didn't pay him any royalties. Shackie took his beef to Harold Ballard and made a lot of noise, and there was a piece in the [Toronto] *Telegram* that I wouldn't pay Ed Shack. For years Eddie embarrassed me at banquets over this thing, saying, 'There's that cheap son of a bitch McFarlane.' One night I handed him a dollar bill at a sports dinner and said, 'Here's about what you earned off the record.' Other than that I never tried to retaliate."

Since that time, McFarlane says, he's talked to Eddie many times and the subject of "Clear the Track" seems to have been dropped. But Eddie has always had other ventures to occupy him. As if there wasn't enough to do, Shack became very successful, and prominent, in the Christmas tree business, and it takes us back to Frank Mayne.

"To give you an idea about that lightning intuitive streak of Eddie's, on a Christmas Eve we were cleaning up the tree lot at Lawrence and Markham Road — Eddie always insisted on cleaning away the trees so there'd be nothing there the next day. Nothing more forlorn on Christmas Day than an abandoned tree lot, is there?

"About 8:45 p.m. a guy with his wife and kid pull up in a pickup, all full of business, and he says to Eddie, 'I'm gonna take a tree, okay? Eddie tells him, 'Sure, for $20 and up.' The man pointed out that we're just tearing the lot down, tossing them into a truck to throw them away. Shackie told him to hit the road, they were his trees and he'd do whatever he wanted with them. I wondered about it, you know, what the hell's the difference, one less tree to haul away, but Eddie said, 'Does he look like he's starvin', a good lookin' truck, dressed that way? The prick probably pulls that stunt every year. He can kiss my ass, the cheap bastard.'

"But another time a little boy about 10 came by the lot at St. Clair and Bathurst, looking at the trees asking how much for this one, then looking at a smaller tree. Eddie said, 'Take this one' and waved off the price as the kid started to dig for his money.

"And the best was the night the minister came over to one of the lots, from a nearby church, looking to buy a few trees. Eddie went outside, picked out a few with him, told us to deliver them, then back in the trailer said, 'No charge, Father, I don't suppose you'd like a beer, eh?' The guy wasn't even Catholic.

"Ah yes, he's a genius," Mayne sighed. "Honest, you'd never think about him that way but he's got his tremendous talent, and I was fortunate to spend time with him and travel the country. That's the way I look at it today. He changed my outlook, made me stop and think, sorta step back and evaluate things. Once, when I'd admitted I'd screwed up badly and was really down on myself, Shackie started laughing and said, 'Well, big boy, you can always un-fuck up, yuh know.' It was one of those moments where you really had to be there, right, but it was so goddamn funny, the logic coming from this guy who was having such a hoot explaining things to me. We musta laughed for fifteen minutes. Whatever it was, the problem was solved and I've often gone back to that piece of advice."

The food and beverage lesson over, Eddie begins to concentrate on his driving, checking both mirrors, then says, "I can sell anything. When I was a kid, I got a job selling candy apples at the circus. I had to learn this little spiel: 'Hey, hey, they're mighty good, they're mighty nice. Good for you and baby, too. Baby cry, Momma buy. Get your candy apples.' The circus wanted me to leave town with it because I was so goddamn good."

I just nod, visualizing Eddie quite easily in a circus.

"Know how old I was?" he asks me suddenly.

I shake my head.

"Eight, maybe nine," he replies.

It prompted me to think about Lena Shack telling me how worried she was, expecting Eddie to succumb to the lure of big money on the carnival tour, and I wondered to myself, Who else can tell a story like that and not be fibbing? Plus the fact he's wealthy today beyond anyone's wildest expectations.

Ron Wicks, the ex-referee from Sudbury, may have explained it best.

"One time Eddie told me anything he can't figure out, or understand on his own, he just calls his lawyer, or his accountant. That oughta tell you how successful he is now."

CHAPTER THIRTEEN

Family

I N THE COMFORT OF THE SHACKS' HOME IN TORONTO I GET THE chance to talk at length with Eddie's wife, Norma, and his two children, Jimmy and Cathy. Norma and I touch on all kinds of subjects, but when I mention Eddie's fondness for the restaurant business, she catches me off guard with the intensity of her feelings on the matter.

"You know," she says, "I was against that Hillbilly Shack thing from the start. Ed's like a bull in a china shop. He sees himself as being the host, everybody having a good time, that kind of thing, but that's not the restaurant business. It's nothing but work and more work . . . and it's a cutthroat game."

The tone and strength in her voice caught me off guard. There was no particular order to her interviews with me. Her part of the dialogue was herky-jerky, helter skelter, as she bustled about her large kitchen, from the phone to the centre-island counter, shuffling papers, searching file folders, checking a daily diary, sometimes talking as if words are ways to buy time until an idea crops up. Pauses become commas, not periods, in her speech.

There were times when I thought a train of thought was over, only to have it resurface after a search through the refrigerator for more cream, or after a rustle through the *Globe and Mail*. The day we talked about Ed's defence being his loudest offense, the thought struck me that Norma, in her own peek-a-boo way, was playing hide and seek with her ideas and thoughts, in effect, editing her own conversation on the go.

"There was a time," she now tells me, "when I refused to go out with Ed. I stayed home for years. I was angry at him, at his antics. Some people can have a drink and carry on a conversation, act normal or happy, be a bit more outgoing and talkative, but Ed would go overboard. During that period he always claimed I'd never go anywhere with him, and it was true, but I wasn't housebound or anything. I always had a lot of woman friends — Sally Baun, Bibs Ullman, Marnie Parrish . . ." She pauses, then blurts out, "Look at his language, the swearing. Yes, there are some people he makes a conscious effort not to swear around. Red Kelly's a good example. But there are too few, and I don't like being around him when he's like that.

"Take the time when I heard they had a moment of silence for Phil Watson at the Leaf alumni meeting and Ed said, 'Fifteen seconds is too long for that bastard.' I was so damn mad, furious with him. I told him how disrespectful. But that's typical of Ed. He's never said he didn't despise the man and he hasn't changed his mind."

"What about the kids?" I ask as she putters around some more.

"The kids' conflict with Ed had to do with his playing hockey, being away so much, more than his personality. Let's face it. I brought them up, I was the one who was with them on a daily basis, I was the one left with the moving, getting them into schools, all that stuff, because Ed was on the road. Ask any hockey player's wife and you'll get the same answer. You have to be independent, and I can't say I didn't like it.

"Ed was too hard on Jimmy. He'd have the kids working all the time. To this day Jimmy says he'll never wash another car as long as he lives. Ed would have them scrubbing and polishing the cars and cleaning the garage. To him sitting around wasn't productive. In fact, I don't think Ed was a good parent. When Jimmy was young, Ed was singleminded. I suppose he pretty much had to be. But he expected too much of Jimmy, not as an athlete but as a child. He was better with Cathy, but that comes from the fact that Cathy learned very early how to get around her father. Cathy could manipulate her dad, while Jimmy just rebelled. But he could also be tough on Cathy. I remember when she was six and we were living off Mulholland Drive in Los Angeles. Ed and Cathy went biking down into one of those valleys. It was hot, and when they started to come up, Ed expected her to climb that hill on the bike like he could. He had to go back in the car and pick her up.

"In Boston the kids regarded the rink as a place to see the other hockey players' kids, eat hot dogs, drink pop, sort of like a weekly picnic. In L.A. they were a little older, a bit more sophisticated, so they looked on the games as a place to socialize and go to dinner, eat lobster, top-shelf stuff. Eventually, though, Jimmy started hating hockey, and it had a lot to do with his relationship with his dad. For that reason, to this day, I know he doesn't like the game. He even dislikes coming back to Toronto, or Canada, for that matter, where Eddie's name is synonymous with hockey.

"Ed was very surprised, probably shocked to find out that Jimmy didn't like him in those days," she continues, almost stuttering, the words tumbling over one another, not coming out fast enough. It occurs to me that she's very nervous but is still trying to be candid regardless of the cost. "Today Ed has mellowed and Jimmy's matured. Ed is happy with Jimmy, especially since our son started selling his artwork, his paintings and pottery. Jimmy's also constantly going to school, and Ed likes that a lot, too. As for their differences, it wasn't all Ed's fault, but Jimmy didn't understand it that way for a long time. Now they have a very close relationship." She sits back quickly, more relaxed after the revelation.

"Jimmy is the kind of man who could fit in with anyone, regardless of their age, 92 or four years old. He'd be happy with the conversation, any conversation. He'd enjoy it. Ed, if he's not interested, he's outta there," she says, laughing. Then, softening, she alters her position slightly. "I believe Ed was always nervous, withdrawn in his own way." I must have a look of disbelief on my face because she waves her hand as if to ward off my unspoken objection. "No, really, it was probably self-protective. He's more confident now, but he comes off as arrogant and abrasive because he thinks he always has to be 'on.' He talks all the time as a sort of defence.

"Yet he has a great sense of humour, which is most important," Norma says, flashing a brilliant smile. " He never complains, he's fair, he's logical, and though he appears rough, he always shows his considerate and good side to us and his friends."

"Now that we're on the subject of childhood, what about Eddie's education?"

"Ed is not dyslexic. I know that for a fact, and regardless of what's said, what's been rumoured, he is definitely not dyslexic. If he came in here now and I asked him to read a newspaper headline, he could do it.

Even the bigger words. He'd sound them out like any other beginning reader. So he's not dyslexic. He told me about the tests they gave him with shaped blocks, triangles, squares, and circles. I asked him how he did and he said he did them in seconds.

"No, if Ed had a problem, it was probably boredom. And don't forget, he was one of those kids who came to school as a late arrival. See, he was born in February and was a little older than most of the others, and big for his age. His education became a series of bad timing, circumstances, and compounded mistakes. In grade 1 he had a serious case of appendicitis, which cost some critical months and set him back. But they continued to push him through the system, even though he'd missed all the essential educational basics the other kids had.

"The result was that he couldn't understand and he became frustrated and angry. So his rescue was hockey. He had a fascination for cars, and those two items — hockey and cars — aren't unusual interests for a young boy, are they? Hey, I've always maintained that hockey was a way for Ed to get out of Sudbury.

"Today he watches TV, not the sitcoms, game shows, or stuff like that, but he likes A&E, motivational programs, the History Channel, and gardening." I glance up at her, and she reads my thoughts, or so it seems. "Yes, I know it doesn't come out in his conversation, but that's what he watches. You know, Ed has a bit of artistic bent in him, too. I pick up on it from time to time. For instance, look up there," she says, pointing to the ledges above the kitchen cupboards. "I come home sometimes and he's rearranged things, put new plates and stuff up there. This side is okay, but the other I'll change, especially that one." She points at a blue platter. "It doesn't go with the wallpaper."

She seems distracted for a moment, then says, smiling, "But we complement each other. Ed's weaknesses are my strengths, and vice versa. Did you know Ed picks up other people's trash? Sometimes van loads?"

I shake my head.

"See down there?" She indicates a small green area on the street side of the front steps. "Ed came home with a large earthenware flower pot with a huge chip in it. He put it in the gap in our rock garden, on its side, threw in some earth to make it appear as if the planter had toppled over, then planted impatiens. The effect was amazing."

I found myself wondering once again how these two seemingly disparate people — Eddie and Norma — had ever gotten together. Certainly I'd heard the story of their meeting on a golf course a number of times from various sources, but that didn't explain what attracted an educated woman of discerning tastes to a loud, rollicking hockey player who had trouble reading stop signs.

Eddie's take on the subject is, as usual, matter-of-fact and not very revealing. The way he sees it is that he was 25, at the Maple Leaf training camp, Norma was a super person, and he wanted to get married and raise a family. But Norma has a different slant on the beginning of their relationship.

"You know we met on a golf course, right?" she asks. "Well, I wasn't very excited about spending the day golfing. Ed was loud, aggressive, just awful all day, and I took offence a couple of times, and wondered what I was doing out there. But later we were at Red and Marion Sullivan's house, although Red was away at the Ranger training camp, and the table chitchat brought out another side of Eddie."

Next I talk to Jimmy, who is visiting his parents. Even a superficial observance of Jimmy Shack would draw the conclusion that he's Ed's son. The resemblance is so striking that he reminds me of his father's pictures as a rookie New York Ranger, or a young Maple Leaf.

"I don't recall there being a 'first' time when I became aware my father was a hockey player," he tells me in the Shacks' living room, "or just when I felt he was away a lot. In fact, I was glad when he was gone, because my memories of my dad were different from Cathy's. I discovered we didn't get along when I was very young. In L.A., when I was five or so, Cathy and I enjoyed going to the games. We enjoyed the junk food, but we didn't know or care about hockey. I just liked running around and playing with the other kids."

"Was your father strict?" I ask when he falls silent.

He fixes his gaze on something to the left and behind my ear, then says, "He wasn't real strict. He was too self-involved to find out what I wanted to do or what I liked. But from the age of three to my mid-teens I didn't like a lot of things he did. Today it's all changed. I see a lot of things I do like about him. For instance, one of my strongest memories was when we went to an old-age home to see one of his friends."

I know the friend was Tommy Naylor, the retired longtime Leaf assistant trainer, skate sharpener to the stars of the world's fastest game, and equipment innovator who was years ahead of the manufacturers. Just then Eddie ambles into the room. Jimmy and I look at each other while Eddie stands there for a moment, his eyes darting around the room, crestfallen to discover he's "interrupting" something in his own home.

"We were just talking about Tommy Naylor and the time you visited him in the old-age home," I say to break the tension.

Eddie blinks. Relief passes over his face, and thoughts of intruding vanish as he launches himself into a volley of words. "I went there to show that Tommy was important, you know, that he was a Leaf. I was arranging a bus tour for him and some others to go to the Gardens, a little trip to see a practice. I was goin' to get Ballard to come out of his hole and say hello, that kind of stuff.

"I even got Rimmer to write about Tommy. He was a great guy, great with skates, and the needle, and he really looked after the players. One day he was walkin' from the Gardens to the parkin' lot up Church Street and froze his foot. Poor ol' Tom. I guess he had bad circulation or somethin' and they had to amputate. He'd lost his wife, lost his foot, nobody knew who the hell he was at the home. He got really depressed and said he didn't want to live anymore. I told him, bullshit.

"That's why I was going to arrange a bus trip for them old turkeys to go to the Gardens, see a practice, see for themselves how the players and the people there knew Tommy. But I had to go to Europe, Pop Shoppe in Vienna, and when I came back he was gone, passed away. For such a little guy he was a big man for the Leafs, and he never got any recognition. Can you believe it? He never said anything to those oldtimers, about the Stanley Cups and stuff, and I just thought they should know."

After his father returns to the kitchen, Jimmy says, "I was more impressed with him that day than I've ever been." We can hear Eddie laughing and kidding with someone on the phone. "He brought Foo-Foo, went around joking, signing autographs, talking about the Leafs and Punch, making them all laugh. You could see they were knocked out, thrilled, that we'd made their day. And it turned out to be such an interesting time for me because I wasn't looking forward to even going, but this was a great chance to see another side of my father and I remember being happy with the whole day. It's a memory I'll always keep, that he's able to give a lot to older people, and people in need. I sort of wish I'd have seen more of that earlier."

"I've heard that you've had problems with unwanted and unsolicited recognition because of the Shack name. Is that true?" I ask.

Jimmy nods. "Cathy's much better at it than I am. I remember when I was a teenager and a kid at school said, 'Your dad must be so funny around the house.' I just thought that there was nothing funny about him at home. In the 10 years I've been in New York, not one person has ever asked me about the name. But here the extent of the notoriety still amazes me. Coming into Toronto recently the customs officer looked at my form and asked, 'How's Eddie?' The first thing that hit me was, I'd never get asked that question in New York."

Eddie's har-har-har rings from the kitchen as he explains to the caller that he's checking his "notes," prompting me to say that all the time I'd been out speaking with his father I always admired his technique, since he couldn't use notes like the rest of us.

"No notes?" Jimmy says, snorting. "No microphone, either, with that voice."

I smile. "I'm told you and Eddie didn't get along when it came to washing cars."

For the first time in our talk Jimmy grins. "For all I know they print how-to books about the different ways to wash dishes, and there's got to be a few ways to wash a car. The problem is there's only one way *he* wants it washed, and there's no room for give-and-take, no room for dialogue. When I was a kid, he'd never take a reasonable approach, like 'Jim, it works a little better if you hose the car down first or soak the wheels.' It would have been nice to have had some kind of interaction or some indication that he had a clue that I might not understand how to do it his way. No, there was always an argument, and that's why we all dreaded it — me, Cathy, and our cousins.

"When he was living at home, it was like walking on glass. They say he was never depressed, but the way he dealt with his difficulties and tension was wrong. For him expressing it was just putting it out there. There was very little process involved. When it comes to street smarts or just ordinary smarts, he's way ahead. He catches on to things very fast, but sometimes not being able to read is very difficult for him to accept. Take the vacation we took in Mexico. He got frustrated. I felt his frustration there. But this time he handled it in a different way. He stayed composed."

I think of the photo Norma showed me of the four of them vacationing at an exclusive section of villas on the outskirts of Acapulco. There's a swimming pool overlooking the bay and the city below in the distance. It's one of those feel-good photos in which everybody is smiling and you know they mean it.

To me it has become obvious that Jimmy and Eddie do have one thing in common: both rebel against authority. But I can also see that as they grew older together they began to treat each other with graduated respect, discovering each other as peers rather than opponents. With time growing short I ask him, "If you had to describe your father to a total stranger, what would you say?"

"Besides loud?" He laughs. "Definitely eccentric, a little over the top, in some ways a genuine humanitarian. He might not know the true definition of that term, but he really is one. He'd be there to help the underdog. I don't believe he's prejudiced against anyone, which is commendable."

"Is there anything else you admire about him?" I ask, expecting Jimmy to say something about hockey.

"Have you ever seen him sharpen a knife?"

A scene flashes through my mind of Eddie at a prosciutto plant and impressing the workers with his deft handling of a wicked-looking boning knife.

"He's better than chefs," Jimmy insists, bringing me back to the interview. "You can do all the fast stuff you want and your knife is duller than when you started. The trick is to make it sharp. I've worked in a lot of kitchens, worked with a lot of chefs, but I've never seen anyone sharpen a knife better."

Late in the afternoon I take the opportunity to talk to daughter Cathy on her arrival from work, leading off with, "What was it like with your dad when you were a child?"

"He was rarely around," she says quietly. "We spent most summers in Keene [Ontario] with my mom's parents and we loved it there. We were very close to them, but as for going to Sudbury. We were never able to get close to Lena and Bill. It was difficult. We got the feeling Bill didn't want to be close to us, and while he was there Lena didn't have much input into the situation, and we didn't really get to know Lena until after Bill passed away."

I'm surprised that Cathy refers to her grandparents by their given names, as though they were next-door neighbours.

"When we were in Pittsburgh, Lena came and took care of us for a short while but we were distant grandchildren, and it made it uncomfortable for everyone. It got to the point where I can remember when I was in high school and being told we were going to Sudbury for Easter. I dreaded that trip, and I was miserable for an entire week before we left Toronto.

"In our teen years our father wasn't our favourite man. He seemed to think we were there to work. Other kids on the street had time off, but not us. Anytime he was around the house we were the only ones who had to work. We had to cut the grass a certain way, trim in a certain routine. We had to wash the car the same way every time, use a certain technique. And he wouldn't put up with a half effort, either. Jimmy and I had a similar teenage period."

She sat up quickly and brightened.

"Knowing him as I do, I realize it had to be humiliating for my dad to be dependent on other people to read for him. He has very little patience. He's not very orderly in his relations with other people. He doesn't like to abide by rules, and he absolutely hates any kind of structure. My father is very vibrant, very extroverted, and I think he worries about the nonrecognition factor. I know if it ever came to not being the centre of attraction, he'd miss it.

"We were at a game in the alumni box at Maple Leaf Gardens and he stood behind the seats, watching the game, but only superficially. He doesn't go to games to rehash the old days or to compare his era to the present. He doesn't try to second-guess the management, the coach, or the players. Yes, he has his opinions, but he usually just lets the guys in hockey know what he thinks, the buddies he played with. In that respect I don't think things have changed since he left the Leafs more than 20 years ago. My dad goes to games because he enjoys the company, the attention, the social contact, not to watch hockey."

I can only nod at that comment as I remember the time Eddie told me that he never followed hockey but just played it.

"After a game, outside there was always a swarm of fans trying to get his autograph," Cathy continues. "It was uncomfortable standing to one side, waiting, but I knew that's what he had to do. He has to be visible, do business, and that doesn't bother me that much. The thing I dislike the most about being a Shack, though, is when people within my hearing say things like, 'Do you know who she is?' Like it mattered. It's embarrassing, and it happens a lot. My brother just couldn't take it. He hated being around Toronto for that reason. One time I got into an argument with a fellow employee. He laughed and said my dad was terrible. Actually he said he was a brutal hockey player."

I rhyme off her father's statistics and several endorsements from his prominent contemporaries to dispel any doubts she has about her father. She listens politely, nods, and says, "I understand all that, but this fellow was the same age as me. How would he know anything about my dad or how he played? He was going by my dad acting like a comical character, the way he does in the ads and things."

Cathy slumps a little on the couch. The gesture says volumes about the futility of changing perceptions or attitudes, and I wonder about the burden this young woman had to shoulder. But the same could be said of Jimmy and Norma, and before their emergence on the scene, Lena and Mary Shack.

Cathy seems to realize that she should say something else, and so she does. "He's a good man, very thoughtful, always helping people. He'd get up in the morning and go down the street to this elderly woman's home, and we watched from our kitchen window as he helped her with the lawn or her flower beds. He'd gab with her, make her laugh. You could tell he was genuinely having a good time, as well."

Then she snickers. "On the other hand, he can be a real piece of work. I was going out with a guy that my dad had no time for. He simply refused to acknowledge the man was in the room. We'd be in the kitchen, and my dad would talk as if my friend wasn't there. But my boyfriend didn't catch on. He just kept talking to my father like they were actually having a conversation. It was incredible. This poor guy even went out to sell Christmas trees at one of my dad's lots. But as far as my father was concerned, that didn't make it better. It made matters worse, in fact. To my dad, if the guy wasn't a gifted salesman, then he was nothing. My father couldn't stand him and made no effort to hide it, but this person chose not to see it that way.

"Then weeks later we were at a function of some kind and Dad came to me and said, 'You have my words.' At first I didn't understand what he was talking about, then it came to me. I realized he meant, 'You have my blessing.' I wasn't serious about the man, but it was enough that Dad thought I was. He just wanted me to know it was okay with him, that he'd accept it if that's what I wanted." Any question I had about the relationship between father and daughter was laid to rest by her smile.

I nod and say, "One of the things that's always intrigued me is how completely opposite Norma and Eddie are in a lot of ways."

That prompts another grin. "They say that girls marry men who are like their fathers. In this case it's not true. My mother's father was from an English-Scottish background. He was quiet and passive. It must have been a tough sell for Mom to convince her parents about marrying a guy who was Ukrainian, illiterate, and a rowdy hockey player."

I can only nod in agreement.

CHAPTER FOURTEEN

Friends

Iᴛ's ʟᴀᴛᴇ ɴᴏᴠᴇᴍʙᴇʀ ᴀɴᴅ I'ᴍ ʙᴀᴄᴋ ɪɴ ᴇᴅᴅɪᴇ's ᴠᴀɴ. ᴛʜɪs ᴛɪᴍᴇ Shackie is driving and Jim Patry is in the copilot's seat. We're on our way to Buffalo for a game between the Sabres and Leafs.

"Arthur!" Eddie yells back at me. "Know what I always wanted me and Patry to do? A contest. Take the place of a bum for a week. We were gonna make a bet — whoever panhandled the least money had to buy the other guy dinner. It'd be great. I'd change places with a goddamn wino and the other poor asshole would have to be me for seven days. But see, I'd have to go to Germany or Holland, somewhere like that. Everybody knows me here. Oh-oh, I just thought of somethin'. I can see some Canadian tourist over there sayin', 'Hey, Shackie, Jeezuz, you're a real piss tank, big boy. You've come down a long way.'"

I can see Patry smiling.

When we reach St. Catharines, we stop at Jack Astor's for lunch, and Eddie is drawn into a conversation at another table with an acquaintance who is now in the construction business. The man is pitching yet another money-making idea at Shack. Left to ourselves at a back table, Patry and I are thrown into a situation that crops up often when travelling with Eddie. We end up talking about him. And as usual the person telling me the stories indulges in a kind of free association, bouncing from one anecdote to another.

"My home is on the Rouge Valley, near the zoo," Patry tells me. "Eddie and I were sitting by the pool one afternoon and a great big toucan was sitting in the tree, obviously an escapee. Eddie spotted it, got the long-handled skimmer off the rack and, whooping and hollering, started chasing this bird. There were feathers everywhere. Finally, out of breath and panting, Eddie gave up and flopped down in his chair. 'I like coming over here,' he said, as if I had the whole thing planned as recreation, like some kind of lawn game. 'You got some really neat birds around here.'

"A few years ago I was involved in publishing a book by Sheila Morrison called *Back to Basics*, if I remember correctly, and got her and Ed together to see if her theories worked on him. They didn't. So much for writing books about how to read. But, according to her, his only problem is that he didn't want to learn, and probably after all these years didn't even think it was necessary. She claimed he didn't want to waste the time. You gotta admit, Eddie has absolutely no attention span. He also has no lack of intelligence, but when he doesn't want to understand something, that's it. He can be very obstinate. I think it's this stubborn streak that most often gets him into difficulties.

"There's a very unusual human being in that body. Keep in mind, because he's illiterate, there's a dimension missing. I've never seen him depressed. Pissed off, yes. Angry, sure. But never depressed. Take something as ordinary as golfing. He loves golf, but he can't even scan through golf magazines. You know, the stuff we do so casually, sitting around doctors' offices, hanging around airports, leafing through a book while relaxing in the living room, you know, to pick up tips on the game? These are everyday things we take for granted. He can't do it, and it's gotta be so frustrating to have all this information just sitting there out in the open and it's simply not available to him."

Perhaps because we're in a restaurant, or because we can see Eddie in action with his construction business crony, our conversation turns to Eddie's revived interest in the bar/restaurant racket.

"I told Eddie," says Patry, "to stay away from the bar business. He gets in there, roots around in the kitchen, checks this and that, looks over their shoulders, tells everybody what to do. I said to Ed, 'For cripe's sake, the first time you come into the bar the staff love you. The second time they're not sure. The third time they don't want anything to do with you.'"

Eventually, though, Patry and I touch on the subject of friends, and naturally, the name of Eddie's most cherished buddy, Paul Rimstead, comes up. "Rimmer," Patry says, "controlled Eddie. But it wasn't a bad thing. It was in a positive way, explaining, talking to him, keeping him on track."

Patry goes off to talk to Eddie about something, and I fall into a kind of mental free association of my own. I think about Eddie and some of the friends he's had, particularly those I can't speak to, the ones who have passed away. Two spring to mind immediately — Paul Rimstead and Bill Parrish.

From the neighbourhood rinks of Sudbury to the pages of the *Toronto Sun*, Paul Rimstead kept Eddie foremost in his everyday actions. The two maintained a lifelong companionship and were inseparable, particularly once Shack's hockey career was over. Rimmer was the trusted friend Shack turned to when he needed an adviser. The newspaper columnist was someone who blocked and ran interference for Eddie in a world full of moneygrubbers. One of those who had the best seat to watch the dynamic duo in action was Paul's second wife, Myrna, the famous "Miss C. Hinky" of Rimstead's columns.

"They shared the same birthday," she told me. "Both were Catholics who grew up within the same block. I think the fact that Eddie didn't have to explain himself to Paul had a lot to do with their common background. You see, they knew each other from day one. Paul, who was a couple of years older than Eddie, once told me he had given Eddie his first pair of skates. They treated each other as extended family.

"They'd walk down the street, cowboy hats and boots, big belt buckles and, of course, Eddie could be spotted a mile away. They looked like Abbott and Costello. You couldn't miss them if you tried. When people walked up to Paul and asked for his autograph, too, Paul would be polite, asking whether they liked his column or the subject matter, where they were from, just small talk, very appreciative. Then he'd write something meaningful, personal, about the fan.

"But Eddie, having already signed his name, which as you know was his limit, always wandered away saying, 'C'mon, Rimmer, let's go,' signifying that he was impatient and wanted to move on. But Paul would continue in his gentle way, dealing with the next person, saying, 'Hi, how are you? What's your name?' I knew he was touched when people asked for his autograph, because he was forever amazed when someone wanted his signature or was interested in talking to him. He was like that, but when he and Eddie were together, there was this special sort of bubble that separated them from everybody else.

"Eddie liked to play, needed a pal to play with, and that's another reason why they were so close. I tell you, when I first met Paul I was amazed. Eddie called every morning at 8:00 a.m. to find out what had happened the night or day before. You see, Eddie was there to protect Paul from the gold diggers, both men and women, and he wasn't too sure about me," she laughs.

"On the other hand, Paul had patience with Eddie, and a lot of tolerance. When Eddie said certain things, it might upset some people, but it wouldn't faze Paul. He knew Eddie, and he'd always point out that Eddie had a heart of gold and didn't think the same way most people did. 'Eddie doesn't have any hidden agendas,' Paul would say. 'He can't connive. There's no facade.'

"So Paul understood what Eddie meant without all the asides and other issues and baggage. He'd never be offended no matter what Eddie said. In fact, he'd laugh because a lot of times it was dead-on, something other people would never consider blurting out in a million years. Eddie cut right to the heart of a situation. It didn't matter to him how hard he might be on your feelings, and Paul understood that. Even when they bickered, Paul would turn to Eddie and say, 'You — please be quiet.'"

I was reminded of Bill May, back in the Pop Shoppe heyday, and a story he told that fit right in with Myrna's description of the two "big kids" at play.

"The three of us went to up-scale Winston's for lunch," May said. "Rimmer and me dressed in our usual office outfits, jackets, ties, loafers, and Eddie dressed to the nines, a nice sport jacket, tailored slacks, cowboy boots, and naturally the waiter comes over and presents the menus. Of course, that's Eddie's cue since he can't read, and he says he's going to the top, he's going back to see the chef, and Rimmer, of all people, was concerned.

" 'Eddie, this is Winston's,' he said, looking around at the other patrons, all Bay Street tycoons in blue suits and red ties. Yeah, if you can imagine Rimmer being embarrassed about anything, but next thing I know Ed comes back with a plate of raw, randomly selected steaks, asking me to make a choice, then he held it in front of Rimstead, and took off again into the kitchen happy as a lark. Paul looked about two feet tall, really flustered, which for him may have been a first. Eddie? He didn't care, he was having a good time, joking with the kitchen staff, the waiters, the customers. And everybody knew who he was, too."

Myrna chuckled at the image. "Well, I can't imagine Paul showing how mortified he was or getting upset at Eddie going into the chef's domain, because he'd think that was just great. Paul used to love to do the same thing. The fact that Eddie had shaken up those bigwigs would be just fine with Paul, because this was the establishment, Paul's enemy, so it would be wonderful, and he'd do stuff to egg Eddie on. He'd know it wouldn't take much, because all you have to suggest was that Eddie not do something. It'd be done."

When I told Myrna I was writing a biography of Eddie, she said she was happy. It pleased her that somebody was finally doing it. To her Eddie was a true character who held a special place in the hearts of Canadians. I mentioned to her that I had told Eddie right at the beginning that if Rimmer were still alive I wouldn't be writing the biography. To me he was always the obvious choice to tell Eddie's story. But Myrna shed new light on that subject.

"No, no, you're the right man. Paul didn't have enough commitment to write other people's books. He could never seem to settle down. You have to remember Paul was a going concern. In a lot of ways they were similar in character. Paul was honest, very honest with his feelings, and about expressing them, very much like Eddie. In that respect Eddie doesn't pull any punches."

While Eddie talked about Rimstead from time to time, he never addressed the subject fully. Instead his remembrances of Rimstead came in bursts, delivered in the middle of conversations on different topics with little continuity.

Driving down Avenue Road in Toronto one time, he suddenly remarked about a car he used to loan Paul without reservation. "I had a red Cadillac and Rimmer asked to borrow it. I said sure, and any time he wanted it after that. Why? The guy took care of the car like he owned it. Better. He never smoked in it, always brought it back washed and cleaned, inside and out, leather gleaming, windows all shined."

Another time as we sat in a bar near the Toronto airport Shackie started another line of thought for no apparent reason.

"He drank Cointreau," Eddie threw out.

"Who?" I asked, looking behind me at the near-empty room.

"Rimstead, ya stupe. He used to call it a square meal. When he wasn't drinkin' that stuff, it was Black & White Scotch. When he was off the drinkin', he once told me, 'I feel so good I wouldn't take a drink if they forced me.' Later, when he got back on the bottle, he tried to bullshit me that the doctors made a mistake, that he didn't have sclerosis. Hell, I know what he was told. If he stopped drinkin', he'd live seven more years. If he didn't, he'd live six months. I mean, in that kind of situation, even if someone ordered me to take a drink, I wouldn't. But Paul, he was an amazin' guy. He drank, anyway, and he lasted seven years."

Still another time, as we drove along a street searching for a suitable place to eat, Eddie remembered a trip Paul and he, or the Booze Brothers, as one of Rimstead's fellow columnists called them, took to their hometown. "We went to Sudbury together for some goddamn reason, and before we started back we stopped at Casey's for lunch. Next thing I know I'm shitfaced, and I tell him I can't drive. So he did. He was unbelievable. I know he wasn't any better than me, but he smartened up as soon as he got behind the wheel. He even made it all the way back without stoppin' for a piss. He was a rock-steady kind of guy who never got excited."

I recalled an observation Milt Dunnell once made at rinkside when the scribes of the day gathered after a Leaf practice long after Eddie had retired: "In his column Rimmer announced Eddie Shack was going to 'write' his next *Sun* column. What it turned out to be was an account of a car trip to their hometown of Sudbury, supposedly with a drink in each hand. It was certainly one of Paul's most responsible pieces, and one that would never make it into print today."

Sometimes it seemed Eddie had a million Rimstead yarns, and all of them were delivered in his inimitable scatter-gun style: "We were gonna take over the Leafs for a dollar, and Rimmer drew up a proposal and sent it to Ballard, but that old son of a bitch didn't even give us the courtesy of an answer. We were gonna take a different approach, eh? Sit around after the game, a little team meeting with the boys, relax, couple of cocktails, shoot the shit, have some fun. What the hell? They couldn't do any worse. You and me were in Saskatchewan, on tour with the Labatt's Original Six, remember, and Rimmer called me everyday to report on the 'progress of the negotiations.'"

And then just as quickly as Eddie dredged up the story of "buying" the Leafs, he was off in another direction: "I don't remember where we got the idea, but me, Rimmer, and Ronnie Hawkins got into a limo and started out at some restaurant to sample chicken wings."

"I remember where. I do, I do," I sang out, snapping my fingers like a kid trying to get the teacher's attention because he finally has a correct answer. "It was at Wheels, Mr. Shack. That's where you hatched the plan," I said smugly.

The plan was conceived at ex-Leaf Brian Glennie's bar on Church Street, just south of the Gardens. It was a converted gas station, complete with two bays with roll-up doors and a pair of pumps in the front yard. In the beginning the fun thing for the regulars lined up along the bar was to watch the unsuspecting pull up, then rate how long they'd sit and wait for service before realizing the pumps were bogus. If the driver impatiently blew his horn, it was considered an automatic 10.

"Yeah, right," Eddie said, pleased the mystery had been solved. "Rimmer was gonna write a column about it. We started at some place on the Queensway. Don't ask me where. I can't remember. I know we ran into Brucie Gamble there. I remember that much. Then we kept goin' to Oakville, Burlington, Hamilton, I think, but I don't goddamn know . . . St. Catharines, some dump in Niagara Falls, and ended up at the Anchor Bar in Buffalo. By that time we were just wahooin.'" Eddie laughed that hearty laugh of us, then settled into a subdued mood.

"Rimmer was good at gettin' people together even when they were pissed off at each other. He'd say, 'Okay, I know you're angry, I know you're upset, but we gotta get on with it, you know? So let's just do it.'"

That was Paul Rimstead. Tim Horton was another kettle of fish. But when I talked to Tim's widow, Lori, she had some interesting comments to make about her experience with Shackie. "Eddie has one of the biggest hearts you'll ever find," she told me. "When Tim died, Norma and Eddie took me under their wing, and I spent most of my time with them going places, or they went with me. He was always special . . . once I learned how to handle his sense of humour. Eddie has a gentleness about him that just isn't apparent to other people. Then again I'm sure there are a lot of people who can say they've seen that side of him, because if you're ever in trouble, he'll be there.

"In the recent lawsuit I had with Tim Horton Donuts, Eddie gave me financial and moral support. All the endorsement I needed came from Eddie. I just love the man. He was supposed to speak at my grandson's hockey banquet [Eddie is the godfather] and he forgot. I located him by phone in the bar at the Devil's Pulpit, and he jumped in his car and drove down to the banquet in time to speak. Apparently the people, the adults, enjoyed him, but the organizers of the event weren't too thrilled with his speech." She laughed. "But that's Eddie.

"You know, he can be tough both ways. They say he's a tough interview." She chuckled. "My lawyer said he couldn't get anything out of him in a telephone conversation. And physically, Eddie and Tim were kind of equal in strength, and the two of them would always wrestle. Nobody got too close to them when they were playing like that. But Eddie's the most loyal person I've ever met. That's why he was at my side through the Horton corporate thing, because he knows I was treated badly."

Eddie remembered the situation Lori referred to this way: "Back when she was having a tough time I loaned her a lot of money. She said she'd get it back to me when she was 65. So one day I asked her, 'Hey, did you forget about the loan?' She said, 'No, I told you I'd repay you when I'm 65.' And I said, 'Well, don't look now, but let's have it,'" he roars laughing. Of course, that was Eddie's 'tactful' way of reminding her.

Bill Parrish was one of Eddie's most cherished friends, one he misses deeply. Marnie, Bill's widow, once talked with me at length about their relationship.

"We met Ed and Norma back in 1967 at some event when Eddie was with the Leafs. We got along very well. Bill and Ed were very much alike in that they were both fun-loving and a little aggressive when it came to having fun. In fact, Bill was as nutty as Eddie, which I'm sure some people found odd, because Bill was a pharmacist and president of the Yonge-St. Clair Businessmen's Association. I'm sure that was as far removed from Eddie's lifestyle as a pro hockey player as you could get. We'd run into each other from time to time, but it wasn't until 1973, when Eddie returned to the Leafs, that we got to be very close. Bill came home one day and said, 'Guess who's moving in across the street?' And sure enough it was Norma and Eddie.

"Bill had a sense of humour, but he could be serious, too. Eddie always came to Bill for advice with any problems he had because he trusted him, and if you got to know Eddie well, you saw this generous and kind man. When Bill died [in 1980], he had just turned 47, and I saw a side of Eddie through Bill's [pancreatic] cancer that no one ever saw. He'd come over on a daily basis, carry Bill from the bedroom to the sitting room, rub his feet and legs, trying to get some circulation back. Eddie would get so emotional that tears would stream down his face, and Bill would look surprised and say, 'Marnie, look at Eddie.'

"Bill died in December, and in April Eddie volunteered to appear with that Maple Leaf dune buggy of his in the Cancer Society's Daffodil Parade. Later he came over to see me, and the police followed him to the house. Eddie was already inside when the cop came up, parked, and waited for him. Eddie knew what it was about because he mentioned he didn't have any plates on the car and he felt they had followed him all the way to my place without pulling him over.

"It was a very emotional day for Ed. I know that firsthand. But when he saw the cruiser he said, 'Screw this,' and went outside to talk to the policeman. He tried explaining what he had done, and why, and the reasons, but the officer really didn't seem to care. He wasn't buying any excuses. So Eddie asked, 'Why didn't you stop me when I was in the goddamn parade?' From there it escalated into an argument. Well, Eddie took off and a chase ensued until they stopped him under a Highway 401 overpass. I heard that the cop eventually backed off and cooled him out, but Eddie was really upset over the whole thing, and I felt so bad because he was trying to do a good thing."

Purists would say that, good intentions aside, Eddie was knowingly breaking the law, but as far as Eddie was concerned, he wasn't an escaped convict or a bank robber on the run. No doubt this fine line between what was a misdemeanour, a minor indiscretion, and an act of help was more proof that Eddie found it difficult to accept society's rules. However, Marnie Parrish gave credit to Eddie for his people skills.

"He's very astute at pegging people in a hurry and he's very seldom wrong. It's interesting in the way he will take an instant dislike to someone. He'll meet them, chat for a bit, put his head down, and shake it, as if to say, 'Oh-oh, no, not for me.' In a matter of minutes he can dislike somebody, but it usually turns out that he's got the right reason for making those decisions.

"He'll make you welcome, but if you're going to be around Eddie's place, you'd better be prepared to wear an apron and be busy. But I've seen him angry. Yes, it's scary, because people don't think he can be hurt, but he can be very easily. One time at a fundraiser at Inn on the Park [in Toronto] the MC singled out Eddie in the crowd and said, 'There's crazy Eddie Shack.' Eddie roared right back, offended, 'I'm not crazy. I might do some silly things, but I ain't crazy.' The MC was really shaken and embarrassed. I mean, I don't think it was ever his intention to hurt Ed. It was just a figure of speech, I suppose. But I've always remembered how hurt Ed was for the rest of the evening."

I told Marnie about the time Eddie and I were at an Original Six game in Sarnia when a well-oiled fan came up and said, "Eddie Shack, you're crazy." Eddie shot back, "Hey, shithead, I got a medical certificate that says I'm not crazy. Do you?" She laughed and nodded at the story, then continued. "On the other side of the coin, there's the time we were in Manchester, Vermont, and Eddie came down with a viral infection. We found out later it was called Benign Positional Vertigo. We had to take him to this clinic, Norma on one side, me on the other, great big Eddie in the middle with his arms over our shoulders, reeling this way, then that way. Jeez, we were bouncing off the walls. He was very sick. When the doctor came in, he was a big Ranger booster from New York. Eddie Shack! He couldn't believe it, and he started talking to Eddie like a starstruck fan, asking him really dumb questions. Meanwhile Eddie's heaving into a bucket between his feet, trying to be nice to this guy.

"But Eddie was someone Bill always loved to see, even if it was just for ten minutes or so, right up until the end. And I bet Eddie's said a million times how much he misses his old golfing buddy. That's why I love Eddie with all my heart."

Which is another side of Ed Shack, this charm of his that allows him to garner true affection in friends like Marnie Parrish and Lori Horton.

And also along that protective line, Marion Sullivan, Red Sullivan's wife, the godmother of Cathy Shack, is an example of a lady who not only goes to church several times a week but is about as quiet and genteel as you can get, relating the story about standing up for Eddie, who was having a few beers and acting up at a New York Ranger alumni party long after his hockey career was over.

"In came Bill Chadwick [former NHL referee, now in the Hall of Fame]. Chadwick's wife had passed away a few years before, and Bill was with his girlfriend who wasn't a hockey person. Of course, Eddie was already into his usual carrying-on and clowning with the occasional swear word thrown in for flavour. Well, she took an instant dislike to him and a bit later said, 'If my ex-husband were around, that man would be on his back, out cold.' Nothing we could say changed her mind and finally, trying to explain, I said, 'Oh, for goodness sake, relax . . . that's just Eddie.' "

As I sit at Jack Astor's in St. Catharines, watching Jim Patry, Eddie,

and the construction guy kibitzing, it strikes me that despite being surrounded by hockey buddies, business associates, and casual acquaintances, not to mention the attention of a hefty share of the general
populace, Eddie is still basically a loner. Rather than develop and grow
with friendships he allows others to befriend *him*. In many cases those
he calls friends haven't seen him in years. And that might be some sort
of self-protection on his part.

Rare is it when people can understand or put up with Eddie's roughhouse personality for very long. Almost everyone likes Eddie, but not all
the time, and even those who say, "Well, that's just Eddie being Eddie,"
have their reservations and their distance. Does Eddie care? Not on the
surface, but deep down you'll find one of two things: a respectful backing off as in the case of Red Kelly, who admits we see a different Shack in
his company, or an I-don't-care resentment, which usually indicates a
waning of the association.

Exceptions to that premise are Jim Patry and Bill May, but that has
more to do with their acceptance of Eddie's ground rules, their less
combative stances, than it does with Eddie catering to considerations.
Most others are friends from a distance, drop-in-on buddies, people he
has an occasional telephone conversation or meeting with. In many
cases he treats total strangers with as much consideration and understanding as he does longtime associates. But then there's Paul Rimstead
and Bill Parrish, and suddenly I realize the emptiness Eddie must feel
now that these two partners in fun and games are gone.

Finally Patry returns to my table, and we chat a bit more about this
and that. Then he says something straight from the heart, something
that sums up better than anything I could muster about the kind of
friendship Eddie commands.

"I consider Ed Shack my closest friend. I know, absolutely, that if I
were in need, or my family, money — anything — he'd be there with
just a phone call."

CHAPTER FIFTEEN

The Pension Fight

On December 17, 1987, the *Toronto Star* reported:

> Former Red Wing great Gordie Howe still recalls those heady days in the late '40s and '50s when $900 of his $6,000 annual salary was put into the pension fund, an amount he thought would set him up for life.
>
> "I was 19 years of age when the first NHL players' association was launched and at the time Leo Reise (the driving force behind the organization) told me the pension wouldn't be worth the paper it was written on by the time I received it," Howe recounted.
>
> "I wondered how he could say that. I knew the pension would pay me at least $50 a month. Now I have 32 years of professional hockey behind me and my pension wouldn't suffice if I was living in a cabin."
>
> A picture of Howe, sports broadcaster of the day Dick Beddoes, and Shack appeared over the story of how Larry Regan and the latest group to bring up the pension issue was going to approach the NHL to find out why their retirement incomes were so low. "We have a real lack of information about what money is in the fund, where it came from, and where it's being distributed," he explained.
>
> "We're not a rebel organization. The idea is not to be confrontational but to get together and work out an agreement. I think there will be some compassion from the owners, and today's players, for the players who built the game."
>
> But Reise, who helped build that first association 40 years ago, isn't sure how much compassion the association should expect.

Many people go through their lives without having left any mark on the world, good, bad, or indifferent. Some leave behind a business, a building, a discovery, a legacy of entertainment, a life of public service, or they just plain survive, while others can point to family, the simple act of raising children to become contributing citizens of the world. The gamut is wide and depends entirely on the individual. Then there are others who have the opportunity to take part in one of those momentous "defining moments" we hear about so often.

By the time Ed Shack was 30 he had already left a mark — his name was on the Stanley Cup four times. Since only 20 or so individuals in the entire world get to have their name etched on its silver sides each year, such a feat, for many, would be the ultimate crowning achievement, a moment in the sun that beats the hell out of Andy Warhol's 15-minute theory.

But the measure of a person is more than being blessed with certain physical skills, and when the opportunity to do something for his fellow man presented itself, Eddie accepted the challenge, took the gamble to make things better, stood up in the interest of making things right. Shack refuses to call it a philanthropic, or benevolent, act; he simply doesn't have the vocabulary to attach a handle to the subject, nor does he care. But one facet of his character is a dogged streak of fairness, a frontier justice way of making things right that prevails each time he's presented with two sides of a situation.

There are those who maintain he's rude, crude, unthinking, and unfeeling, that he's inflexible and insensitive. At various times, superficially at least, all those terms can have a ring of truth. But only a few things can get a self-righteous rise out of Ed Shack. Phil Watson is one; the NHL pension surplus is another. Watson was a nemesis, a personal, unforgiven foul-up that time hasn't painted over, while the pension surplus became a burning passion that took four years out of the lives of both Ed and Norma Shack.

The NHL Pension Society was incorporated on May 12, 1948, with original members Clarence Campbell (NHL president), John Reid Kilpatrick of New York, and Conn Smythe of Toronto. From the society's inception until 1990, several groups purporting to act on the retired players' behalf have come and gone. None enjoyed much in the way of success; most were merely watchdogs, figureheads lacking the necessary expertise, organization, and unity, let alone a single, galvanizing goal. This confusion, and in varying degrees, empire building, fragmented the "overseeing" to only a few individuals, while leaving the players' representation splintered and divided.

As in every game, and every war, there are the victors and the van-
quished. The champions call the shots, and the defeated get to ask,
"What if?" In the case of the NHL pension battle there were "war
crimes." A few of the people involved, directly or indirectly, were considered guilty of nothing more than being disinterested, not having the
foresight to line up on the side of their peers, or simply not reading the
situation correctly. In the beginning a few were deemed disloyal; in the
extreme, some saw these individuals as traitors.

As wars go, the pension issue was a low-key affair, nothing like the
major-league baseball strike, or the NHL's most recent lockout, walkout,
cop-out involving active players and ownership. It was a tame affair,
plodding its way through the legal system, surfacing annually to garner
a few headlines. Some of the people involved compared the struggle to
the long, drawn-out process of a death row inmate fighting to the final
writ, waiting for that eleventh-hour telephone call.

The National Hockey League was the last team sport to be nudged
into fairly attending to the needs of those who had made the game a
viable business. Never before had a major-league game treated its grey-
ing greats with such blatant disregard. At no other time, certainly in
North America, had athletes' pensions been battled over in a lawsuit, a
tooth-and-nail fight for benefits, that had been their legacy to begin
with. What it came down to was that former players were being treated
shabbily, and nobody cared, including the present-day players who were
the recipients of misinformation.

Which brings me to the game of hockey's status in Canada. There
were ex-players and members of the hockey-watching public who felt
that challenging the NHL was heresy, that those who had been skilled
enough, talented enough, to have even pulled NHL jerseys over their
heads were indeed privileged, and now greedy. To many inside and outside the game it was more than a dispute over money; it was a trashing
of the colours, a stomping on the flag. It's important to remember that
in the beginning of this paper-and-money chase the problem didn't
seem to be as great as hindsight now indicates. With the salaries of current players climbing in leaps and bounds, with their quarter-million-

dollar payoff at age 55 for having played in 400 games, the pension plan of the 1990s players was viewed as substantial, if not extravagant.

The public misconception was that this windfall applied to the game's elder greats such as Rocket Richard, Alex Delvecchio, Glenn Hall, or Ed Giacomin. Lost in the reality shuffle between then and now were those who played the game when $4,500 was the annual salary for a star like Ted Lindsay, or the fact that Norm Ullman, a Hall of Fame member who toiled in the NHL during the prime 20 years of his life, had an annual pension of $11,000.

Most of the players who were victims of pension mismanagement were around when there was no "international money," few endorsements, little marketing of logos, not much in the way of retail goods or rights fees, and virtually nothing to speak of in the form of television contracts to supplement the flow of rewards. For the retired rank-and-file players the only support from the best years of their lives was pension money set aside and expected to grow, to accumulate earnings, as all these plans are supposed to do. In reality, though, the NHL was using the lion's share of the accumulated surplus to fund its assigned premiums and other benefits accorded to the newest players. The older players on pensions were mystified when they thought about their stagnant, even shrinking, remuneration.

For the retired veterans the upcoming fight offered odds no more unequal than those they had faced throughout their careers. They had reached the top of their chosen profession, overcoming all the obstacles and roadblocks they encountered and despite bigger, better, and more talented opponents. That premise is nothing more than the lead paragraph in a professional hockey player's job description. It came down to winning or losing, nothing more than they were accustomed to, no less than it had ever been. When you won, you reaped the benefits; when you lost, you stared defeat in the face and went on.

If there's a continuous thread in Ed Shack's character, it could well be his nonacceptance of titles, diplomas, or positions of authority. Since not one of these facets are important to him, they carry little or no value. Whether it was a coach, a teacher, a millionaire mining magnate, or one of his doctors imparting knowledge that was above and beyond his understanding, it was only the character of the person that mattered to him.

Eddie was, and is, a study in quick-draw jurisprudence. He brooks no interference, doesn't suffer fools lightly, follows no guidelines, and adheres to no rules except his own code of loyalty. Whether he admits it or not, it was these principles that drew him inexorably into the pension war. Above and beyond the consideration for money, it was the injustice of the situation that attracted him to the fight.

"Carl Brewer came to the house to see Norma and me," Eddie told me by way of an introduction to the pension saga. "He said there was $42 million in surplus and it was ours. Carl felt we should get the right guys together and suggested that we hire Mark Zigler as our lawyer."

The "right guys" included seven contributors to a lawsuit: Carl Brewer, Andy Bathgate, Leo Reise, Allan Stanley, and Eddie Shack. Keith McCreary's contribution wasn't in money or as a signer, but his help was tangible in the form of his offices and business equipment and intangible in his political experience and levelheaded counsel. While Orr threw in money and his autograph, he stayed in the background, perhaps wisely, considering he was already involved in a lawsuit against Alan Eagleson and didn't want to cloud the issue. After the initial seed money was dropped into the pail, like any war, the pension battle became an organization and logistical entity.

Through the grapevine I discovered the pension fight was Norma Shack's "baby," a crusade she had taken up with considerable determination. After all the years of being in the hockey sideshow, pulling up stakes and moving, getting Jimmy and Cathy in and out of school, managing a house and all the finances, not to mention being Eddie's travelling secretary, the only one who could keep notes and a calendar for her hither-and-yon husband, Norma had finally gotten to take up the flag and use the paramilitary experience all wives and mothers possess. In short, she had marched off to the wars.

Now, in her house in Toronto, Norma sits primly on the edge of her living room sofa. She appears to be much more petite than five foot five while becoming animated and excited as she goes through the two full boxes of pension files stacked on the floor. Her eyebrows rise dramatically when she suddenly remembers hot points of the fight, then she grimaces at the typewritten names on some documents, grins and laughs at another piece of paper once deemed crucial, now relegated to a long-gone concern. Her reading is done to the exclusion of any distractions, and over the course of the next few hours I often get the feeling I'm alone and unnecessary. After only a short time, I'm convinced Norma's powers of concentration could accomplish the same thing sitting in the middle of Toronto's Don Valley Parkway during rush hour.

Without warning she slaps a sheaf of paper down, startling me. "Here it is! There was an original pension group consisting of Andy Bathgate, Carl Brewer, Dave Forbes, Gordie Howe, Bobby Hull, Bobby Orr, Dennis Owchar, Rene Robert, and Al Stanley. It was going nowhere, and even before that there was a move afoot by Bobby Baun, Al Stanley, and Larry Regan. Their agenda was to try to find out why we didn't have more pension money. But it didn't come together. Larry Regan had the idea that you never sued the NHL. You worked with them. He said he knew a lot of people in Ottawa political circles and that there were going to be laws made to deal with the situation. But the problem wasn't political. This wasn't an issue that could be decided by any politician. It was an issue for the courts, an out-and-out legal matter. Regan couldn't be convinced of that option."

She settles back with yet another handful of legal-size correspondence and hands me a newspaper clipping to pore over. It relates how the "issue" hit the fan. According to the news item, the critical point of the matter occurred when the NHL decided to use the players' pension surplus to give itself a "contribution holiday." In effect, the league took the accumulating money earned and used it as their payments into the plan of the retired players. This was the crux of the dispute brought out in subsequent trial testimony, and it involved Alan Eagleson as head of the players' association, who implied the league had the right to employ this method.

"Shortly after Carl Brewer came to our house and told us about the pension surplus," Norma continues, "an initial meeting with about a dozen or so players was held at the Chick 'n Deli on Mount Pleasant Road. Ed came home from the meeting and didn't really say much. He wasn't very impressed. But the situation remained the same whether anybody liked how the meeting went or not, so I called Carl and said this had to be made into a bigger issue for a larger group of people, including the wives. I asked who else other than wives would be more concerned with an income? Carl agreed.

"We booked a hotel meeting room at the Ramada Inn at Highways 400 and 401 and started phoning. We lined up 40 to 50 players and wives this time. Rich Winter was there. So were Ed Garvie, who represented the NFL players' group, and Mark Zigler. In my mind there was only one of them, Zigler, we had any reason to consider, because he was a pension lawyer and knew pension law inside and out."

"What do you mean by absolute certainty about Zigler?" I ask. "Was anything said about Winter or Garvie before the meeting?"

"No, nothing. It was just a gut feeling. When his turn came, Mark Zigler said he felt that we had a case and that we should get a group together. I can still remember everybody continuing to talk as if nothing important had been said. They all nodded in agreement and wondered how we were going to spend the millions we had coming. I said, 'Hold it! Are you all deaf?' God, nobody got it. That's a lot of money. Our piddling little $30,000 up front would only cover Zigler's written opinion.

"Sure, Eagleson was the man who always maintained the money belonged to the NHL, but he never circulated any information to that effect. It was just his word that the money was the NHL's. No one ever saw such an opinion and, of course, we were sure there never was one, that he was just siding with the NHL. It was pointed out in 1967 or 1968 that Eagleson sent a letter to the NHL, saying the players weren't objecting to the use of the money from their pension. But none of the players had even heard of this issue. He just gave the NHL the rights in a letter and obviously the Ontario government didn't ask any questions.

"Later in the trial, affidavits were presented to a man by the name of

Marcus Gracyk. He was the U.S. attorney who said the NHL could take the players' money and use it, and he was cross-examined by Mark Zigler. When he was shown a document in our pension correspondence that refuted his position, he got very huffy and said, 'Well, I never saw that. It was never in anything I saw.' As far as I was concerned, that proved he was only given what the NHL wanted him to see."

At the Ramada Inn meeting the issue of trying the lawsuit in the United States was brought up for the first time. The reason? There was a feeling that triple damages allowed by U.S. jurisdictions would be more lucrative. "They also thought we should go after the NHL on collusion, too," Norma says, displaying a touch of irritation. "We'd have still been in the courts right now, probably for another five years, probably till we were all dead." She waves her hands over her head in a kind of dismissal. "I felt we should go after what we could get. We had a good chance to win the pension battle, but collusion is much more difficult to prove. I'm not saying other people who felt that way were wrong. They could be right, but you can't waste your entire life on this stuff. The pension, not the damages, was the only way Ed and I would get involved."

Then, shuffling through wads of paper, she shows me bills and statements, laughs nervously, and says, "Look at this. They never seem to end." Leaning back for a moment, she lets the words tumble out almost on top of one another as the enormity of the task comes home to roost again. "What if no one had taken the bull by the horns? What if the bills just kept arriving and nothing came in? It was a frightening prospect because you have to know the NHL would come after payment or damages if they won. It could have cost the signers a fortune.

"There were times when I thought, My God, we're crazy. Yet I felt so confident in our position that I sometimes worried I was going overboard. Even on the days I went down to listen to the proceedings, I never came away with the feeling we were losing. I was always absolutely sure we were winning. I knew we were right, and I had a lot of confidence in Mark Zigler. He never made a rash prediction. He did say we had a good chance, but he'd add that things can go so wrong, so fast."

"How were the seven signators corralled?" I ask, to change the time frame if not the subject.

"I called Andy Bathgate out in Whistler, B.C., although he said he'd never be a part of a lawsuit. I told him Ed and I would be, and he said he'd talk to Merle [Bathgate]. The very next day he called and said, 'We're in.' It wasn't until then that I told him Gordie and Colleen Howe had met with Mark Zigler and said they were with us, too.

"Red Kelly came by shortly after that and said that from his standpoint, 'If you proceed, you must go through to the end.' At the time Red was into legal proceedings in his own business, and the one thing he warned was no matter what happened, stick with it. Red was also of the opinion that Mark Zigler was the man we should deal with, and he was the one who recommended Leo Reise from the older days. Andy Bathgate called Leo and he agreed. Because Leo had been on the first players' pension committee, he was an excellent choice. You couldn't get a better person. His expertise on the subject and his incredible memory for all the details of what went on before were very helpful.

"Then there was Bobby Hull. I was nervous about asking Bobby to come in with us. You see, any time we approached someone, we were asking for a lot, because the losses could be huge. But I asked Bobby if he'd be willing to sign up, warning him about the consequences, and he just said it was all okay."

Norma mentions she never asked Hull for $5,000, nor did she know if he was aware all of the signators had put in that amount. "It didn't make much difference at the time. The case wasn't going to be won or lost because of $5,000, and he would have had to put up money if the case was lost, anyway. It was enough that he was in with us.

"One of the reasons Bobby was around was his strong position on the tactics. I remember him saying in an earlier meeting that the only way we'd ever get the NHL's attention was to bring a lawsuit. Larry Regan, on the other hand, still thought the way to get this overturned, or put in place, was through politicians in Ottawa, or by waiting them out. Good Lord, did he think the NHL was going to think it over, then agree to fork over $40 million to a lot of old guys? I mean, come on, when it's put that way, straightforward, doesn't it sound silly?

"And another thing about Bobby Hull. He came to every fundraiser. He might have had his own paying date booked, but that didn't mean anything to him. He'd cancel it and come to our event. He was always there from the outset.

"The last piece of the puzzle was Keith McCreary. Al Stanley had gone to Florida for the winter. Andy had gone to Whistler, but he suggested Keith McCreary because someone had to help organize things, and as it turned out, we made all the decisions. If Mark Zigler was going to need a cheque, he called either Keith or me."

McCreary was a 10-year NHLer with Montreal, Pittsburgh, and the Atlanta Flames before retiring in 1975, More important, he brought business acumen to the table from his real-life job as a general insurance broker and investment dealer, along with 12 years as a politician. As such he rose all the way to Peel Region councillor, a job that governed the municipal guidelines of 900,000 people, including the booming metropolis of Mississauga and his own growing mini-city of Bolton.

"Andy Bathgate said Keith was a tie-in guy who would take the time from his job," Norma continues. "Andy asked Keith to do it and he said he would. Without Keith McCreary involved in this lawsuit we'd have been dead in the water. We wouldn't have had a case because it would have fallen apart long before. I don't know if a bill would have been paid or an event arranged. Heck, I needed some help, and Keith was there from day one."

The plot began to thicken with the emergence of the new Group of Seven and its intention to take the case to the courts. Charges and countercharges were traded in the media. Then, on May 15, 1991, the NHL brought a libel lawsuit against the *Toronto Sun*, Gordie Howe, and Billy Harris, charging "the [*Sun*'s] article erroneously states that proceedings pending in the Ontario Court of Justice allege that the claimants [NHL] have misappropriated millions of dollars from the funds of the NHL Pension Society."

In a companion article Billy Harris articulated the ludicrous position the player participants found themselves in: "Our lawyer, Mark

Zigler, started asking questions about the money and was told it's none of his business. In essence, Brett Hull and Mark Howe will receive one quarter of a million dollars at age 55 because of money contributed by their respective fathers, Robert and Gordon."

"That summer we had two golf events," Norma recalls, licking fingers and fast-forwarding through more documents from the second carton. "The first one at our course [Vaughan Valley] on July 9, 1991, was bedlam. Keith and Ed sold most of the teams, Carl was still involved at the time, and a lot of people and a lot of work went into getting our feet wet in the fundraising business. It was the most glorious day of the summer, a complete sellout, and we were able to pay off the bill for the opinion. By the way, here's a copy of the Zigler opinion," she declares triumphantly, slapping a thick, stapled file dated June 1991 onto the coffee table. "It was so clear, wonderful, really worth reading."

Then, reaching into another file, her attention returns to the first golf tournament. "To give you an idea of how little funding we had, before we even got off the ground, we were under a pile of bills — $35,000 worth," she announces, producing the proper piece of paper. "And at that first tournament we'll be forever grateful to a guy named Charlie Bennett. He must have spent $20,000 buying auction items from the players." Bennett, a general contractor in heating and air conditioning, was a pure hockey fan. "Two months later he came to the next one at Huntington and did it all again. In fact, he bought an around-the-world-vacation trip. He saved our bacon."

She rifles through more files, lost in the correspondence for long periods, sometimes reading aloud, rehashing and reliving a time in her life that was both frightening and, given the outcome, exhilarating. It was an expending of effort that provided a sense of accomplishment few others get the opportunity to experience.

For the signators it was an act of courage, an all-or-nothing gamble that they were right, based on a belief that justice wore a striped shirt and red armbands much like the many officials who had governed their hockey lives, and that the foul was so obvious the referee had to blow the whistle. They not only risked the personal loss of their homes and savings, but gambled with friendships, the wrath of peers who felt the status-quo system was fine. Plus there was the considerable risk of rejection by the public whose perception might be shaped by the lobbying interests of a high-profile and powerful business entity like the NHL.

There aren't any known dissenters to the statement that ex-Leaf Carl Brewer was the one who blew the whistle on the pension plan, on the discrepancy between what was being done, and what was supposed to be going on. Also, there wasn't any misreading of the sparks between Brewer and Eagleson, as was noted in a Toronto newspaper quote from the ex-Leaf: "Al Eagleson dusted me off, the way he dusted off all retired players."

The battle lines had been drawn; the ranks of centurions were lined up on either side.

After talking to Norma, I sought out Eddie to get his perspective on the pension battle. "I said let's put on a golf tournament," he tells me, still relishing his role in the affair as if he were an oversize Mickey Rooney in one of those films where the kids put on a garage musical. "Some of the guys said it was too early, that we didn't have enough time, all kinds of goddamn excuses, but we did it, anyway, and raised $50,000. That first time we just said to people that we were suing the NHL, and the players said, 'Stick it in their crease,' but the lawyers wanted to see how much support we had, and we got guys to sign a petition.

"Next we got our lawyer [Jim Garvey] involved, and at one of the early meetings Brewer wanted to know what Garvey was doing there, like Carl was the king or somethin'. He knew goddamn well what Jim was doin' there. He was our lawyer for the card deal we were considering at the time to raise money. So Carl had to make a big exit. He walked out, him and his girlfriend, Sue Foster, yelling and screaming about suing us, and he did, but just for expenses, going back over six years. But we paid him off, anyway," he says, dismissing the annoyance with a thump of a big hand on a table, "because we were all reimbursed."

"We did the golf thing again, September 18, at Huntington, Vic Hadfield's place, where I ran into Jim Gregory and asked him about the lawsuit, what chance we had to get the money for our pensions. He said we didn't have a hope in hell. I figured he works for the NHL, so what else is he gonna say? Then, as I was walkin' away, I thought, Without the players what the hell would he be? So I went over to ask Darryl Sittler about supporting us, and he said, 'You don't have a chance.' He was sure we were just standin' on the corner with our dicks in our hands. He even said if we won I could keep his share.

"That really pissed me off, that kind of attitude, because I could remember goin' to an all-star game us Legends played for some charity the NHL dreamed up, and John Ziegler [a former NHL president] and Eagleson came rolling along in their stretch limos, dishing out big tips like it was their money. Yeah, they got all the perks. Meanwhile we came to the rink in a goddamn smokin' bus, and we were the guys puttin' on the show. The money they were tossin' around came from us, not them. The players got screwed so bad. Nobody's ever gonna know how bad.

"Clarence Campbell [a former NHL president] was another bullshit artist. He'd come to practice when I was with the Leafs, get the team in the dressing room, and give us the company line, all that crap about us havin' the best pension in the world. Then us dummies would go out and have a few beers, whackin' each other on the back, happier than pigs in shit."

Eddie's eyes skip around like laser beams for a moment, angry and sparkling, then his face crinkles into a big grin. "Arthur, did I tell ya about when we were at the Devil's Pulpit, a member/guest thing, and who was there? John Ziegler was one of them. I got him into the locker room and ate his ass out, both cheeks. He couldn't go anywhere, so he had to sit there and take it."

Red Kelly was Eddie's guest that day at the Pulpit, and he remembers the confrontation between Shack and Ziegler with a lot less invective: "It was at the time they were going through the court battles over the pension. The tournament organizers made two mistakes. First, they invited John Ziegler, and second, they put him in the same bay where Ed had his locker. Eddie came in after his round, found Ziegler there trying to get dressed, and Shackie went up like a volcano. He stood in the doorway cussing him out, really giving him what for, tearing a strip off John that I don't think he'll ever be able to forget. It was quite a scene, and Ziegler had to take it. Where was he going to go?

There was no way out unless he wanted to go through Eddie."

Sometime later I arrange a meeting with Norma Shack and Keith McCreary, the two pension lawsuit quarterbacks, at McCreary's office in Bolton. "I can remember the day when we went to Mark Zigler's office and he said you can expect to have to come up with at least $5,000 a month," Norma begins.

"We didn't have five cents at the time," McCreary adds, swivelling from side to side behind his cluttered desk, an occupational hazard he blames on the approaching income tax deadline. "And that didn't take into consideration that we were set up as a nonprofit organization. We had our own lawyers, our own accountants, and we had other costs on top of that. So the number wasn't just $5,000. That was Mark Zigler's number."

For some reason the conversation leads to the early meetings and Leo Reise's no-nonsense attitude toward the machinations of Carl Brewer. "Leo was great in some meetings," McCreary says, laughing, "including the ones with controversy. There was the time Carl wanted the books opened. Leo straightened out Alan Dick, sitting in at Carl's request, when Dick implied we were bad people."

Norma agrees. "We had an audit done every year, and everything was on the table, but Brewer's lawyer hinted that it wasn't. Leo said, 'Are you saying we're dishonest?' I think Alan went away that night very red-faced, and in my opinion I don't think he bothered with Carl much anymore, either. See, Carl was saying all these things, and Leo said, 'Show us where we've done anything wrong.' Of course, Carl couldn't. And there was also the night Leo put down Colleen Howe. He told her to be quiet."

This time McCreary picks up the story. "Colleen was speaking about how Gordie felt, and Leo said, 'Wait a minute. These are the applicants, and I don't see your name down here as one of them.' That was also the meeting where Gordie brought up that I had done a lot of business with Eagleson, which wasn't true. I asked him who'd told him that, and Colleen, as usual, answered for Gordie. She said, 'Well, Carl just told us.' Brewer was out of the room, so I gave a yell for him, and his excuse was that he had overheard it somewhere. The fact was that it didn't matter whether I had or I hadn't. That wasn't part of our program that night, but I never have dealt with Eagleson and didn't intend to." He shakes his head at the thought of the mercurial Brewer.

"We were walking on glass in the Brewer situation," he continues. "Hell, everyone recognized that without Carl Brewer there wouldn't have been an application before the courts. Without question Brewer was the guy who spearheaded the whole pension issue. He got the players up in arms. But later I suppose we were hopeful he might soften his stance, because the group could have fallen apart at any time."

"He only attended the first golf day, and that was it," Norma explains. "He walked away from the meeting at Huntington when we were planning the second tournament, he and his cohort Sue Foster. He said he'd make sure we got bills from everybody. And we did. Huge bills from people who had nothing to do with the actual lawsuit. Rich Winter, Ed Garvie, Ed Ferrin, the lawyer who filed the case in the States for Reggie Leach and Bob Dailey. I never understood how come they suddenly ended up on the bandwagon."

"Did Brewer sue the signators?" I ask McCreary.

"Yeah, and though he didn't pursue the matter past expenses, it still cost us legal fees and a lot of aggravation. You know, it's a funny thing, but I don't hold any malice toward Carl. He did a great service for a lot of people getting this thing going, but you have to understand that he's an individual, not a team player. He can't play on a team. It's either his way or it isn't any way at all. For instance, we were just going nicely on our lawsuit and he wanted to fire Zigler and move the whole issue to the U.S. That was another strain on our group that took countless hours of discussion. The pension issue was here in Ontario. It operates under the Ontario Pension Commission. Why in hell would you want to try it in the U.S.?

"He even lobbied our group to fire Mark Zigler, the guy *he* brought into the lawsuit. And Zigler knew about it. But Mark also realized he had a good affidavit, a strong one from Carl, and he didn't want Brewer withdrawing from the case. See, if Carl bolted, the affidavit went with him. From Carl's side, if he pulled the plug he wouldn't have had the pipeline to the inside, the opportunity to be able to call Mark whenever he wanted and ask, 'What's the latest?' Zigler gave him countless hours of time, which were all billed to us. So that was a wedge between Carl and me, and an issue that broke the back of the relationship."

"Did Brewer participate in the later fundraising, the events that provided support for the lawsuit fund?" I ask.

"Not with us. He never involved himself in any event or appearances, nothing to support what we were doing. The truth of the matter was, three years later when the final verdict came down, he hadn't done dick since he'd taken off. That's the kind of person he is, but I also think there's no doubt about the fact that Carl had two agendas. He had a great distaste for both Harold Ballard, for the Leaf organization to a certain extent, and a burning hatred for Eagleson. What created it? Only Carl knows, because in the early days they were friends. but that changed. Al was someone who represented the owners and the way they did business with the players. To Brewer, Eagleson was in bed with the owners."

Norma is called away to the phone, which gives me an opportunity to question McCreary about Ed and Norma Shack. "The Shacks were very strong in this whole matter," he tells me, "and Ed was involved all the time. He made up for his lack of formal education with his people skills. He knew when to jump in, when to get involved, and brought a positive spin to the project, an enthusiasm that rubbed off on everyone else. Plain and simple, Eddie was a key player in the pension issue, although there are a lot of people who won't see his contribution from the same angle we did on a daily basis. He didn't make any bones about who he was or what he was doing. He walked around with his chest stuck out, saying, 'Here's the pension situation and I'm on this side.'

"With Norma and Eddie, despite the handicap of his illiteracy, their sincerity and dedication to what they saw as right and fair overcame shortcomings in that department if, in fact, there are any. They look good on each other. Eddie's had a great career. He's hit all the top scenes — Toronto, L.A., Boston, New York — and she's supported him. And this pension issue rounded out Norma's portfolio in terms of confidence, because she has talent and she's accomplished a lot. Yes, Norma was a very hard worker and a loyal friend through it all."

After Norma returns to the room, I mention how difficult communication among a group of scattered players living in all four corners of North America, and some in Europe, must have been. Given the lack of finances, the limited facilities, equipment, and manpower, I ask McCreary if it's fair to say this was a Mickey Mouse, Band-Aid, helter-skelter operation.

He laughs and nods. "Nah, it was a guerrilla operation. It had to be that way."

"You're right. Communications *were* a big problem," Norma adds, after almost losing her tea thanks to McCreary's flip reply. "Heck, every time we did a mailing it cost us $500. But any player who had an interest in this case who says he didn't know what was going on is taking the easy way out."

"We couldn't talk to any major sponsor," Keith explains, leaning forward to make the point. "They were either doing business with the NHL or the Leafs, and many of the players were still working in hockey. We even had our pals telling us to shut it down, that the NHL had been good to all of us. A lot of the scouts didn't want to be seen talking to us. Our first letter didn't even ask for money. It just asked them to sign up. Geez, it became a cloak-and-dagger operation. I got a lot of calls, and I'm sure the others did, too. Guys would say they wanted to be with us, but they had to keep a low profile. Some of the alumni took forever to deliver the money after promising and promising it was in the mail."

Norma points at me and shakes her finger. "And don't forget, any of the big cheques we received, like the alumni ones, were sent in *after* we won the first round."

The fact was that very little in the way of support money came in from anywhere other than what they developed on their own until the lower court had found in the signators' favour on October 21, 1992. At this point in our talk I figure it's a good time to explore the role of the alumni organizations in the battle.

"I've heard some of the alumni organizations that contributed toward the end of the legal battle wanted to remain anonymous for their own reasons," I say. "I suppose it had something to do with a hat-in-hand relationship with their team owners. But apparently the strongest and most supportive alumni group was the one in Montreal. Is that true?"

"Right," Keith says, jumping in, "and this was after Billy Harris, Eddie, and I had gone to Montreal to get a commitment from their alumni. Rejean Houle was the president of the Montreal oldtimers, and we were there for the All-Star game, spreading the word. A good representation of years and players were there — Maurice and Henri Richard, Elmer Lach, Murray Wilson, Pete and Frank Mahovlich. After I made our pitch, Houle said it would be a good thing to help us, so a figure of $5,000 came from the floor. Then Jean Beliveau got up and said the Canadiens' alumni had always been a class organization and he felt the figure should be $25,000. Then he said, 'If anyone has a problem with that, let's hear it now. All in favour . . . carried.'"

McCreary, however, suggests things weren't as rosy and easy as it might have seemed after the Montreal windfall. "When we came back to Toronto with that cheque in our pocket, we thought it would be a breeze to get the same out of the Maple Leaf alumni. Man, though, it was tough, even with Billy Harris, a Toronto oldtimer, on our team. Some days it was two steps forward, three steps back.

"The guy who'll say very little about his role is Eddie. He brought a lot of people to the party, going through the whole process, negotiating deals for the tournaments, bringing corporate people in with us. He was there on a 12-month basis every year. Eddie was the turning point in the Montreal alumni meeting because nobody has the presence he has. No one else can talk about a subject in that straight, direct, no-holds-barred way he has. And when he looks you in the eye with that logic of his, you listen. He spread the gospel to the Montreal group and kept them on side."

I had to think about that for a moment. It's a tough picture for me to conjure up: Eddie Shack in a conciliatory moment with the regal Jean Beliveau, the beady-eyed Rocket, and the coco-bonked Henri.

"The result was that the Montreal alumni were as well informed as the people here in Toronto," McCreary continues. "No one can underestimate the value of having the Canadien oldtimers on our side. If you don't place value on that statement, consider the different attitude that would have prevailed had they not been in the fold. Eddie kept taking the message there. You won't get Ed to go to the front of the line to take any credit, but from where I sit he deserves a lot of praise."

Later, as Norma and I make our way to McCreary's front office door, she has a final thought on the pension saga, a note of vindication, nostalgia, and sadness all in one. "I remember when I told my father what we were getting into. He was really worried and told us not to do it, that we were making a big mistake. He felt that you just didn't take on people like the NHL. My father passed away after the Supreme Court ruling, two days after we'd won the case."

Aside from the mounting costs of the lawsuit and the never-ending shortage of money and support in those early years, nothing was more hurtful to the cause than the internal bickering between Carl Brewer and the others directly involved, a fact already stressed by McCreary and Norma Shack. The ripple effect had started early, as far back as the initial meetings, and continued to the very end and beyond, as others involved in the dispute can testify.

Andy Bathgate, who was thoughtful about his entry as a signator, remembered the difficulties in lining up support. "Hell, in one day I called five Original Six players and asked them to come in and have their pictures taken for the card series. I said we'd give them $1,000 each, which was more than fair. I was literally told to fuck off by all five. Three of them were inside the NHL at the time. One said what we were doing was completely wrong, that hockey had been so good to us and we should be grateful. When I asked if he thought he was getting a fair return on his money, he said, 'I've been looked after very nicely, thank you.' Sure, because he still had a job in hockey. See, we were always told we had the best pension in all of pro sport, but what we actually discovered was far from the truth, and the most disappointing part was we were all going through this rejection shit, except Carl.

"I'll tell you what was a real eye-opener. We met with football, basketball, and baseball players in California, and these people knew what they were talking about. They told us to make sure we worked with the press, said we should be honest, that we shouldn't criticize the game, that it was important to have one spokesman, and that our people shouldn't come from different angles and badmouth hockey. Basically that's what we were afraid of with Carl Brewer. If I was gonna pay Mark Zigler big money, I wanted him to make the statements.

"We never had a beef against the NHL but rather with the pension people, whoever ran the pension money, because it wasn't properly administered back then. Today's administrators had nothing to do with it, and we didn't want bad statements being made that would take away from the game. That's exactly what we were concerned about with Brewer. Meanwhile we were out there wearing out our welcome, doing autograph shows, golf tournaments, collecting memorabilia for auctions, just to survive. We had Norma and Keith damn near full-time for free. Eddie was running around browbeating people for golf prize items, the wives and Keith's daughters were doing mailings, stuffing envelopes, all that sort of necessary work. And Carl wanted to run the show, with an office, a secretary, and all this other guff. We were talking maybe $100,000 a year. Like I said, his telling me he was looking for a goddamn job absolutely floored me."

Another of the outside observers was Bobby Hull, and he relates a story about an early meeting: "I can't remember where it was, maybe the Old Mill, but Brewer was there, Shack, Baun, Stanley, Eagleson's boys, Larry Regan, who was representing our Alumni Association, the NHL people. What struck me, though, was that we never seemed to be on the same page. We weren't cohesive, we had more of a shotgun approach, and it played into the NHL's hands. I remember saying after the meeting that the only thing these people were going to understand was a lawsuit. We'd be doing something the NHL would never expect from a bunch of hockey players, and I asked, 'So who's willing to put their names and their heads on the block?'

"Well, there was Carl, Gordie, Leo, Orr, big Sam [Allan Stanley], Andy Bathgate, who's gotta be the salt of the earth, and Norma and Eddie. Bob Pulford [the Chicago Blackhawks' general manager] was against it, along with others in the same position because they had jobs on the line. But with the exception of Pulford I never ran into anyone who was negative, but I wasn't in the Toronto area where most of the guys were located. I never had anyone say anything to me other than 'Go get 'em.'

"This group accomplished what the NHL had tried to keep us from doing all our careers. They didn't want us to be unified. They didn't want us to know anyone else's business, or even our own. Seven of us from different teams and different eras saw that we had a valid position, and nobody was going to sway us.

"Without banding together we couldn't have done it. The money required was raised through golf tournaments and things like that, but I don't think any of us realized how much money it was going to take to get it done — up there in the neighbourhood of a million.

"But I was confident once we got started with the fundraisers, and no, I never worried about putting my hand in my pocket. Norma Shack was a tower of strength, and it's not likely we would have succeeded without her. I'm very impressed with Norma, her tenacity, and the work she did. She was tireless, her and Keith McCreary. Without his contributions, his office, his dedication to the cause, our group might have lost the case.

"I'm also impressed with Eddie as a human being, as a guy who cares, one who'll give you the shirt off his back." Hull lets out a gravelly laugh. "Now I'm not saying he'll give you the money out of his pocket . . ."

All that remains are the facts. In March 1991 the seven signators, represented by Mark Zigler, filed their application with the lower court. On July 28, 1994, the Supreme Court dismissed the NHL's submission to appeal. In March 1997, six years after the first court appearance, the NHL Pension Society began to distribute the money awarded by the courts to the players.

CHAPTER SIXTEEN

Life Today

FOR THE PURPOSE OF OBSERVATION I OFTEN ASKED EDDIE SHACK TO meet me at Maple Leaf Gardens, take in a practice, hobnob with the media people and the core of characters surrounding the morning work-outs, especially on game days when the visiting team swells the numbers. Eddie resolutely declined, not with an outright no, but with the usual dip-ping and diving I've come to recognize over a lot of years. In addition, several times Eddie himself suggested we attend a game together and visit the alumni box, where I would theoretically be able to trade lines with other members of the hockey fraternity. It never happened.

But persistence usually boxes Eddie in, so I make much of the point that we have to spend more time together and press him for yet another meeting at the Gardens. He dodges the issue, changes the subject, some-times blatantly ignores the question, and goes into his eye-darting rou-tine, seeking a way out like a recently singed survivor of a house fire checking for all available exits. But by December and the arrival of our designated day at the Gardens, Eddie has a parallel reason to meet me: he has to buy a half-dozen Maple Leaf jerseys in the souvenir store.

And there he is, as advertised, waiting in the parking lot. We walk together across Church Street to Carlton. Eddie's western boots, black leather pants and vest, string tie with a turquoise clasp, and Hockey Legends team jacket are topped off by a cowboy hat that would have made Hoot Gibson green with envy. The lid is crisscrossed with a multi-tude of silver signatures. "Look at this, Bobby Hull, Bobby Orr," he tells an interested scalper who greets him outside the shop doors. "And look here, Walt McKechnie, Jim Dorey," he adds, as if the latter are somehow in the same league, prestige-wise, as the former.

Inside he stands at the cash register, big hands palm down on the counter, decked out in two large rings, the one-carat diamond Stanley

Cup ring suitably matched by the other bit of finger jewellery. Customers in the store stop, gawk, and whisper, while the clerk tries hard to be nonchalant and overly businesslike, only succeeding in being abrupt to the point of rudeness.

An American couple, honeymooning Ohioans judging by their his-and-her Cleveland Indian baseball caps, hold hands and stare at this large man in the strange outfit. Sensing they are in the presence of a celebrity, they ask his identity of an equally enthralled older man wearing a Leaf jacket over a porky frame, the dome fastener at the middle straining to keep him from spilling over into another aisle. From the side of his mouth the man whispers, "That's Eddie Shack."

"Who's Eddie Shick?" the young man whispers, desperately wanting to know.

"SHACK," the portly one corrects loudly.

Hearing his name, Eddie turns, smiles, nods, and quietly says, "How's she goin'?" Then he glances back at the clerk. Mr. Big appears vindicated, while the honeymooners are the ones who now appear enthralled. It's a study in cause and effect, this bigger-than-life man who can command curiosity and attention regardless if his name is Shick or Shack.

Upon getting to rinkside and seeing the full-gear, one-hour game-day practice, Eddie is incredulous. "What's *this* bullshit? This is crap. Have a little meeting, put on some sweat pants, pair of gloves, just a little skate. Hell, I used to come out, waddle to the net, put my arm on the crossbar for a while, lean on my stick a couple of times, you know, bend it like I knew what I was doin', and head back to the dressing room. You don't need this stuff. You know who started this routine? Rudy Pilous in Chicago." The big grin begins to spread. "What the hell was he thinkin', eh? That Hull and Stash Mikita we're gonna forget how to skate overnight? This," he repeats, waving at the young Leafs behind him whirling through line rushes and drills, "is bullshit."

As often happens when former players visit the scene of their crimes, they gather together and take the opportunity to relive their adventures. Today is no different as Denis Dupere, who played with Eddie during his last two seasons in Toronto, is joined by another old teammate, Jim McKenny, in the southeast corner. Dupere good-naturedly absorbs the jabs about carrying a few pounds over his belt buckle but bridles at the suggestion his salt-and-pepper hair is a sign of aging. "It's not grey," he corrects McKenny. "It's sun-bleached."

When Denis tries to tell a story, claiming he occasionally had a few beers after a game, Shack turns away in mock disgust, waves him off, and groans. McKenny sets the record straight. "Dupey, you used to take down a six-pack on the goddamn bus to the airport."

Ignoring the bare-faced truth, Dupere continues. "One time right here," he says, managing to point while his hands are still in his pockets, "we came in on a two-on-one, and Shackie busted for the net, yelling, 'Give it to me. Give it to me, big boy.' But I held it and held it. I even winked at Shackie before I took the shot myself." They both break into guffaws. "And scored."

By now they're cackling. Dupere, catching his breath, continues. "Eddie made the big turn, shook his head, and said, 'Aw, shit.' You could hear him in the fuckin' greys." Shackie and Dupere break into full-fledged howling, causing the steely-eyed, drop-dead-serious Leafs sweating on the other side of the glass to turn and look for the source of the commotion. Tie Domi fixes our group with his practised, award-winning, beetle-brow glare.

Shack flings himself against the glass as if he's been boarded. "Tidy-Didy," he whines, and starts laughing. "Tie Die-Oh-Meeee," he howls, causing the young Leafs to snuffle into their gloves and the butt ends of their sticks.

Domi grins, too, but the look says, "Take it easy, Eddie. I'm working out here."

Dupere, caught up in the warmth of reminiscing, lurches on. "We were in Oakland. I wasn't playin', just sittin' in the press box. And the Seals had one of their bigger crowds . . . about 2,500. So they let Eddie play. He hadn't dressed in two weeks, so you knew when he got out there, he wasn't comin' off. Well, on his first shift he picked up the puck in our end and took off like a rocket, the whole way. He got a shot on goal and headed back. Then the same thing all over again. He got a pass and tore down the ice. It happened about four times. Every time he tried to get to the bench another great pass would come and he'd have a clear path to the goal.

"Upstairs I was poundin' the table, laughin' so goddamn hard, hackin' and coughin'. I couldn't even talk, watchin' him tryin' to get off the ice. All I could do was point. It musta been a four-minute shift. Finally he got one last pass as he was makin' his way to the bench. It musta hit him in the fuckin' skates, and he just waved it off, as if to say, 'The hell with it.' He nearly skated over his tongue. I never laughed so goddamn hard in my life. Oh, Shackie," Dupere wheezes, shaking his head as he joins Shack and McKenny to wipe away tears, "I thought I was gonna piss my pants."

Later, across the street at Gardoonies restaurant, Shack and I sit at a window table facing the Gardens' blue-and-white marquee, which Eddie points to for some unknown reason. As we look at the Gardens, I ask, "Was the competition as intense between the Canadiens and Leafs as the CBC-TV show *Forever Rivals* claimed?"

"Naw, the people used to get more riled up than the players. The fans used to go completely fuckin' bonkers. But I'll tell yuh somethin'. You can't play this game with no people in the crowds," he states emphatically, not realizing he's just created another Shackism. "When you got no one in the crowds, that's when nobody wants to boogie. You need that stuff, you know, when they talk about conditioning. They say it's — whadda you call that shit? Drem-alim?"

"Adrenalin?" I translate.

Shack bobs his head in agreement. "Say the guy has a cold, an itchy ass, maybe a headache, comes to the rink and gets an extra shot of drem-alim from the people. That's what it's all about." We watch two workmen, one on a ladder, the other holding the base, replacing coloured bulbs on a tree perched on the facade.

He points again. "Ballard once called me up and said he needed a dozen Christmas trees — on the clock over centre ice, in the Hot Stove Lounge, on the marquee in front, that kind of shit. He promised me all kinds of advertising on the message board, or the clock, one 'a them, but I know it never happened. I'd bug his ass all the time, but like every-thing else, he never paid that bill, either. That's exactly the kind of stuff that got him in the joint in the first place. Dumb, eh?"

Just then Susie, a waitress with a Maple Leaf logo painted on her cheek, arrives. "Is it permanent?" Shackie asks.

"Yep," she says. "I put it on for every home game."

Eddie is excited because he can go one better. "I know guys who have those on their bums."

Next comes the manager, Allan, to pay his respects. He's tall but slim by any standards, and Eddie asks, "Now pay attention you two. This here's my Arthur, and I'm tryin' to impress him. Allan, would you care to twist wrists for a hundred?" Allan goes 150 pounds at best, including the big key ring. Shack is 235 without the hat.

"You gotta be kidding. Susie and I together don't weigh as much as you," Allan replies, and walks away, the welcoming ceremonies over.

Sometime later the cross-street view of the Gardens leads to a another conversation about life with Ballard. "When I came back to Toronto, I had the dune buggy, right? What the hell? It was mine. Jack Kent Cooke had it painted gold and purple when I was in L.A., but it was my car, so I still had it and I tried to make the same deal with Ballard. Paint it blue and white and I'd zip around town, promote the Leafs, eh? Pittsburgh Paint said they could do the job perfect, and it was . . . beau-tiful. Maple Leaf stripes, the works. When the bill came to Ballard, the cheap bastard backed out. He refused to pay it and said I should put up the money." He makes a face. "Don't forget. It was good for that old bugger, too. I drove the goddamn thing everywhere. I used to take Foo-Foo for rides, sold beer out of it on my golf course. Even took kids for rides when I had the hockey school in Rexdale.

"That goddamn Ballard, eh?" Eddie says, his pale green eyes squint-ing through the noon sunshine at the historic building across the street-car tracks. "I don't give a shit. He still owes me $500 for painting my dune buggy." Then he grins. "Ah, I went overboard, too, yuh know, but he was a goddamn chiseller." Surprisingly I hear an admiring chuckle escape his lips. "Took out all the good seats and replaced them with them smaller ones. Sold all the private boxes himself. Didn't trust any-one else to do it right. Besides, he liked to push big shots around. He'd always say, 'You never know when someone's gonna do it to yuh.'

"When I came back to Toronto from Pittsburgh, Ballard was talkin' to me in the hall during trainin' camp just when Salming came out of the dressin' room. Ballard called him over and said, 'Borje, I want you to take a look at this Stanley Cup ring. You ever think you're gonna win one of these fuckers?"

Eddie har-har-hars just as a couple of teenagers walking by slip on an ice patch. Furious windmilling plus a few double toe loops save them from falling. Flustered, they look around and discover a big guy in a big hat laughing. Now crimson, they shout obscenities, which just makes Eddie pound the table and double over with laughter, causing Tattooed Susie to come running, thinking Eddie needs another draft beer.

"One time I told Ballard if he ever fell off his money, he'd get a charley horse." Eddie shakes his head, ignoring, or completely forget-ting, the kids, who continue to yap and point accusingly on the other side of the window. "I went up to see him at his cottage after buyin' a car in Midland. He showed me the bridge he put into the property, steel fence, birdhouses, birdbaths, lions at the gate, a waterin' system for the lawns and flower beds, all that bullshit, and crowed about it, too, as if nothin' had happened. I told him that's how he got charged in the first place. 'Aw, fuck 'em' was all he could come up with. And when I was leavin', he asked about the car and I told him it was for my daughter. He said, 'Don't bullshit me. That car is for some broad.' See, he thought like that all the time with everybody.

"You know somethin'?" he asks, now unsmiling but continuing to stare out the window at the Gardens. "I can't remember ever having tough times. For me 'tough' was having to go from New York to Springfield, no, make that Springfield to New York. Phil Watson was always waitin' in New York. Other than that I always had it good."

A week later we're in the van with Norm Ullman, who is quiet and unobtrusive as always. We're heading along the 401 eastbound on our way to a pair of oldtimer games in Cornwall and Ottawa. The cellular phone rings, and the two of us are treated to one of the frequent one-sided conversations that are part and parcel of life on the road with Shackie. This one's from Vancouver. "Whatsa matter with you? You got something there you're harpooning? Naw, I'm deliverin' two tough old turkeys to a hotel. Yeah, hardworkin' Normie Ullman and an unemployed guy who's writing a book about me. Yeah, he's an Arthur. That's right. No free books. Okay, I'll try to get somethin' for New York. Wait a minute. That's Gretzky, yuh know. It's a tough ticket."

Stopping for lunch at a 401 service centre near Kingston, Shack draws elbow-nudging amusement from the knowledgeable hockey patrons, as well as the usual blank and suspicious stares from the uninformed.

"Jeez, and I used to be a waitress," he chides himself loudly, bringing three glasses of water to our table and spilling most of it on the floor. "Holy sheepshit, no wonder I never made any tips." Everybody gets a kick out of that one, including two elderly couples sitting near the window. "G'day, g'day," Eddie says, almost bowing in respect for their age. "Hard to get good help these days," he adds, acknowledging their gracious, snickering acceptance of a known fact.

A second after finishing his soup, Eddie goes back to the counter and asks, straight-faced, for more. "He didn't fill it up, you know," he insists, pointing to the cook, who only grins and heaps vegetables into a new bowl while the cashier and two real waitresses hide their giggles behind hands.

That night we find ourselves in the Cornwall arena, unusual in its interlaced yellow ceiling girders and wide concrete walkways between the boards and the elevated seats. For Eddie it's a quick change. The black hat and jeans remain, but he adds silver-spurred skates and a striped shirt with a "Clear the Track" nameplate and the familiar 23 to his costume.

Red Storey, he of the Hall of Fame and a master of the game in this show business environment, is dressed in complete official garb. He handles the mike and does a skillful and professional play-by-play from ice level, while Eddie, wooden train whistle in hand, simply floats around like a big seagull, unnecessary and redundant, leading a few cheers, mostly moving to the opposite end of the ice from the play like a counterbalance, without infringing on Storey's act.

Between periods Gil Perreault, in fine form, does the macarena to music that blares out of speakers in the dressing room. The Big M, Frank Mahovlich, was held scoreless in the first period, and Eddie says, "Jeezuz, Frank, take a fuckin' double benny. Take Geritol, somethin', anythin'. Public skatin' is on Wednesday. All these goddamn people came to see ya. Shit, even I could do this routine." Mahovlich puts on his best Mona Lisa smile, sighs, and turns to cross his shin-padded legs and sit on the other side of his pants, facing away from Eddie.

Shack gets going on the French spoken in the dressing room. "No more of that ding-dong in here!" he roars at Gaston Gingras, Perreault, Pierre Plante, and Mario Marois, whose young son is with him and seems to take offence. "Maybe *you* should learn some ding-dong," Marois challenges.

But Shack is oblivious and turns his attention to Storey as the players begin to tie their skates. "Red, loosen up out there. Get away from hangin' on the glass and stop worryin' about fallin' down. Just relax. I'll pick you up. Don't be out there slippin' and slidin' like a calf in yer own shit."

The traditional postgame get-together for both teams is put on at the downstairs pub in our hotel. Only one woman sits on a stool at the bar, which is completely lined with men in baseball hats and team jackets, winners each and every one.

Eddie sits at the other end of the bar, holding court. More than the occasional swear word litters the conversation he delivers in a voice that clings to you like lint all the way to the men's washroom. When he spots a gentleman's chestful of souvenir team pins, he asks, "What the hell are those? Medals for all the broads you've harpooned." Raucous laughter is joined by happy grins as the woman looks at her boyfriend with a knowing smirk.

"Lookin' good, Shackie," a man in a painfully tight baseball cap yells from the other end of the bar.

"Built like a moose, hung like a mouse," Eddie roars back.

The woman grimaces, obviously not impressed while her boyfriend laughs uproariously, going along with the crowd.

"Havin' a good time in Cornwall?" the man at the other end bellows, four shooters and six drafts worth of sincerity and concern crossing his face for this famous visitor.

"Not yet," Shack replies for all to hear. The woman excuses herself and marches to the powder room. The man at the far end shouts an incoherent sentence, and even Eddie seems to tire of the ruckus.

"This ain't a goddamn game-day skate. You don't have to work on your yappin', pal. You're already good at it. Put a chastity belt on your mouth, okay?" The woman has missed the best-received putdown of the night.

For my own information I now decide to ask Eddie about this outlandish behaviour pattern in what is arguably an outlandish setting: a smoky basement bar with a noise level equivalent to a steel mill, filled with a volatile mixture of celebrities, local hockey players, and any number of area tough guys and their girls. A real hockey night in Canada.

"Eddie, are you aware, or do you care about the fact that a woman is sitting here right in the middle of this campaign debate?"

"Nah, I'm just having fun, and so is she. Tomorrow she'll be telling everybody how crazy I am, and how much fun *she* had. She's only makin' out she's embarrassed to suit herself, to show these clowns she's not used to this kind of behaviour, and that's bullshit. Look at the horny asshole she's with!"

Disinterested, Eddie gets off his seat again and wedges into the doorway of the side room where the main body of the team sits with their hosts. There is a visible split of expressions, from assorted grins down to resentment, as Eddie barks some obscenities. Cherubic Gil Perreault comes right back with a remark in French that ignites howls of laughter, none harder than Shack's. "Oh-oh," he snorts, "they're givin' me the ding-dong. I'm goin' back in this room with these other shitheads. You Pepsi's are too tough," he tosses over his shoulder.

We leave Baseball Hat and the woman to their own devices and retire to our room well before the bar closes. For the next few hours, over some excellent red wine Eddie has in his bag, The Entertainer opens up.

"Do you think you had respect as a player?" I ask. "Or did that matter to you?"

"Respect? How can you have respect when you're associated with people like Ballard or Eagleson? Hey, I can bullshit them as much as they bullshit me. My problem has always been the same. I can't read and write, and some people don't have any respect for me on account of that. Take cars. I could buy the cars and sell them, no problem, but I couldn't do the paperwork. I was totally fuckin' euchred. I got screwed in the travel business. I had trouble in the restaurant business. You know, if some people had had faith in me, like Bob and Amy Watson, for instance, shit, we could have bought Huntington Golf Course. Certain people might have made a lot of money with me, but they couldn't deal with a guy who can't read or write. They couldn't live with it."

Even though Eddie doesn't really answer my question, I'm still surprised at his sudden willingness to talk, to examine his thoughts, to put them out on the table. It's the kind of discussion where he isn't looking for any assistance, and I try to figure out why he's gracing me with this welcome burst of cooperation. Still, this isn't the time to question his motives, and while many of the topics are the same old tunes, they're obviously the major concerns in his mind right now. So, although there isn't an order or a structure to our talk, which I chalk up to the wine, I let him ramble, deciding to interrupt or prompt only when the silence drags on too long.

"Take Vomit Valley [Vaughan Valley Golf Club]," he says, obviously wanting to continue the subject of golf. "See, back then I didn't know fuck all about golf courses, but I learned, and I knew about people and selling. I changed the nines around, and everyone got into a dither, yappin' about how I was gonna screw up the course. Yeah, I was gonna change the layout, but did they think I was gonna change it for the worse? We had a short par 5, then a par 3, another par 3, then a short par 4. This wasn't Augusta, eh? The goddamn golfers were always backing up every day and twice as much on weekends, so I brought in the bull-dozer and put the blade down. Next was the 12th hole. I got them to shave it down, makin' the course better. Then I filled in a few sand traps, 'cause some of them poor hackers were moving more earth per round than the goddamn miners in Sudbury.

"At first the course could handle foursomes, but after, I could put out fives, ride around with a couple of cases of ice-cold beer, and keep 'em moving. The difference is $25 extra a round, plus carts, plus beer. I'm the manager, and I liked it. Yeah, I fired a few people, but the course was pro-ducing more rounds, more people, more sales on everything. What, am I stupid? You sell four hot dogs, or you sell five. You sell four beers, or five, all the way down the line, practice range, new balls, everything."

Scribbling furiously, I only catch up when he takes a sip of wine. He sits on the the edge of his bed in shorts and cowboy boots, occasionally scratching his arm or preening his eyebrows. In the break I write, "Never have a camera when you need one."

Then he starts again, this time frowning as he puts his wineglass on the night table. "So here's the lawyers now, I'm givin' them orders. Me, because I'm the best promoter. Shit, I put in music, waitresses, gave a T-shirt away now and then, and all the while I was a nervous wreck from my partners drivin' me fuckin' bonkers. They wanted to take it further, get another bulldozer, and I'm tellin' them, 'Whoa, put the brakes on. I'm the one who knows how far you can stretch this thing.' You know, if you treat people half decent, you'll get more out of them. See, they got greedy. All I know is I did more work than anybody else. Piss break," he announces abruptly.

"Some people say you've got a bad habit of sticking your nose into the business too much, you know, looking over your manager's shoul-der," I observe.

Eddie's face darkens. "I look at it this way. I've been out there in the garbage findin' knives and forks, cutlery, the shit that costs money. Those assholes just threw it out. They were too goddamn lazy to sepa-rate the slop from the silverware 'cause it cut into their smokin' and bullshittin' time. You're fuckin' right. I stick my beak in there. It's the way I was brought up. Yeah, I've fired a few people, the ones that challenged me. They think they've got you by the balls, eh? But they're costing me money. Don't forget. I'm the one with the goddamn jobs. They're working for me. I'm good enough to hire them, and if they decide they don't wanna work, then they can kiss my ass goodbye."

"You shouldn't tap-dance around the question," I say, straight-faced.

Eddie only smiles wanly and turns his attention to the art of being a coach. "Peter Pocklington called me, and I went out to Edmonton, the Oilers, and sat down with him and Glen Sather in his office. I told him I didn't read or write, and I guess Peter Puck said, 'What do I need with a guy who can't read?'"

"You mean he didn't know or didn't believe you were illiterate?"

"Yeah," Eddie snorts, "but that's happened before. I've met a lot rich dopes who don't wanna believe it. Hockey is still fucked up, still got its head up its ass. I used to tell Punch he shouldn't be running the practices. Up and down, up and down, the same borin' shit forever, and they're still doin' it. Who says a coach has to be the one who gets the boys in shape? You can't coach and run the practices. It's two different things. Hockey has to come up with some common sense, because winnin' and losin' aren't that far apart, you know. There isn't enough money to play hockey this way for 84 games. It's fuckin' borin'. It'll drive ya cuckoo.

"Take a look at a horse trainer. He knows he's got to get the horse in shape, then he puts another guy on top to ride the goddamn horse and steer it. Right? Same thing in hockey. You have to ask yourself why guys are burnt out. Look at Dougie Gilmour, the poor little bugger. He's had it by the third period. Yeah, he's tryin', but he hasn't got anything left for Christ's sake. The coach is the guy who has to realize it, but that's how stupid hockey's been lately."

He places his wineglass on the night table again and counts off points on his fingers. "You only run two lines, the best two. Let the bastards go, turn 'em loose and let 'em buck. As for goalies, if they're fair with you, play 'em. But if they start playin' games with you, park their asses. Tell me, why does a goalie gotta stay in the game no matter what the fuck happens? How come you can't take these guys out without hurtin' their feelings? You got two goalies, right? One's usually better, but who knows? So you get a lead, 7-2 goin' into the third. What the hell's the big guy gonna gain hangin' on to a win? So you take him out, put in the kid, and give the guy some experience.

"What's wrong with that? You're the coach. You can do what you want. But some of these goalies have t'play every minute of every game, or they're gonna pout and sulk. Bullshit. You know, you can practise all you want, but it doesn't count at game time. So you get the two guys workin' together, gettin' hot together, winnin' and playin' better together, keep them up for the games. How else are yuh gonna get experience? The worst goddamn thing in the world is sittin'.

"Take a forward who's got two goals. Double-shift the guy, put him on the goddamn power play, let him get a hat trick. Try somethin' different when the score is 7-2. Put a forward on defence, stick one of them defencemen at centre, let 'em learn how the other half lives. It'll goddamn sure as hell help them play better.

"You got a big guy who likes to drink a bit, you work him, make him puke a little. A little guy who stays in his room, gets his rest, and stays in good condition, you don't work his balls off. Lookit Gil Perreault, a big guy, he needs to work regularly. A good workout doesn't hurt him. But in a game you just turn him loose, work his ass off, double shifts, power plays, and he's only gonna get better. Forget about comin' back. He'll put the show on for you. Whoever's playin' with him, just get their fat ass into position and tap in the rebounds. There's nothin' difficult about playin' with Gil."

The room is completely quiet. Only the mute TV even suggests noise. Just as I'm about to prompt him, Eddie starts again. "When I was 19, with Eddie Bush and the Biltmores, that's when I got serious about playin' hockey. If I'd been that serious in the NHL, I woulda been perfect, eh? No, I woulda been fuckin' dynamite. But what happened? I got Watson and guys like that to work with in the NHL. If there was somebody, a goddamn coach behind me, it would have been much better. See, you're a kid, you're from up north, and all those bastards can say is you're lucky to get out of Sudbury. They knew they were runnin' your life, and that's exactly what they did. I didn't want anybody to run me.

"You know, a player like me is pretty goddamn easy to figure out. Tell me what colour we're wearin', show me how to put the equipment on, tie my skates, give me a stick, point out where the goal is, let me know when they're gonna change directions every period, then stand back and turn me loose. But coaches, eh? Any dope coulda told me I can skate good. If a guy can skate, then put him on the ice, ya fuckin' stupe. Let him burn off some of that energy instead of runnin' the ass off him in practice, makin' him jump through hoops, doin' things to aggravate him. Coaches. They try to come off as smart, but they're the dumbest bastards goin', bar none. But I liked Imlach. I always had respect for him. He didn't stop me from actin' up. I liked Eddie Shore, too," he adds, staring moodily at the television, unseeing, still caught up in his thoughts. "I hated Phil Watson. Didn't like Hal Laycoe, either."

He pauses to stare some more, and I think how he must have felt like a rodeo rider, always hanging in there for eight seconds, never winning a dime.

"Do you know what my most embarrassing moment was?" he suddenly blurts out. "I stopped at a little motel. I was drivin' by myself, absolutely baffed out. I'm so goddamn tired, and I can't fill out the registration card right. I tell the guy the information and he gets all pissed off. He was dumber than me, working this piss-ant fuckin' job at two in the morning. He wouldn't do it for me, thought it was some kinda trick. And he told me I can't stay there. I could say all the right stuff — telephone number, address, the works — but he didn't give a shit. That's what I learned. If you teach somebody the right way, even if they're not too smart, they'll learn," he says, defensive, then laughs nervously.

"Yeah, I'm honest all right. I never bullshitted anybody about not being able to read or write. I never hid the fact. Look, when I'm on the ice, even tonight, people know I'm very honest. They might get that 'he's not very sensible' look on their faces, but at least they know I'm honest. I'm a salesman, one who's up front and honest. There's too many crooks out there."

"Did you *really* want to learn to read and write?" I ask, not for the first time. "And don't shrug this question off again."

"I didn't shrug it off before. It's a dumb question."

"That's my job. As an 'Arthur,' I have to ask dumb questions. The dumber the better."

Eddie snuffles a soft laugh, then takes a sip of wine.

"Well?" I persist.

"Are you shittin' me? Of course I did. I tried in Guelph, New York, Toronto . . . several times. Private tutors, homework, the whole thing. Like I said, all my life I wanted to run a car dealership, but without an education the only thing left for me was stuff like the golf course, Christmas tress, straight selling, nothing that involved paperwork."

The phone rings. It's Norm Ullman. He wants to know about breakfast arrangements, wake-up calls, estimated time of departure. Hanging up, Eddie says, referring to Ullman, "Another borin' guy. Jeez, I asked him one day about livin' in that great big condo. 'Normie,' I said, 'can you wash your car?' He said no. I said, 'Well, what the fuck do you do all day?' But what a hockey player, eh? Look at him even now with the oldtimers. He works, and works, and works. He wants to win, and he wants to play, all the goddamn time. Single games, doubleheaders, day after day on the road, and he never complains. Just like when he was a kid."

"Several people have told me they don't think you're dyslexic," I say out of the blue, figuring two can play Eddie's game of disconnected dialogue.

Obviously surprised, he replies, "Well, what am I then? You know, I was always up front. I made a point to put it forward, about not being able to read. A lot of people can't read, but they don't say anything. In fact, I was too up front with it."

I nod and smile. Seated in our "palatial" hotel suite, I notice Eddie has his elbows on his knees, a familiar pose for a hockey player, as he stares down at the floor between his boots. The wineglass is a boxcar-style coupling for his fingers. "Was it hard to bring yourself out in the open like that with all the teams you played on?" I ask quietly.

He remains immobile.

"Many players told me they'd heard," I prompt, "but nobody ever went right up and asked you. Was that your way to handle the situation? Did you want to get it out in the open?"

"Yeah, I guess I did, right? But I think it would have helped if I'd shut my big mouth so that nobody knew."

The quiet interludes are getting more frequent. Fatigue is painted on his face and the slope of his shoulders. His moustache seems to droop like a Fu Manchu, and he rubs his eyes as I close my notepad. "What time do you want to roll out?" I ask, standing, but Eddie isn't listening.

"You know," he says, "when I first came to the NHL, I was scared to be on radio and TV because you could be manipulated. I was petrified. That's a word, isn't it?"

I nod, sit down, and open the notepad again.

"And later, when I got better at it, I knew I had to be a person. Ross, do you understand what I mean?"

This is the first time he's used my real name in weeks, and I realize his next statement is going to be important.

"I couldn't be a Wayne Gretzky or Bobby Hull," he almost whispers, beginning to stammer. Then he stops and composes himself. "Let's face it. If you can't read or write, you can't cope with some of the questions, or the words, they're gonna use to trap you. But I wanted to be . . . a person."

The next morning, sitting alone in the coffee shop, I go over my notes, sorting, trying vainly to put them into order, and the thought strikes me that as a subject of observation Ed Shack is a lot like an actor who knows his role but doesn't know the play. He has *his* part down pat, but he doesn't recall anyone else's lines. He'll follow the cues, but only if they dovetail with his own sense of what's good or bad. Seemingly he's wrapped up in his character, without understanding, or in the worst sense, caring about the other players in the production.

It's a matter of taking care of himself out of necessity. We'll never know how often he's been faced with decisions, important choices, on his own. For example, I think about him catching the wrong train on his way to the Guelph Biltmores' camp. It would have been just as easy to abandon the journey and return to Sudbury. There was the time he left the New York Rangers. Or when he was sent down to Rochester and stood on the brink of bucking Imlach and the system in an age when those actions were unthinkable. Ed trusts himself; he has to. Some might say he's selfish. If you know Eddie, though, you'll agree he's one of the most unselfish people you'll ever meet.

The next day we arrive in Ottawa, and while driving down a main street, Eddie rolls down the window at a stoplight to blare at a man wearing a Toronto Maple Leaf jacket in the next lane. "You like them turkeys?" he bellows. "Buncha goddamn stiffs." Eddie laughs while the man points happily in recognition and tries to find the button to roll his window down. It's too late, though, and the light turns green. But another happy fan has a story for dinner conversation.

Eventually we pull into what is obviously an empty stall at the market in the downtown core, a collection of indoor and outdoor shops festooned with Christmas decorations, lights, and sparkling trees. "This isn't a parking spot," Ullman says quietly. Those are the first words he's uttered in 50 miles.

"Why not?" Shack asks, landing his cowboy boots on the pavement. A woman, all smiles, dressed for the chill in a heavy coat and a 12-foot scarf, stands in a display of fresh tree bough garlands and door wreaths and sings out, " 'Allo, Shack."

"How's it goin'?" Eddie asks. "Movin' them things?"

She makes a so-so sign. " 'Ow's business for you?" she shoots back, pointing at the racks of trees on display along a makeshift back fence.

"Ah, I got out of it. I'm retired. I'm an old turkey. Too goddamn old to freeze my ass off. You gotta be one of them young buggers now, full of piss and vinegar. Like you."

The woman bursts into snorting giggles.

Moving along in a search for a restaurant of choice, we pass a panhandler who's too drunk to keep his head steady, but through the bobbing and weaving he spots Shack. "Shackie, hey, bro, you got any green?" the man slurs as Eddie strides by.

"Naw, I used to, but I kept givin' it to you assholes and now I don't have a pot to piss in."

The panhandler frowns and shrugs. "So be it," he mumbles philosophically.

Later, we pull up to the rear of the Civic Centre, and Eddie parks in a "by permit only" spot and waves at the security guard, who scurries over to place us in handcuffs. But he's pulled up short by Eddie's foghorn voice. "It's okay there, eh? Normie Ullman here's got a pulled groin." Ullman emerges from the back of the van, walking gingerly because of the crackling ice on the roadway, and even I have to admit he looks "hurt." The guard puts away his pen and grudgingly waves us through. On reaching the door Eddie holds it open for Ullman and his large equipment bag, saying, "Jeezuz, Normie, what the hell would you do with your life if they didn't have rinks?" And, laughing, the two ex-opponents and ex-teammates enter yet another arena in their long careers.

That night as we made our way back to Toronto in a sporadic sleet storm, one particular line stuck with me. Between the second and third period I had sat in the corner of the dressing room, "Hall of Fame row," in a right angled line with Guy LaFleur, Marcel Dionne, Storey, me, Gil Perreault, and Norm Ullman. Directly across the room was a group the others referred to as the "Wall of Shame," Shack, Jim Dorey, Jimmy Mann, goalie Richard Sevigny, and Mario Faubert. In the salty way of hockey players, in which nothing is beyond ridicule, all exchanged slurs and cast aspersions on each other. But as the players rose to file out of the room, with only the familiar creaking of tight skates, the whisper of nylon pants, and rustle of straining equipment for background noise, Storey leaned over, nudged me, and said in all sincerity, "If we all put out as much goodwill and effort as Eddie, we'd sure as hell have a better country."

It is a month later when I learn that Ed Shack, on his way to Cornwall and the Nation's Capital, exchanging barbs with a Cornwall bar crowd, trading trade secrets with the market tree seller, giving an Ottawa bum the bum's rush, joking with Frank Mahovlich and Red Storey, was by then aware he was going head-to-head with cancer.

Epilogue

THREE WEEKS BEFORE EDDIE'S SCHEDULED PROSTATE CANCER surgery we meet for a late lunch in a place called Graffiti's in Toronto's west end. Standing at a high table, I'm amazed at how reserved he's become since I last saw him. The familiar cowboy hat and boots are in place, but in between is a royal blue track suit, which gives him the look of an Olympic weight lifter from Dallas.

He offers the battling of a slight cold as a reason for his mood, but his movements and step appear considerably slowed, like a player who's gone through a tough seven-game set of the playoffs. He's also very meditative and pensive, shrugging as he answers my question about being continually "on" as a player.

"I looked at myself as an entertainer," he says, "somebody having fun, good in the dressing room with the players, acting up, that kind of stuff, you know, honest. I could get the pot stirred, loosen the boys up."

"Some people I've talked to say your brand of honesty is the kind that fires from the hip," I say. "You know, brutally frank, no-holds-barred."

"Yeah, I guess, but I was also honest about my lack of education. I think I could have been a coach, maybe even one of those motivator guys, but I was honest, maybe too honest, and I know stuff I said sometimes hurt people, but . . ."

It's a familiar rationalization, and I'm just about to add that many of the same people I talked to feel he's fair, doesn't pick his spots, and that he believes in good for one, good for everybody, with no one exempt, when the waitress appears and Eddie turns himself "on" again.

"¡Ariba! ¡Ariba!" he exclaims, making heads turn. "Sumbitch, that's a good Ukrainian drink." He wipes down his moustache in appreciation of the extra-spicy Bloody Caesar she's delivered.

In the general discussion that follows about how to make a proper "larynx burner," I watch Eddie perform and wonder if he's mellowing.

Perhaps, but it's more likely he now has to stare immortality in the face. He's watched his father go, and Billy Parrish. He's also lost his close business associate and best friend of all, Paul Rimstead.

When I consider Eddie's newfound reticence, I realize he has to come to terms with a new outlook, and for a guy with the energy, the zest for life he's always represented to anyone who's met him, that has to be a humbling prospect. But while the knowledge of his cancer stirs up feelings of anger, the frustration of dealing with the predestined, and a sense of something slipping away, it also elicits an all-out determination, the kind hockey players display when they glance at the clock and see they're one goal behind late in the third period. No matter what the digital numbers read, they always believe there's time to get it done.

A few days later, sitting down to lunch with Shack and his neighbour Ben in a place called the Bow & Arrow at Davisville and Yonge, Eddie lets it spill over. It's the last week in January, and his surgery is scheduled for Valentine's Day. Eddie is decked out in his black cowboy hat, blue sweater vest, denim Hillbilly Shack's shirt with "Saloon Staff" embroidered on both sleeves and is preparing himself for the worst. "All I know is when they operate and they tell me I only got three months to go, every bastard who fucked me over is in for it." The remark is delivered with some venom.

As the presurgery days dwindle to only a few, Jim Patry and I meet at the Chick 'n Deli. He's already there when I arrive, and as I look around the entire room, I see something I've never noticed before, a sign that reads: "You Are Not Drunk If You Can Lie on the Floor Without Holding On." The pithy saying is attributed to Dean Martin.

Spotting Patry, I climb into a window seat and watch the light dusting of snow settle on the parking meter I've just jiggled clear a few minutes before.

"I went for that prostate test, too," Patry says over his cup of coffee. "When I told Eddie, he asked, 'What for?' I said if I had it, maybe we could get the surgeon to give us a two-for-one deal. He laughed like hell."

We talk about the sense of finality, of what most people assume when they hear the word *cancer*. I tell him that Norma first made me aware of Eddie's cancer late in December, and that a lot of thoughts raced through my mind at the time, not the least of which, I'm ashamed to admit, was how much time we might have to finish the book. We also talk about how incongruous it seems to have this bigger-than-life character, a man who's "up" every day, handling the seriousness of one of life's blindsiders. Then the talk switches to how Norma was taking it.

"I think they'll bicker less," Patry says, chuckling quietly. He sits back in his chair, then briefly looks out the window. "Norma is all the things Eddie isn't. She's shy, private, very intelligent, has a certain order to follow. But I think Eddie is the 'unknown' she needs in her life. Everybody needs a little mystery. In this case she has a big one. Don't worry. Norma will be great, and so will Eddie. He's tough.

"I'll tell you something about Eddie. I had a close friend, Billy Kearns. We started hanging out together as kids, and though we went in separate directions, we were always in daily contact. Billy was a singer with choirs and groups around Toronto, and eventually he became the head of Kanata Records. I remember Shackie, Rimstead, and I got into this fire log business and we were going to do a series of radio commercials. Of course, we called on Kearns, and he made some studio time available. Rimmer was there writing, Eddie was acting up, and before long we had a few commercials. But guess who was in the next studio recording an album. Anne Murray. In our state it was too good an opportunity to pass up. We just had to drop by and say howdy. Lucky we got out of there with our ad tapes.

"It wasn't long after the studio session that Kearns contracted cancer, necessitating the removal of his tongue. And despite not knowing him that well, Eddie would drop in to visit and they became friends. The day Billy passed away Eddie and I were on the golf course at Devil's Pulpit, just coming through nine, when he took a telephone message from Bill's wife, who knew I was out there with him. Nothing was said and, of course, I didn't know what the call was about. It could have been anything, right? We completed the round, got into our bathing suits, and went to the deep whirlpool, the kind you can stand in. Suddenly

Eddie grabbed me, hugged me hard, and said, 'Billy's gone. Billy's gone.'

"I suppose since Eddie was a club member, the staff knew how to reach him on the course. He accepted the message, and in doing so, took on the responsibility of breaking the news to me. So he played the last nine holes, wrestling with how and when. I can imagine how hard it must have been for him to get to the point of telling me, and I often think about that day. It showed me a side of Eddie I hadn't seen before."

There is a ring of concern in Patry's voice that belies the brave face he's putting on the situation. Lost in our separate thoughts, we both look out the window at the falling snow.

My next meeting with Eddie is five weeks after our lunch in the Bow & Arrow. For the past while our only contact has been by telephone. It's now the end of February, and Eddie has had his operation and has recently returned home, and I've come to see him at his house early in the morning. He's in a sky-blue robe and ragged terry-cloth slippers, Twiggy is in the sink, looking embarrassed, forlorn, and betrayed all at the same time, as only dogs can when getting a bath. I ask Eddie, as everyone else does lately, "How's it coming along?"

"They gotta check my cells, or grasshoppers, or whatever those things are. And I get X rays every three months. Ah, those bastards are just guessin'. Some guys last this long, some guys last that long. All they're sayin' is they did their best. What the hell? It's a fifty-fifty thing, and I gotta take their word for it, right?"

"The doctor said he had blood vessels where nobody else did," Norma remarks, explaining they had used all three pints of the blood he'd donated.

Two weeks after his surgery Eddie is up and about. We're on our way to take down Shack's pictures from the walls of a former Eddie Shack's Donuts location just north of Toronto. Eddie's other, more important objective is to have a face-to-face encounter with the present owner to remind him he's had more than enough time to remove the Shack sign as agreed to in the contract. Eddie is no longer involved in the donut shop, but the sign doesn't convey that idea at all. I'm the "muscle" along on this trip of enforcement. In reality my muscles are there to carry the large pictures to the van. Eddie's not allowed to lift anything heavier than a 10-ounce draft beer.

As we motor up the four-lane street, Eddie works his cell phone. The first call is to his lawyer, Jim Garvey, and is answered by one of the firm's secretaries. "You went to the game? Who paid? Make them cheap mothers pay. Yeah, I saw that. Listen, you got more balls than Sunbeam. Yeah, I'll wait." I wonder if Mats Sundin, or "Sunbeam," realizes he has just made Eddie's mispronunciation hall of fame along with Inge Hammerhead and Ian Trimbrill.

"Jimmy? Yeah, shit, I'm happy to be alive and drivin' around." The conversation shifts to a jumble of stock prices and then settles on the wayward donut shop owner who hasn't removed the offending sign. "Well, fuck him. I'm gonna go in there and tell him I'm not tryin' to put him outta business. All I want is the goddamn sign down. And if he don't wanna do it, I'll go back and paint the bastard black. I'm tired of bein' a good guy."

In a twinkling, about the same time the phone hits the floor between the front seats, the topic of conversation reverts to his membership at the Devil's Pulpit golf club. "Nah, I don't play golf every day. Just like a regular goddamn job to me, five days a week." He laughs. "Golf is boring. I just like to shoot the shit with the boys and have some fun."

Then he's back on the phone, this time to Gerry Paxton, a longtime associate and the former used car manager for a local dealership Eddie worked for while playing with the Leafs. Gerry Paxton is at home, facing terminal cancer, and time is getting short.

"Hi, Marg. Good, good. Yeah, you know we're gettin' old when we go out and don't even drink, eh? How's the big guy feelin'? Oh, shit. Yeah, yeah. Okay. Well, I'll call again when I get close. No, don't wake him up. I'll call back in a little while."

Eddie gets off the phone again and asks me, "Did I ever tell you about trading Gerry the hockey skates for the car? Gerry said he needed skates, and if I got him a pair, he'd give me a car. Deal! I got the skates. The toes were scuffed and the blades were almost gone, and he gave me this clunker. But I already knew Jim Boylen needed a shitbox for something or other. So I went over and we made a trade. Boylen said, 'You get me a car and I'll give you that pipe you like.' He had this old European pipe. It's one of those big bent ones with the ceramic bowl, really different. So I gave him the car for the pipe. A goddamn pair of skates for a fuckin' car for a pipe. It was a quick flip. The skates are history, the car's in the junk pile, and the pipe is on my downstairs rec room wall. It's worth a shitload of money, too." For some reason Eddie finds this stroke of good fortune comical, and another big har-har-har fills the van.

The next call reaches Gerry Paxton. "Hi, how ya doin', buddy? Hangin' in there like a bird dog? Great. Do you wanna see me for about five minutes? Ten minutes? Okay, I'm comin' over. Yeah, don't be afraid to kick me out. Just say, 'Big boy, I'm tired. Now get the fuck outta here.' Okay?"

When we arrive at the donut shop, the sign is still on the outside wall, and the owner is outside the walls, too, meaning he's unavailable at the time of our visit. But, according to the two young women working the shop, he might be back anytime. The lone patron stares at Eddie, who asks if he likes the chocolate donuts. The answer sounds like "Yolp" through a mouthful, but before the man can choke it down and carry on a conversation, Eddie has stepped outside to look at the offending billboard for the third time.

Over a coffee at a small side table I pick up a nearby *Toronto Star*, with a *Sun* beside it, and know I'm good for 30 minutes. Flipping through the pages, I glance at Shack, who stews, gets up, walks past empty tables, peers at pictures of himself, looks out the window, studies the rows of donuts briefly, and you can see the wheels turning. He sits down, then, ants in his pants, gets up and goes through the same routine. To Eddie the give-and-take of wheeling and dealing is a welcome distraction, a form of relaxation, the way the rest of us watch television or collect stamps. It's fun, and biding his time is not.

It's as if stopping to relax is out of the question. Rarely does anything catch his attention for any sizable length of time, with the exception of the company in the immediate vicinity. He categorizes them quickly, sorting out the "fans" from the simply curious, judging who can be taken into a verbal joust, and how far, while dismissing those who are either resentful or ambivalent.

For other people, waiting rooms, airports, bars, and restaurants are places to take a break, sip coffee, or knock back a drink. They're respites where people-watching or browsing the paper can be enjoyed, but with Eddie it's either conversation, as long as he can swing it to something in his range of interest, or the telephone. If Eddie was ever asked what the greatest invention benefitting mankind was, he would rate the automobile first, followed in a heartbeat by the cellular telephone. As I watch him in the donut shop, I realize he's a study of controlled aggravation, so I flip the page and continue my reading.

Later, though without seeing the owner, we drive to the Devil's Pulpit golf course. The van is full of framed photos, but the Shack sign is still in place back at the donut shop. In the Pulpit's bar we find a small group of staff members poring over a photo album.

"What are you girls lookin' at?" Eddie bellows. "Dirty pictures? Hey, would you please look up a couple of telephone numbers for me? I can't read, you know. Thanks very much." Then, turning, he observes, softly, "Notice how fuckin' polite I am since I got out of the hospital?"

The lone club member sitting at the bar chokes on his drink, then wipes his chin and asks sympathetically, "How's it coming along?"

"Great, great," Eddie responds cheerfully. "When ya get to be 60, the whole goddamn bottom falls out."

As those around him fight advancing years, Eddie seemingly enjoys them, making jokes about aging in a self-deprecating style, which he uses as both a jovial entry, or exit, at any scene or in any conversation. He's the only celebrity I know who can walk into a room and, when confronted by a well-wisher inquiring about his state of health, is more likely to announce, "Jeez, how the hell am I supposed to remember? When ya get to be 60, you forget a lot of shit, eh?" Very few others, particularly the celebrities I know, ever bare themselves in this fashion.

At one point in our talk Eddie rises quickly and leaves the bar, answering my concern about where he's bound by saying, "I'm takin' my bag for a piss." He's still on a catheter, and I'm jolted out of the "just like old times" mood Eddie is portraying and am reminded how serious the situation remains.

On his return Shack continues the levity to dispel any notion he's not his usual self, A new arrival in the bar inquires, "How's it comin'?"

"Holy sheepshit," Eddie says, assuming an injured look. "Never say 'coming' to a guy who just had his pross-crate cut. Say, 'How's it going?'" This time 10 people laugh at the new Shackism.

Just before we leave, Eddie tells me about his most recent visit to the doctor, who cleared him to make a scheduled reunion trip to Los Angeles, where the old Kings are getting together. "The doctor said, 'You're okay, big boy.' And I said, 'Put 'er there, Doc. I'm outta here to L.A.' I got a buddy that's gonna leave me one of them rich-bitch cars, a Bentley, to drive around town. Now I'll be cruisin' the streets, laughin' and wavin', happy as a goddamn lark, sayin', 'Hi there, shithead.'"

Six weeks later Gerry Paxton passed away.

Eddie shack is one of the truly great "characters" of sport. Certainly the greatest "character" the NHL has ever seen, unquestionably head and shoulders above a contemporary by the name of Harold Ballard, a man who conspired and contorted to be a headliner. There is no contriving in the persona of Eddie Shack. He was a character as a boy, teenager, and hockey player, and is still one of a kind to this day. Even from the advantage of his lofty position in a city like Toronto, it took a daily effort on Ballard's part to remain in the limelight. His "tools" were farcical statements, spiteful badgering of people on slow news days, self-serving plots and plans, the smirking dismissal of his jail sentence as part of his mystique, and the use of his position and assumed wealth to threaten himself into public acceptability.

On the other hand, Eddie accomplished his distinctive character traits by being himself, both on and off the ice, and hasn't spent a day in jail. By all evaluations of ex-player recognition, he's up there in the Big Five of national hockey notoriety. In the fame game he rivals Bobby Orr, Gordie Howe, Bobby Hull, and Jean Beliveau. The only other face of merit is Don Cherry, although purists say he never really played in the NHL, therefore he can't be in the group. But theories and bench-marks aside, Don Cherry is "hockey" and a figure of immense popular-ity. Within that context he has a different, singular, and personal read on Shack.

"The first time I ran into Shackie was at the Ranger training camp," the man they call Grapes tells me, looking casual in a T-shirt and shorts, sitting amid a pile of newspapers in his sun room off the backyard. "I was with Springfield and had driven down from Kingston in my car, not a new one or anythink like that, eh, but okay. Up comes Shack in a brand-new red convertible, top down, golf shirt, muscles, everythink. A car I woulda killed for, and this guy's just out of junior.

"That night it poured rain, and I looked out the motel window and there was Shack's car, filling up with water 'cause the top was still down, and I thought, What a waste, lettin' a guy who don't care have a car like that one.

"For the rest of the camp we had to listen to him and Phil Watson argue like hell in the hotel lobby, in the rink corridors, all over the place. Can you figure that out? This guy is out of junior and he's arguin' with an NHL coach." Cherry shakes his head and raises his eyebrows at the audacity.

"The next time I caught up to him he was sent down to Springfield, for gettin' outta line. They'd send guys down to get a taste of Eddie Shore. For us career minor-leaguers Springfield was Alcatraz, the Devil's Island of hockey. But Eddie came to town and enjoyed himself. Why not? He knew he was there for two weeks. The rest of us had life sentences with no paroles. Shore and Shackie got along like a pair of beauts. The rest of us were scared to death of Shore. We had to be. He had ahold of our paycheques. Still, I think it backfired on the Rangers. Shackie went back worse, more cheesed off, than when they sent him down.

"Next time I saw him was seven years later in Rochester. The Leafs sent him down, too, you know, to do some penance. One night he got cut, I mean cut — 30 or 40 stitches, like that." Cherry runs a big finger around his eye from top to bottom. "Eddie came right back and never missed a game. Today they'd be out for a week. I've never forgotten that cut. Oh, yeah, he was tough and he could play. Geez, when you hit him, it was like running into a bag of anvils, all elbows, knees, stick, an' every-think. After, you'd be skating away, limpin', hurtin' worse than him." Cherry gives the obligatory thumbs-up to the accomplishment, negative though it might be. "I'll tell ya, Eddie was somethink. As a hockey player, he was a lot more than an entertainer."

In writing Eddie's biography I was often struck by several things I'd previously taken for granted about him. First, after all this time, I thought I knew Ed Shack. But I wasn't even close. Like most everyone else over the years, I'd fallen into the mistake of considering him comic relief. Second, I let that murky image cloud over his abilities as a hockey player. Milt Dunnell, Don Cherry, Bobby Hull, Jerry Toppazzini, John Ferguson, Red Kelly, and a host of others all indicate that there was more to Eddie than The Entertainer. And as Billy Harris put it so aptly to me, "Today's teams have a goon and a backup goon. But all 52 goons in today's NHL couldn't score 25 goals in total. Eddie and John Ferguson were *players*."

To describe Eddie Shack as a "brutal hockey player," as Cathy Shack's workplace colleague did, couldn't be further from the truth. Despite the mismanagement of his talents in New York, Eddie has never cried about life's deal. He has always played the hand he was dealt and has never said he was short-changed on aces or wild cards. And with the exception of his initial disgruntlement at moving along, a normal reaction with most players, he was rarely bitter about being traded. He just went on to a new city, did his thing, and didn't rail at the system.

Some people said it took 25 games for each new club to find out he wasn't the player he was purported to be, and a lot of that had to do with his irreverent attitude toward the game. Perhaps, because when you look at his statistics, the assists versus goals, he certainly wasn't a playmaker. But that part of the game was never his job. When you hit town and score 20 or 25 times, how much more can be expected? And if he wasn't given the chance to play, to score, to pull the trigger, then he was really hamstrung.

People looked for and expected too much of Shack when he was with bad teams, and when he was with a good one, they downgraded him and his play and made light of his worth. On the one hand, he was expected to be an entertainer; on the other, he was forced to be a leader. And when he didn't lead in the acceptable manner, he was often put down for it. The big misconception, the lasting image of Ed Shack's career, flavoured and fuelled by his own actions since he retired, is that all he did, game in and game out, was jerk around. Perhaps Eddie brought a lot of the country bumpkin, Forrest Gump, Gomer Pyle image on himself, even perpetuated it.

But you don't last 17 seasons in the NHL by being a fool.

Going back over our interviews, I realize there were many moments and occasions when Eddie volunteered his thoughts so that I didn't have to lever them out of him. But I also remember how exasperating he could be. There were times when he made me wish I were one of those television drama prosecutors who could ask a judge to grant permission to treat his star witness as "hostile." But caution prevailed, and in the face of Eddie's inability to express himself, he frequently allowed me to relate a story, only correcting it if absolutely necessary, bobbing his head in agreement if it was even close to being right. He neither added nor subtracted, relying on the third-person hearsay I repeated, thereby becoming the unseen fourth person in the anecdote.

Only on rare occasions, particularly in the hotel room in Cornwall when he sat on the edge of the bed, stripped down to shorts and a glass of wine, rubbing his face like an archaeologist scraping soil from a rock, did he open up and try to describe his feelings. In a painstakingly slow process he explained his vision of himself and related the many chances that wouldn't have been missed if the people involved had only displayed faith in his ability to pull off the deal in question.

Each and every time he allowed me to get a look at his inner self he was as open and forthright as it was possible for him to be, and I realized that I, much like the interviewers he'd faced years ago when he first arrived in the NHL, wasn't his buddy. At that point I was one of *them*. Once I accepted that concept I fared much better.

Toward the end of the writing of this book I came to a juncture where speculation got the better of me. I'd wonder how life might have been for Eddie with an education. I even took it further and pictured him with a university degree, and found myself trying to make the result of that education fit the free spirit that evolved, the one I knew.

I wondered, If sacrifices and alterations were made with respect to language, etiquette, protocol, decorum, and propriety, what changes would occur in exuberance, personality, and the abrasive exterior of my subject. Would we be left with a reasonable, compromising Ed Shack, a man capable of diplomatic statements, small talk, and observational comments on current events? In other words, another glib, faceless clone in the cookie-cutter tradition.

Try as I might I couldn't envision Eddie wearing anything from Roots or Ralph Lauren, and I realized I didn't ever want to see him wearing a backward Nike baseball hat.

Nobody, but nobody, had as much fun playing hockey as Ed Shack. Yes, his career had its ups and downs like everyone else's, but within Shackie's big picture they were merely momentary aberrations, like New York. With that notable exception he had good times everywhere he played, and created good times for those who watched him perform from Guelph to Los Angeles, from Buffalo to Pittsburgh. And in Toronto he had twice as much fun.

For some people Ed Shack is a Canadian tragedy. He's a boy who went away from home to play hockey, which is true, but so did Bobby Orr, Wayne Gretzky, and Bobby Hull, and no one considers them national mishaps. In the hockey world the best of the crop are always going away, whether it be to a junior team, posh prep schools like Ridley or Upper Canada College, or on to university. Going away has always signified getting better.

The adversity faced by Eddie Shack isn't that he went away so young; it's that he couldn't read or write. Having made that distinction, he's the Canadian hero we keep searching for, a walking, talking, extraordinary success story rather than a cross-country calamity.

So, if I had to go back through the scores of stories and vignettes I've recorded about Ed Shack and select one that spelled out chapter and verse how he can be simultaneously as curious as a kitten and as clumsy as the proverbial bull in a china shop, it would be a tale from our days in the ranks of the Labatt's Original Six.

In those days, not so long after his retirement, Eddie would occasionally get out of sorts and be moody and morose. We knew better than to push the matter with him. In fact, left to his own devices, he would be back to his old self within an hour. Still, when he became publicly surly, I'd caution him. One time, when we were in Vancouver, I remarked that he was "being obtuse," and you could almost see his ears point upward, like those of a Doberman when faced with a burglar.

"OB-JUICE," he repeated. "OB-JUICE."

"OB-CHUICE," I corrected. "Or the Rosedale pronunciation might be better suited to Your Grace, as in OB-CHOOSE."

But Eddie preferred the garden-variety "OB-CHUICE," which sounded suspiciously like a surprise sneeze. After several attempts at getting comfortable with this incredible new attention getter, he wanted to know what it meant.

"Obtuse means not making yourself clear, lacking smarts, being a big pain in the ass," I said.

Eddie nodded sagely, then went about happily calling anything and everybody "OB-CHUICE" for the next hour.

The following morning we sat down to breakfast in Hotel Vancouver where the silverware was silver and the waiting staff, regardless of the hour, was starched and painfully pressed in black and white. A cheerful waitress approached our table with a gleaming urn of fresh coffee. "Good morning, sir," she said to me. Then, turning to Eddie, she breathed, "And good morning to you, Mr. Shack."

"She's being OB-CHUICE," Eddie snorted. I only shook my head.

"Would you care to order?" the waitress asked. I made my selection, then she turned to Shack, pen and paper poised.

"Now, first of all, I want an omelette, but I gotta warn ya, I like 'em my way," he blared.

The waitress nodded, as if to say nothing was too difficult, too good, or too much trouble for a celebrity.

Eddie cocked his head, took on a serious look, held up his huge hands as if to slow her down, and said, "Tell the cook in the back I like my omelette runny . . . in the middle . . . like snot."

The woman blanched, then she gasped as if ready to heave. Finally she put the unfinished order list to her mouth and bolted toward the kitchen. I gave Eddie my all-time, career-best, pained expression.

"See, I told yuh she was bein' OB-CHUICE," he sneezed, totally unconcerned.

Somewhere in British Columbia there's a woman with a story that is less than flattering of Eddie, and undoubtedly he has often fallen into the category of aloof and/or impolite celebrity. Lots of other notables have; it's a common pitfall, and one the famous person has to come to grips with if he or she ever expects to have some sanity or privacy. In Eddie's case he's sometimes loud, ill-behaved, and unpolished, and he's seldom politically correct and possesses few, if any, inhibitions.

What's even more intimidating is that Eddie often invites the label because he lives on the edge, but it's his edge. He's funny and outrageous, but on his terms. He'll join the parade or the show, but he'll lead the parade and steal the show.

Either that or he's outta there.

I'll go back to the lady with the fight-night mentality in New York who thought he needed a good thrashing, and Marion Sullivan's poised rebuke of this ramrod dowager.

"Oh . . . relax," she gently scolded, the reprimand of a dignified and gracious lady providing security and haven for an unruly street urchin. "That's just Eddie."

Index

A

Adams, Jack, 102
Adams, Weston, 126, 136
Alexander, Claire, 7, 167
Anderson, Dave, 69–70
Apps, Syl, Jr., 153
Arbour, Al, 34, 47, 80
Armstrong, George, 34, 84
Ashley, John, 122
Austin, Al, 53–54
Awrey, Don, 123

B

Balfour, Murray, 82
Ballard, Harold, 140, 160, 161, 195, 236, 245–47, 251, 267
Balon, Dave, 82
Bathgate, Andy, 67–70, 82, 225, 226, 229, 239–40
Baun, Bob, 78 79, 108, 179, 226, 240
Baun, Sally, 199
Beddoes, Dick, 160, 221
Beliveau, Jean, 83, 238, 267
Bennett, Charlie, 231
Bentley, Max, 16
Biggs, Al, 24, 182–87, 189
Biltmore Hat Company, 4, 45, 57, 126
Bionda, Jack, 62
Bizar, John, 50
Blake, Toe, 13

Boivin, Leo, 79, 96
Borovich, Adam, 35
Boston Bruins, 111–12, 115–26
Boutette, Pat, 167, 168
Bower, Johnny, 97–99, 107–8
Boylen, Jim, 264–65
Boylen, M. J., 80
Brewer, Carl, 78–79, 82, 225, 226–27, 231, 232, 234–36, 239, 240
Broda, Turk, 58
Browning, Kurt, ix–x
Bucyk, John, 118, 181
Buffalo Sabres, 139, 142–52
Bush, Eddie, 46, 54–58, 60, 61, 254

C

Cahan, Larry, 155
Campbell, Bryan (Soupy), 35, 37
Campbell, Clarence, 76, 222
Canadian magazine, 113–14
Carroll, Dink, 72
Casey, Ron, 36
Cashman, Wayne, 124–25
Cedarburg, Fred, 73
Cerone, Smokey, 62
Chadwick, Bill, 219
Chambers Meats, 182
Cheevers, Gerry, 123
Cherry, Don, 55, 96, 172, 186, 267–69
Chicago Blackhawks, 75–76, 101–2

Christie, Frankie, 145, 151

Clancy, King, 103, 161

"Clear the Track, Here Comes Shack," 5, 194–95

Cooke, Jack Kent, 127–29, 133, 135, 137, 140, 246

Copper Cliff (Ontario), 34–35, 37

Crawford, Johnny, 62

Creighton, Dave, 154

Crozier, Joe, 151–52

Crozier, Roger, 91, 121, 143

D

Dailey, Bob, 235

Davidson, Bob, 26

Desjardins, Gerry, 7, 130, 158

Dick, Alan, 234

Dionne, Marcel, 259

Dixon, Tom, 25

Domi, Tie, 244

Dorey, Jim, 161, 259

Douglas, Kent, 35, 77, 79–80

Dryden, Dave, 150

Duff, Dick, 14, 34, 78, 82, 139, 142, 143

Dunnell, Milt, 88–91, 127, 154–55, 214–15

Dupere, Denis, 243–45

E

Eagleson, Alan, 184, 185, 225–27, 232–34, 236, 240, 251

Eddie Shack Golf Course, 179–80

Eddie Shack (racehorse), 80–81

Eddie Shack's Donuts, 263–66

Eddie Shack's Top Secret Steak Sauce, 182

Edestrand, Darryl, 7, 157–58, 165–66

Edwards, Marv, 7

Ellis, Ron, 18, 105, 161, 173–74

Esposito, Phil, 112, 116, 121, 125

Esso. *See* Imperial Oil

F

Facelle, 178–79

Faubert, Mario, 259

Favell, Doug, 7, 163, 168–69

Ferguson, John, 12–15, 68, 99, 269

Ferrin, Ed, 235

Flaman, Fern, 65

Fleming, Reggie, 76, 96, 101, 143, 155

Flett, Bill, 130, 133

Fontinato, Lou, 40, 58–59, 79

Foo-Foo (Eddie's dog), 150–51, 159, 177

Forbes, Dave, 226

Forever Rivals, 245

Foster, Sue, 232, 235

Francis, Emile, 89, 90

Frayne, Trent, 167–68

Friday, Bill, 90

G

Gadsby, Bill, 71, 102

Gamble, Bruce, 36, 215

Gare, Danny, 133

Garvey, Jim, 179–80, 232, 264

Garvie, Ed, 227, 235

Giacomin, Rollie, 35

Gilbert, Rod, 69, 90

Gillis, John, 43–47, 57

Gilmour, Doug, 253

Gingras, Gaston, 249

Girard, Ken, 58

Givens, Phil, 84

Glennie, Brian, 7, 215

Globe and Mail, 58, 103, 155–56

Goegan, Pete, 76, 96

Goyette, Phil, 90, 143

Gracyk, Marcus, 228

Gregory, Jim, 161–62, 166, 176, 232

Gross, George, 89, 99–101, 170

Guelph (Ontario), 17, 41, 46

Guelph Biltmores, 16, 33, 41–42, 44–46,
    54–56

Guelph Mercury, 53–54

H

Haddow, Jack, 33, 44

Hadfield, Vic, 232

Haggert, Bobby, 96

Hamel, Pierre, 167

Hamilton, Al, 145

Hammarstrom, Inge, 165

Hannigan, Pat, 73

Harris, Billy, 8, 54, 75, 78–79, 83, 94, 152,
    179, 230–31, 238, 269

Harris, Ted, 13, 90

Hawkins, Ronnie, 177–78

Hewat, Jane, 170

Hewat, Ron, 169–70

Hewitt, Foster, 113

Hillbilly Shack's, 50–51, 198

Hillman, Larry, 34, 76, 96

Hockey News, The, 157

Hockey Night in Canada, 113, 140

Hodge, Ken, 112, 121, 125

Hoganson, Dale, 130

Horn Provisioners, 180

Horton, Lori, 216–17, 219

Horton, Tim, 34, 35, 37, 78, 94, 98, 99,
    120, 124, 216

Houle, Rejean, 238

Howe, Colleen, 229, 234

Howe, Gordie, 16, 68, 71, 74–75, 79, 96,
    117–18, 174–75, 221, 229–30, 240,
    267

Hull, Bobby, 10, 36, 64–65, 68, 76, 79,
    125, 229–30, 240–41, 267

Hull, Dennis, 7

Humphreys, Jack, 53, 55, 60

Huntington Golf Course, 231, 232, 235,
    251

I

Imlach, Punch, 6, 62, 73–74, 76–79, 81,
    82, 90, 97, 103–5, 107, 109–12,
    126, 130, 139, 140, 151–52,
    170–71, 253

    feud with Eddie Shack, 86–88, 92–94,
    98–101, 142–47, 149

Imperial Oil, 92–93, 177

Inco, 21, 28, 34

Inglis, Billy, 145, 149–50

Irvine, Ted, 130

Ivan, Tommy, 66

J

James, Gord, ix–x

Johnston, Ed, 123

Joyal, Eddie, 130, 133

Joyce, Ron, 39

Junior hockey, 42, 44

K

Kearns, Billy, 263–64

Kelly, Red, 69, 71, 88, 91, 102–3, 109, 125, 152–54, 158–67, 176, 199, 220, 229, 233–34

Kennedy, John F., 81

Keon, Dave, 78–79, 84, 89, 93, 98, 104–5, 109, 119–20, 156, 161

Kilpatrick, John Reid, 222

Krake, Skip, 134–35, 145–47

L

Labatt's NHL Old Stars, 6–9

Labatt's Original Six, 215, 218, 272–73. *See also* Labatt's NHL Old Stars

Labine, Leo, 71, 140

Lach, Elmer, 238

Lafleur, Guy, 259

Lapard, Frank, 48

La Rosa, Julius, 47

Lavar, Emile, 52

Laycoe, Hal, 6, 127–31, 133–36, 138, 255

Leach, Reggie, 235

Lemieux, Real, 133

Ley, Rick, 161

Lindros, Eric, 6

Lindsay, Ted, 88

Litzenberger, Ed, 64

Lloyds of London, 188

London Nationals, 157–58

Lonsberry, Ross, 126, 130

Los Angeles Kings, 112, 126–31, 133–39

M

Mahovlich, Frank, 13, 34, 36, 54, 58, 82, 84, 92, 98, 107, 125, 150, 238, 249, 259

Mahovlich, Peter, 150, 238

Maki, Chico, 7, 10, 11

Mann, Jimmy, 259

Mann, Larry, 136

Mark's Work Wearhouse, 178

Marois, Mario, 249

Marotte, Gilles, 112, 125

Marshall, Donny, 143

Martin, Pit, 7–8, 112

Martin, Rick, 150, 152

Mason, Roy, 42

Mason, "Swat," 42, 54

May, Bill, 7, 183–85, 187–90, 212–13, 220

Mayne, Frank, 190–93, 195–96

McCarthy, Jay, 34

McCarthy, Tommy, 54

McCauley, Bill, 194

McCreary, Billy, 56

McCreary, Keith, 8, 156–57, 225, 230, 231, 234–41

McDonald, Jiggs, 128–29, 133

McDonald, Lanny, 163

McFarlane, Brian, 194–95

McKechnie, Walt, 158

McKenney, Don, 82

McKenny, Jim, 7, 163, 170–73, 244, 245

McKenzie, John, 121

McMahon, Mike, 139

McMillan, Mickey, 41, 45, 110

McNaughton, Ron, 49

McNeill, Billy, 71

Mellanby, Ralph, 140

Mickey, Larry, 8

Mikita, Stan, 7, 36, 76, 79, 82, 156

Miller Lite, 179

Minnesota North Stars, 112

Montreal Canadiens, 16–17, 82–85, 103

Montreal *Gazette*, 72

Montreal Royals, 45

Morrison, Sheila, 210

Mr. Dressup, ix

Muller, Kirk, ix–x

N

National Hockey League, 230

Naylor, Tommy, 90, 203

Neale, Harry, 36

Nevin, Bob, 8, 34–37, 58, 79, 82, 179

New York Rangers, 36, 53, 55, 60–71, 82

New York Times, 69 70

NHL Old Stars. *See* Labatt's NHL Old Stars

NHL Oldtimers, 7

NHL Pension Society, sued by ex-players, 222–41

Niforos, Van, 14

Norris, Bruce, 102

Norris, Jack, 112

O

Oakland Seals, 112, 244

O'Connor, Carroll, 182–83

Oklahoma City Blazers, 162, 167–68, 175

Oliver, Murray, 111–12

Olmstead, Bert, 68, 76, 80, 104, 109

Orr, Bobby, 118, 121, 125, 166, 181, 225, 240, 267

O'Shea, Kevin, 145, 150

Owchar, Dennis, 226

P

Paice, Frank, 67

Pappin, Jim, 8, 34–37, 49, 75, 81

Parrish, Bill, 59, 211, 217–19, 220, 261

Parrish, Marnie, 199, 217–19

Patrick, Muzz, 55, 60–62, 65, 66, 68, 70, 71, 72

Patry, Jim, 180–82, 209–11, 219–21, 261–63

Paxton, Gerry, 59, 264–65, 267

Pelyk, Mike, 7

Perreault, Gil, 143, 145, 147, 150, 152, 249, 250, 254, 259

Philadelphia Flyers, 112, 117

Pike, Alf, 45, 72

Pilote, Pierre, 7, 76, 101–2, 179

Pilous, Rudy, 79, 243

Pittsburgh Penguins, 112, 152–60

Plante, Pierre, 249

Pocklington, Peter, 253

Podborski, Steve, 20

Popein, Larry, 67

Pop Shoppe, 7, 182–94

Portland Buckaroos, 78

Pratt, Babe, 148

Pratt, Tracy, 145, 148–49

Prentice, Dean, 8, 67, 86

Pronovost, Marcel, 108–9

Proudfoot, Jim, 86–87

Providence Reds, 62

Provost, Claude, 105

Pulford, Bob, 92, 94, 240–41

Q

Quality Inn, 179

R

Rain, Dan, 28–32

Ramsay, Glen, 46–47

Ratelle, Jean, 68

Regan, Larry, 136–38, 221, 226, 229, 240

Reiner, Rob, 182

Reise, Leo, 221, 225, 229, 234, 240

Richard, Henri, 79, 82–84, 97, 193, 238

Richard, Maurice (Rocket), 16, 71, 84,
    103, 238

Riley, Jack, 152, 158

Rimstead, Myrna, 211–13

Rimstead, Paul, 35, 37, 113–14, 131,
    177–78, 184–86, 188–89, 203,
    210–16, 220, 261

Robert, Rene, 152–54, 226

Rochester Americans, 87–89, 105

Rolfe, Dale, 130, 134

S

Salming, Borje, 164, 165, 247

Sanderson, Derek, 8, 112, 115, 118,
    120–24, 155, 158

Sather, Glen, 153, 253

Sawchuk, Terry, 98, 108–9

Schinkel, Ken, 154, 158

Schmidt, Milt, 66, 111–12

Schock, Ron, 154, 158

Schulz, Charles, 7

Selke, Frank, 84–85

Selwood, Brad, 161

Sevigny, Richard, 259

Shack, Bill, 19–21, 25–26, 28, 33–34, 59,
    206

Shack, Cathy, 27, 80, 114, 147, 180, 198,
    199, 204, 205, 206–8

Shack, Eddie
    battle with cancer, 59, 260–63
    as a Boston Bruin, 115–26
    as a Buffalo Sabre, 143–52
    business interests, 50–51, 154–55,
        179–82, 195–96, 198, 210, 251–53,
        263–66
    childhood of, 21–26, 29–31, 33–34
    commercial endorsements, 7, 14–15,
        177–94
    feud with Phil Watson, 62–64, 66–67,
        69–71, 268
    feud with Punch Imlach, 77–78,
        86–88, 92–94, 98–101, 111,
        142–47
    as a Guelph Biltmore, 17–18, 33, 38,
        41–42, 53–58
    illiteracy, 25, 30, 69, 72–74, 157,
        200–201, 210, 253, 255–57
    junior hockey career, 41–58
    as a Los Angeles King, 128–31, 133–39

as a New York Ranger, 63–72

nose insured by Lloyds, 188

as a Pittsburgh Penguin, 152–60

sent to minor leagues, 62, 67, 87–89

sold to Toronto, 160

as a Toronto Maple Leaf, 73–105,
    107–12, 162–75

traded

    to Boston, 112

    to Buffalo, 139, 142

    to Los Angeles, 126

    to Pittsburgh, 152–54

    to Toronto, 73

Shack, Jimmy, 27, 147, 180, 198, 199, 200,
    202–8

Shack, Lena, 19–21, 24–28, 31–35, 197,
    206, 208

Shack, Mary, 19, 20, 26–29, 35, 179, 208

Shack, Norma, 27, 59, 75, 93, 114–15,
    131–33, 138–39, 140, 147, 176,
    179–80, 190, 198–202, 208, 219,
    262, 263

    involvement in NHL pension fight,
        225–32, 234–37, 239–41

Shatto, Dick, 82

Shore, Eddie, 35, 67, 255, 268

Sinden, Harry, 6, 115, 118, 122–23,
    125–26, 130, 155, 166

Sittler, Darryl, 165, 174, 233

Smith, Dallas, 7

Smith, Floyd, 145

Smith, Gary, 158

Smythe, Conn, 87, 109, 222

Smythe, Stafford, 87–88, 94, 109

Spencer, Brian, 129

Spencer, Irv, 35, 70

Springfield Indians, 67

Stanfield, Fred, 7, 10, 11, 112, 118–19,
    121, 125

Stanley, Allan, 77, 84, 104, 107, 143, 225,
    226, 230, 240

Stapleton, Pat, 7, 101–2

Stemkowski, Pete, 108

Stewart, Ron, 81, 82, 109

St. Louis Blues, 112, 176

Storey, Red, 248–49, 259

Sudbury (Ontario), 19–20

Sullivan, Marion, 70, 202, 219, 273

Sullivan, Red, 69–70, 73, 202

Sundin, Mats, 264

Sutton, Sam, 57

Sweeney, Bill, 46–47, 54, 55, 60–63, 72

T

Talbot, Jean-Guy, 143, 145

Tallon, Dale, 7

Team Canada, 155–56, 184

Tennyson, Wilmot, 182–83, 185

Terbenche, Paul, 150

Thompson, Errol, 8, 163

Toppazzini, Jerry, 65–66, 137–38

Toronto Maple Leafs, 16–17, 26, 73–105,
    107–12, 160–75

Toronto Marlboros, 26, 105

Toronto Star, 58, 86–91, 154–55, 221

Toronto Sun, 167–68, 170, 178, 230

Toronto *Telegram*, 73, 89, 90, 99, 142, 195

Toronto Toros, 175

Trainor, Terry, 193–94

Turlik, Ken, 126

Twiggy (Eddie's dog), 1, 16, 52, 263

U

Ublanski, Gerry, 154, 179

Udvari, Frank, 101

Ullman, Bibs, 199

Ullman, Norm, 7, 59, 163, 174–75, 224,
   247–48, 256, 258, 259

V

Valiquette, Jack, 8

Vaughan Valley Golf Club, 154, 231,
   251–52

VentureTec, 192–93

Verone, Joe, 46, 50

Victoria Maple Leafs, 92–93

Vipond, Jim, 103

W

Wall, Bob, 130

Walton, Mike (Shakey), 8, 109

Waterloo Siskins, 55

Watson, Amy, 251

Watson, Bob, 154, 162, 179, 180, 251

Watson, Bugsy, 154

Watson, Harry, 150

Watson, Phil, 6, 36–37, 55, 74, 102, 108,
   130, 131, 199, 222, 247, 254, 255,
   268
   feud with Eddie Shack, 60–67, 69–72

Webber, Brian, 54–56, 72

Webber, Velma, 54

Westfall, Ed, 115, 118, 121, 126

White, Bill, 7, 130, 134, 155, 179

Whitt, Ernie, ix–x

Wicks, Ron, 57, 197

Wilcox, Chester, 28, 72

Williams, Tommy (Bomber), 6–9, 12

Wilson, Johnny, 73, 136, 138

Wilson, Murray, 238

Winter, Rich, 227, 235

World Hockey Association (WHA),
   161–62, 175

Worsley, Gump, 108

Y

Young, Howie, 101

Young, Scott, 155–56

Z

Zeidel, Larry, 116–17, 119

Ziegler, John, 233–34

Zigler, Mark, 225, 227–31, 234, 235–36,
   240, 241